Antonio Maceo

BY PHILIP S. FONER

History of Black Americans
History of the Labor Movement in the United States
The Life and Writings of Frederick Douglass (5 vols.)
A History of Cuba and Its Relations with the United States (2 vols.)
The Complete Writings of Thomas Paine (2 vols.)
Business and Slavery
W.E.B. Du Bois Speaks (2 vols.)
The Fur and Leather Workers Union
Jack London: American Rebel
Mark Twain: Social Critic
The Jews in American History: 1654–1865
The Case of Joe Hill
The Letters of Joe Hill
The Bolshevik Revolution: Its Impact on American Radicals, Liberals, and Labor
American Labor and the War in Indochina
Helen Keller: Her Socialist Years
The Autobiographies of the Haymarket Martyrs
The Black Panthers Speak
The Basic Writings of Thomas Jefferson
The Voice of Black America: Major Speeches of Negroes
The Spanish-Cuban-American War
When Karl Marx Died: Comments in 1883
Organized Labor and the Black Worker, 1619–1973
American Labor Songs of the Nineteenth Century
Labor and the American Revolution
We the Other People
The Democratic-Republic Societies, 1790–1800
Inside the Monster: José Martí on the United States
Our America: José Martí on Latin America
The Factory Girls
The Great Labor Uprising of 1877
American Socialism and Black Americans

ANTONIO MACEO

The "Bronze Titan" of Cuba's Struggle for Independence

by Philip S. Foner

Monthly Review Press
New York and London

Library of Congress Cataloging in Publication Data
Foner, Philip Sheldon, 1910–
Antonio Maceo: the "Bronze Titan" of Cuba's struggle for independence.
Bibliography: p.
1. Maceo, Antonio, 1845–1896. 2. Revolutionists—Cuba—Biography.
F1783.M125F66 972.91'05'0924 77-76163
ISBN 0-85345-423-X

Monthly Review Press
62 West 14th Street, New York, N.Y. 10011
47 Red Lion Street, London WC1R 4PF

10 9 8 7 6 5 4 3 2 1

Manufactured in the United States of America

Contents

"Always, as in the past, I will be on the side of the sacred interests of the people."

—Letter from Antonio Maceo published in *El Yara* (Florida), September 1880

"I have no other aspiration than to see my country sovereign and free. With natural sovereignty we shall obtain our natural rights, calm dignity, and the representation of a free and independent people. . . . When Cuba is free and has a constituted government, I shall request that we fight for the independence of Puerto Rico also. I would not care to put up my sword leaving that portion of America in slavery."

—Antonio Maceo to Anselmo Valdés, July 6, 1884

"Whoever tries to take power over Cuba will get only the dust of its soil, drenched in blood, if he does not perish in the struggle."

—Antonio Maceo to Máximo Gómez, October 13, 1885

"Liberty is not begged for; it is conquered."

—Antonio Maceo, Proclamation to My Comrades of Oriente, 1886

GUANABACOA
MATANZAS
CARDENAS
HAVANA
HAVANA
ARTEMISA
MATANZAS
CANDELARIA
COLON
PINAR DEL RIO
RANCHU
MANTUA
SANTA CL
CIENFUE
SIERRA DE TRINIDAD
ISLE OF PINES
CARIBBEAN SEA

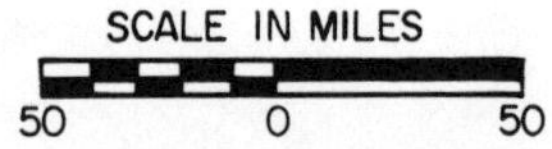
SCALE IN MILES
50
0
50

ATLANTIC OCEAN

TI SPIRITUS

CAMAGUEY

NUEVITAS

CAMAGUEY

HOLGUIN

SIERRA DE NIPE

SIERRA DEL CRISTAL

ORIENTE

BAYAMO

BARACOA

MANZANILLO

YARA

JIGUANI

SANTIAGO DE CUBA

GUANTANAMO

SIERRA MAESTRA

Preface

During a number of trips to Havana, Cuba, I often had the pleasure of visiting the Antonio Maceo Memorial Park. There, the monument to the black hero whom Cubans call the "Bronze Titan" is one of the island's most impressive landmarks, equivalent in impact to the tall marble monument in Havana to Maceo's comrade-in-arms, José Martí—"El Apóstol," venerated as the father of his country.

The Maceo monument stands on an elevation in the vast green park. The work of Italian sculptor Domingo Boni, it shows the warrior on his horse. The frieze relates that Maceo was killed in battle against the Spanish colonialists on December 7, 1896. A section of the frieze says that his aide, twenty-year-old Panchito Gómez, died with Maceo. On another frieze are the words, "Capitán famoso, patriota intachable, caudillo de los valientes. Su valentia igualó a su lealtad." (Famous captain, exemplary patriot, leader of the valiant ones. His bravery equalled his loyalty.)

In revolutionary Cuba today, Antonio Maceo's life, his accomplishments, and his place in Cuban history are almost as well known as those of Martí and Che Guevara. He is honored as an unwavering fighter for independence, an anti-imperialist, and a consistent spokesman for the equality of all Cubans, black and white. He represents today what is considered the very best in Cuban history and society. It is no accident that in 1958, Fidel Castro commissioned his companion-in-arms, the hero of Sierra Maestra, Camilo Cienfuegos, to duplicate the legendary invasion of the western province of Cuba first carried through by Maceo. He named the column assigned to Cienfuegos "Antonio Maceo." After the triumph of the Revolution, the airport in Oriente, that section of Cuba in which the "Bronze Titan" was born, was named "Antonio Maceo."

Of the three individuals most closely associated with Cuba's struggle for independence—Jóse Martí, Máximo Gómez, and Antonio Maceo—Martí is known in the United States through translations of a section of his vast writings and through two biographies, neither of which, unfortunately, is a first-class study of this remarkable man. There are occasional references to Gómez in American history books. But Antonio Maceo is practically an unknown figure. In the May 1931 issue of *The Crisis,* official organ of the National Association for the Advancement of Colored People, Arthur A. Schomburg, who was born in Puerto Rico and was an extraordinary collector of books, prints, and manuscripts dealing with African and African-derived peoples, wrote:

> I know of no man of military standing in the whole of America—white, yellow, or black—that can excel the exploits of Antonio Maceo. Toussaint L'Ouverture had Wendell Phillips to enlighten an English-speaking world to his greatness. . . . Yet the world knows little of Maceo, the ablest and noblest of American-born cavalry leaders, unsurpassed by any which the new world has produced.[1]

Actually, Schomburg was referring only to the English-speaking world. For there is a vast body of literature on Antonio Maceo in the Spanish language. In 1945, on the occasion of the centennial of Maceo's birth, a seventy-two-page bibliography was published, consisting of books and articles dealing with the career of the "Bronze Titan."[2] However, all were in

Spanish. Indeed, apart from obituaries and tributes published at the time of his death, there are only three items in the English language devoted to Maceo's career.[3] The first is a twenty-four-page one-act play by Willis Richardson, which forms part of *Negro History in Thirteen Plays,* by Richardson and May Miller, published in 1935. Ten years later, the second English-language item appeared—*Antonio Maceo: An Historical Sketch,* a thirty-page pamphlet by Luis Rolando Cabrera, originally published in Spanish and translated by Beatrice M. Ash and Elsa Lecrona. In 1954, the first serious and scholarly study of Antonio Maceo in English appeared: Laurence Richard Nichols' unpublished doctoral dissertation at Duke University. Since then, only two articles in English have been published in scholarly journals: my own in the *Journal of Negro History* (1970) and Patricia Weiss Fagen's in the *Latin American Research Review* (1976).

In the second volume of my *History of Cuba and Its Relations with the United States,* published in 1963, and in the first volume of my *The Spanish-Cuban-American War and the Birth of American Imperialism, 1895–1902,* published in 1972, I have dealt with Antonio Maceo in the course of discussions of the long and inspiring story of Cuba's struggle for independence. But the time is long overdue for the publication of a volume in the English language devoted exclusively to the career of this great figure in Hispano-American history.

Antonio Maceo was officially considered a mulatto in Cuba, but in the United States he was considered black. Yet some who admired him tried to deny his color. Just after his death in battle in 1896, J. Syme-Hastings' tribute to him was published in the *Journal of the Knights of Labor.* In the concluding pages of this volume, I have reprinted sections of the laudatory critique by the southern white journalist. Here it is worth noting that Syme-Hastings insisted:

> I have always denied and deny now that Maceo was a Negro, as many of the papers contend. That he was dark, I will admit, but it

> was a bronze-black from exposure—there was nothing of even the mulatto in the fine, shapely head and fine forehead, the prominent arched nose, the thin, eloquent lips or the air of refinement with which he was ever surrounded.[4]

Years later, in 1945, a Cuban historian, Luis Rolando Cabrera, author of the pamphlet mentioned above, echoed the American reporter in celebrating Maceo's heroism on the centennial of his birth. In the course of his brief historical sketch, he mentioned neither race nor color until the last page, where he noted that Maceo was by origin "mulatto and poor"; otherwise, the Cuban hero was described as "browned by the tropical sun."[5] It would seem that Maceo's blackness somehow made him less fully Cuban! As the reader will discover below, this was an aspect of racism in Cuba that Maceo had to endure all his life, even among those who were his compatriots in the cause of Cuban independence. Fortunately since the Revolution of 1959, this is no longer a problem. In such works as Raúl Aparcio's *Hombradía de Maceo* (Havana, 1967); José Antonio Portuondo's *El Pensamiento Vivo de Maceo* (Havana, 1963); and *La Vida Heroica y Ejemplar de Antonio Maceo* (Havana, 1963), by the Cuban historian and leading authority on Antonio Maceo, José Luciano Franco, the point is made clear that in his own mind and work, Maceo identified himself with other blacks and mulattoes in Cuba. Moreover, unlike too many studies published in Cuba, even those of a laudatory nature, which depict Maceo solely as "a great warrior, a man of action but not of ideas,"[6] the new studies show clearly that he made a vast contribution to Cuba's heritage of social and political ideas, as well as to its revolutionary military traditions.

I have received most generous help in writing this book. I particularly wish to acknowledge my indebtedness to the Archivo Nacional, Havana, the Library of the City Historian of Havana, the Biblioteca Nacional, Havana, the Central University of Las Villas, and the Institute of History, Academy of

Sciences, Havana, for placing their facilities at my disposal during several visits to Cuba for the purpose of research. I also wish to thank José Luciano Franco, José Antonio Portuondo, Juan Marinello, Carlos Rafael Rodríguez, Dr. Julio Le Riverend, Director of the Academy of Sciences, Institute of History, Cuba, and Professor Sergio Aguirre, Department of History, University of Havana, for the opportunity to discuss with them various aspects of Antonio Maceo's career. I am especially grateful for the opportunity of spending many enriching hours at the Archivo Nacional discussing with José Luciano Franco both the political concepts of Antonio Maceo and his place in world history. My thanks also to Fabio Grobart and Pedro Serviat for warm hospitality during a research visit to Cuba.

I also wish to thank the National Archives, Washington, D.C., the Library of Congress, the New York Public Library, the Schomburg Division of the New York Public Library, Duke University Library, Howard University Library, Harvard University Library, University of Florida Library, University of Michigan Library, Yale University Library, and the Library at Lincoln University, Pennsylvania. The late Dr. Julio Girona of Havana was extremely helpful in obtaining documents, articles, and books from libraries in Cuba and in arranging for them to be sent to me in the United States. My wife, Roslyn Held Foner, was of tremendous assistance in translating sources from the Spanish, and my brother, Henry Foner, read the entire manuscript and made valuable suggestions.

—Philip S. Foner

Lincoln University, Pennsylvania

1

Prologue

José Antonio de la Caridad Maceo y Grajales was born on June 14, 1845, in Majaguabo, San Luis, in the province of Oriente, Cuba.[1] He was the son of Marcos Maceo, a black, and a light-brown woman, Mariana Grajales y Cuello, both free blacks. Marcos Maceo was born in Venezuela and as a young man witnessed the struggle for independence in Hispanic America. On July 5, 1811, the independent Provinces of Venezuela were established, and from Caracas, Simón Bolívar set out to achieve, together with José San Martín, the expulsion of Spain from the New World.[2]

Marcos Maceo and his younger brother, Doroteo, remained loyal to Spain, and both fought with the Spanish army. With the battle of Ayacucho in Peru on December 9, 1824, the Spanish forces were decisively defeated. The complete overthrow of Spanish rule on the American mainland—north, central, and south—had been achieved, never thereafter to be reestablished. Out of the debacle, Spain managed to salvage only two islands in the West Indies: Cuba and Puerto Rico.

With the defeat of Spain, the Maceo family decided to leave Venezuela and emigrate to Santo Domingo. Clara Maceo, the mother, two sons, Marcos and Doroteo, and two daughters, Bárbara and María de Rosario, arrived in Santo Domingo in

1825. It was a time of great instability in the islands, so the Maceos left for Cuba—Spain's "Ever Faithful Isle."[3] To get into Cuba, however, was no easy matter. In 1817, King Ferdinand VII of Spain, under British pressure, had signed a treaty prohibiting Spanish subjects from "engaging in the slave trade on the coasts of Africa," and that same year he issued a royal *cédula* prohibiting the admission of colored people into Cuba.[4] By the use of money, or perhaps by other methods, the Maceos managed to evade the law. They entered through the port city of Santiago de Cuba and settled in a modest house on Providencia Street. Doroteo continued his military career and joined the Spanish army in Oriente. Marcos started a small business in agricultural products.

In 1843, Marcos Maceo entered into a common-law marriage with Mariana Grajales, who was then about thirty-five years old and whose first husband had died in 1838. (The marriage was legitimatized before the parish priest on July 6, 1851.) Mariana Grajales had had four sons by her first marriage, and was to give birth to nine children during her second. The entry at the time of the baptism of her first son after her marriage to Marcos Maceo—Antonio Maceo y Grajales—lists her as a native of Santiago de Cuba. Marcos was also listed in this fashion. This was due to the fact that he deliberately falsified his records to avoid the decree, enacted after the slave revolts of 1844, in which free blacks were active, which expelled all free colored people who had come from another country.[5]

As Marcos Maceo's agricultural-commercial business prospered, the family added two small farms to their residence in Santiago: "La Esperanza" and "La Delicia." Both were located in a rich agricultural area of hills, valleys, and small rivers on the shoulders of the Sierra Maestra mountain range in the area of Majaguabo, San Luis. "La Delicia" had nine *caballerías* of good land with a stone house and several buildings for tobacco, storage, and stables. It produced an abundance of coffee, tobacco, bananas, and a variety of fruits that formed a part of the regular diet of Cuban families. It also supported a few beef cattle and horses. As his income from the farm grew, Marcos Maceo acquired still other farms and was regarded as an important member of the local rural middle class.

Antonio Maceo was the first child of Mariana's second marriage, but other children followed rapidly: María Baldomera, José Marcelino, Rafael, Miguel, Julio Dominga de la Calzida, José Tomás, and Marcos. While the growing family lived mostly at "La Delicia," Mariana Maceo took her children to the city for private schooling as they each came of age. Antonio Maceo had three teachers for short periods, but received most of his education at home and in the streets. He went to work at the age of sixteen, transporting and marketing fruits and tobacco by muleback. This took him regularly into the countryside and the knowledge he acquired of the terrain of eastern Cuba and the skill he achieved in horsemanship were later to stand him in good stead. So, too, was the instruction he received from his father in the art of handling firearms and in the use of the Cuban machete.[6]

On February 16, 1866, Antonio married María Magdalena Cabrales y Fernández, a light-brown woman of his neighborhood. They made their home at "La Esperanza." In November of that same year, a daughter, María de la Caridad Maceo, was born.[7] At about the time that Antonio Maceo became a husband and father, Cuba was undergoing a crisis that was soon to change the course of its life.

As we have seen, during the years 1810–1815 Spain's colonies in the New World revolted and achieved their independence. Of what had once been the great Spanish empire—including the West Indies, Mexico, Central and South America, and parts of North America—only Cuba and Puerto Rico remained. Of these two, Cuba was by far the more important to Spain. Following the destruction of the sugar economy of St. Domingue (later to become Haiti), Cuba gradually emerged as the world's largest producer of sugar. By 1838, it was the prize of Spain's greatly reduced overseas empire. Its contribution to the Spanish treasury made it an important possession for the perpetually bankrupt Spanish monarchy.

As the sugar economy expanded, slaves poured into Cuba from Africa. Between 1762 and 1838, about 391,000 blacks were brought to the island, and despite the acceptance by Spain in 1817 of the British-inspired agreement to end the slave trade in 1820, the flow of slaves from Africa not only continued but increased. Slaves were imported illegally in greater numbers after 1817 than when the trade was legal.

Cuba's white society was made up mainly of Creoles, born in the New World, and Peninsulares, born in Spain. The political affairs of the island were dominated by the Peninsulares, who occupied almost all of the positions in the colonial bureaucracy and who also dominated commercial life. The Creoles, on the other hand, were principally landowners—cattle raisers, and tobacco, coffee, and sugar planters—and professionals.

An inevitable conflict developed between these two groups that increased in intensity during the nineteenth century. While the Peninsulares were fanatically pro-Spain, as might be expected because of the political and economic advantages that Spanish policies afforded them, the Creoles resented the restrictions imposed by the Peninsulares upon their political aspirations and on their freedom to trade under Spanish mercantilist policies. Although Cuba was emerging as the world's largest producer of sugar, it was still functioning under Spain's backward and chaotic colonial policies. The sugar revolution gave even greater wealth and political power to the Peninsulares, and although new immigrants from Spain were able to participate in the accumulation of great wealth, the substantial investments required for effective sugar production were major obstacles for the advancement of the Creole small producer and landholder.

Again, a leading characteristic of the island's political life was the notorious corruption of Spanish officials. The ideas of the Creoles inevitably ran counter to Spanish colonial policy. Furthermore, as they came into contact, through travel, with conditions in other countries, particularly in the nearby United States, the Creoles increasingly resented the corrupt, inefficient, and frequently repressive Spanish colonial rule in Cuba.

Some Creoles believed that only through independence could Cuba achieve a modern political and economic form of society. Even during the Latin American independence struggles there were Cubans who favored joining the war for independence against Spain and ridding the island of the domination of the home country. In 1825, in order to assist these revolutionaries, Mexico and Venezuela planned an expedition to Cuba. But the United States, fearing that an independent Cuba would bring about an end to slavery, which would have repercussions in the Southern states, let it be known that it would block any move to liberate Cuba. It was also influenced by its belief that in due time, under the operation of the law of political economy, Cuba would fall into its lap. The United States was not only becoming a major market for Cuban sugar, but, despite Spanish restrictions, an important source for its manufactured goods. As John Quincy Adams put it, as long as Cuba remained part of Spain it would in time, like a ripe apple, fall into the lap of the United States.

After the 1820s, independence movements rose and fell in Cuba. The struggle for liberation from Spain was retarded by the fact that the black population grew enormously with the rise of the sugar economy. In 1842, the official census reported a population of 1,037,624 inhabitants: 448,291 white, 152,838 free blacks, and 436,495 black slaves. The danger of insurrections increased with the growth of the slave population, and Cuban planters came increasingly to look upon the Spanish government, and particularly the Spanish military power on the island, as their major safeguard against rebellious slaves.

To be sure, the value of Spanish protection of person and

property in a slave society clashed with the restrictions imposed upon the island by Spanish imperial policies. The Cuban planters demanded the right to buy goods from countries other than Spain and to sell their products in a market larger than that offered by the imperial country. But as long as slavery was the key to Cuba's prosperity, and Spanish power offered protection against the slaves, the Creoles swallowed their distaste for the repressive features of Spanish rule and turned a deaf ear to appeals for the liberation of the island from the home country.

Both the Peninsulares and Creoles opposed any attempts on the part of Spain, spurred on by England, to alter or abolish slavery—the key to Cuban prosperity. It is not surprising, therefore, that whenever Spain appeared to be veering toward the support of the abolition of slavery, there emerged schemes for annexation to the United States, where slavery flourished. But as the fears that Spain might interfere with slavery subsided, annexationist sentiment in Cuba lost its main appeal. This sentiment continued, but with the main initiative for it now coming from the predominantly proslavery groups in the United States. They saw in the annexation of Cuba a vast area for the expansion of "King Cotton" and the acquisition of increased political power to the national government. The annexationist movement in the United States was doomed, at this time, by Spain's refusal to sell the island to the United States and by the opposition of Northern antislavery expansionist forces to the purchase or seizure of Cuba. With the outbreak of the Civil War in 1861, annexation, for the time being at least, was dead.

In 1865, Spain, suffering from internal dissension and political and economic difficulties, and fearing the rise of independence movements in Cuba, adopted a policy of conciliation toward its colonial possession. A royal decree of November 25, 1865, established a Colonial Reform Commission to discuss proposals for reforms on the island. Despite conservative opposition in Madrid, the Spanish colonies in the Antilles elected twenty commissioners, sixteen from Cuba and the remaining four from Puerto Rico.

The election of the Cuban commissioners and the debates in Madrid created a wave of excitement on the island and nurtured the hope that at last the long-awaited reform of Cuban political and economic life was on the way. The complete failure of the reform commission led to bitter protests on the island, but Spain paid no heed to them. Indeed, early in 1867, the Spanish government, without consulting the colonies, imposed a new tax on the island, ranging from 6 to 12 percent, on real estate, incomes, and all types of businesses. The new tax came on top of the enormous customs duties against which the Cubans had continuously complained. Coming at a time of economic depression on the island, the new tax stimulated a tremendous increase in political discontent and brought to a head long-standing grievances. This was particularly true in the eastern, or Oriente, section of the island, where the smaller planters felt the burden of Spanish repression most sharply. Meeting in Masonic Lodges and other political clubs, the rebellious forces planned a revolutionary uprising to liberate the island.[8]

While the Cubans were planning, the Puerto Rican revolutionaries rose in revolt. Puerto Rican revolutionary Dr. Ramón Emeterio Betances had been organizing revolutionary activity on the island since 1863. This activity blossomed forth briefly in the *Grito de Lares* (Cry of Lares) of 1868. On February 24, 1868, a Revolutionary *Junta* was established in the town of Lares and began to plan the immediate liberation of the island. The *Junta* was a revolutionary nucleus led by members of the middle class, but its base was peasant. One of its members was Mariana Bracetti, known as *Brazo de Oro* (Golden Arm), an indication of the important role assigned to women in the Puerto Rican revolutionary movement.

On September 23, 1868, the historic rebellion of Lares broke out, and the Revolutionary *Junta* proclaimed a Puerto Rican

Republic. Unfortunately, Dr. Betances was unable to supply the uprising with the needed arms and munitions, and, despite heroic resistance, the small revolutionary forces were overwhelmed.

The Spanish authorities were convinced that there was close communication between the revolutionaries in Puerto Rico and Cuba. General Paviá, governor of Puerto Rico, wrote to the Spanish Minister of War: "It is not to be doubted that connivance existed between the chiefs of this island and those of Cuba."[9]

Early in October 1868 an event occurred that forced the Cuban revolutionaries to abandon their plans for an uprising on Christmas Eve that year. A telegram from General Lersundi to Colonel Udaeta, governor of Bayamo, was intercepted by a telegrapher friendly to the revolutionaries. It read: "Cuba belongs to Spain and for Spain she must be kept no matter who is governing. Send to prison D. Carlos Manuel de Céspedes, Francisco Vicente Aguilera, Pedro Figueredo, Francis Maceo Osorio, Bartolomé Masó, Francisco Javier de Céspedes. . . ." The conspiracy had been discovered. The wife of one of the rebels, Trinidad Ramírez, had revealed the plan in confession to her priest, who had convinced her that it was her religious duty to inform the authorities.[10]

On the morning of October 10, 1868, Carlos Manuel de Céspedes, accompanied by only thirty-seven men—all planters from Oriente—proclaimed the independence of Cuba in the historic *Grito de Yara* from his plantation, "La Demajagua," near Yara, in the vicinity of Manzanillo. On the same day, Céspedes liberated his slaves and incorporated them into his small and poorly armed forces. He also issued a prepared manifesto stating the causes of the revolt and listing its officers, with himself as general-in-chief.

The manifesto, issued in the name of the *Junta Revolucionaria de la Isla de Cuba*, declared that the revolt was due to arbitrary government, abusive taxation, corrupt administration, the exclusion of Cubans from government employment, their similar exclusions from the Cortés, the legislative body, and the deprivation of political, civil, and religious liberties, particularly the rights of assembly and petition. Explicit references were made to the failure of the Colonial Reform Commission of 1865–1867:

> . . . as great nations have sprung from revolt against a similar disgrace, after having exhausted pleadings for relief, as we despair of justice from Spain through reasoning and can no longer live deprived of the rights which other people enjoy, we are constrained to appeal to arms and to assert our rights on the battlefield, cherishing the hope that our grievances will be sufficient cause for this last resort to redress them and to secure our future welfare.

The announced objectives were the culmination of the demands of Cuban agitators developed over half a century:

> To the God of our conscience, and to all civilized nations, we submit the sincerity of our purpose. . . . We only want to be free and to see all men with us equally free, as the Creator intended all mankind to be. Our earnest belief is that all men are brethren. We respect the lives and property of all peaceful citizens even though they be Spaniards resident in this territory; we admire universal suffrage which assures the sovereignty of the people; and we desire the gradual indemnified emancipation of slaves, the free interchange with nations which use the principle of reciprocity, national representation to decree laws and taxes, and, in general, we demand the religious observance of the inalienable rights of man. We constitute an independent nation because we believe that beneath the Spanish roof we shall never enjoy the complete exercise of our rights.[11]

Following this declaration of independence, the provisional government of the Republic of Cuba was organized at Bayamo.

The manifesto proclaiming independence basically represented the interests of the Cuban landowners in the eastern provinces. They sought an important position for themselves on the island and wished to end commercial restrictions on their economic development—neither of which, they were convinced, could be achieved under Spanish domination. The manifesto's policy on slavery did not differ in any way from that advanced by reformers prior to the reform commission of 1865–1867: gradual emancipation with government payment of indemnities to owners. Both the reformers and the organizers of the revolutionary movement of 1868 proposed a conservative solution to the "social question," a solution which was to follow the achievement of political and economic freedom. The abolitionist section of the manifesto was to be put into operation *after* the revolution emerged victorious. "When we have made the Republican flag triumph," said Céspedes, "and we have forced the representatives of the Spanish government to leave Cuba precipitously, the revolution will take care of this vital question."[12]

Clearly, then, the demand for the immediate emancipation of the slaves played no part in the action taken at Yara. Nevertheless, the momentous decision in the *Grito de Yara* to raise the banner of revolt against Spanish rule was the most important event in Cuban history up to that time. What is especially significant is that this small band of men was determined to pursue the revolt against incredible odds. But victory could not be achieved without involving the black masses, and without allowing them to rise to high rank in the revolutionary army if their services proved essential to the struggle for independence.

It was in such an atmosphere that the career of the greatest man of color in Cuban history—Antonio Maceo—began to unfold.

2

The Ten Years' War: Part 1

At an early age, Antonio Maceo showed an interest in the political issues of his day. He learned to hate slavery, the evidences of which he saw during his trips into the countryside, and, like other members of the Maceo family, he came to view Spanish domination as the cause of economic hardship. Despite the lack of a formal education, he was keen and perceptive and soon caught the attention of Santiago lawyer Don Ascencio de Ascencio, who introduced him to a group of merchants and other friends who were involved in "subversive" political activities. In contrast to the rest of the island, which was dominated by large sugar plantations, society in Oriente was relatively fluid, and interaction between the races was frequent and natural.[1]

In 1864, Maceo became a member of the Masonic Lodge of Santiago de Cuba, and entered the inner revolutionary circle. As a young man, he was already associated with the most anti-Spanish elements on the island. He learned of the revolutionary activity in the first weeks of 1868 through his friend and companion, Exuperancio Alvarez, and a short time later his father, Marcos Maceo, obtained knowledge of the proposed insurrectionary movement and gave it his full approval.[2]

The news of the first clash with the Spaniards on October 12, 1868, at Yara spread quickly, and that night the rebels ate supper at the Maceo house in Majaguabo. After the meal, Marcos Maceo was asked for horses and a contribution. He gave four ounces of gold, a dozen good machetes, two revolvers, four shotguns, and a blunderbuss. The rebels also recruited three black volunteers: Antonio and José Maceo, and Justo Regüeyferes Grajales, half-brother of the Maceo boys.[3] According to a later account by María Cabrales, Antonio's wife, the mother of the Maceo "heroic tribe" was so fired with emotion at that moment that she issued the following command: "Everyone, parents and children, kneel before Christ, who was the first liberal man who came to the world, and swear to free the country or die for it."[4]

Riding his best horse and carrying a machete which he used in his work, Antonio Maceo received his baptism by fire in the village of Ti-Arriba that night. In that very first battle the qualities that were to make him an outstanding fighter and leader of men became so apparent that he was immediately promoted to the rank of sergeant.[5]

While Antonio was fighting, a Spaniard, Tomás Sánchez, revealed to the Spanish authorities the assistance the Maceo family was giving the revolutionary movement. Aware of the danger, the entire family abandoned their home at Majaguabo and joined the rebel forces. Spanish soldiers soon appeared at the abandoned home to burn it down and surprised Rafael Maceo, sixteen years old, who had returned to get some forgotten personal effects. They took him to prison. When Marcos Maceo learned of what had happened to his son, he went to the authorities and offered to substitute himself for the boy. Instead, he was himself imprisoned without obtaining the release of his son. Rafael was able to escape and eventually reached the forces in which Antonio served. Marcos obtained his freedom through the aid of two Spanish friends and joined his sons in the rebel force. Thus, the whole Maceo family was forced to live in rebel camps in the countryside as far away as possible from the policed towns and villages where they might be denounced to the Spanish authorities. Even so, Justo Regüeyferes was captured and executed while trying to visit his wife. He was the first of Mariana Grajales' eight sons to fall in the struggle for the independence of Cuba.[6]

Events moved rapidly in the early days of the Ten Years' War. In Havana, an official Spanish newspaper had dismissed the news of the *Grito de Yara* as inconsequential, announcing derisively that "a handful of deluded, badly armed fellows had uttered a cry of rebellion in Yara."[7] There was good reason for this early contempt for the *mambises,* as the Cuban rebels were called.[8] The first patriot forces consisted of just 147 volunteers who did not even have a weapon apiece; their arms consisted of 45 fowling pieces, 4 rifles, and a few pistols and machetes. Since they were forced into action before their organizational system had been completed, the leaders of the rebellion operated in their respective areas with little more than their former slaves and without any close contact between them. No wonder the Spanish authorities took the rebellion lightly.

But the rebel leaders, with their motley crews of poorly armed patriots, engaged the Spaniards in a series of minor skirmishes, and the revolt developed rapidly. The patriot army quickly grew as the Cuban masses, white and black (free and slave), joined the movement, especially in the rural areas. By October 12, Céspedes already had 4,000 men; toward the end of the month, his army numbered 9,700; and by November 8, 12,000.[9] The blacks were to form a considerable part of the Cuban army throughout the revolution; nearly all were operating without uniforms and with an amazing variety of weapons. The Cuban troops often overpowered an enemy contingent entirely through the element of surprise and with few arms other than their machetes. This heavy, two-foot-long knife was an implement with which the peasants, black and white, were familiar and already well supplied. They were commonly used for cutting sugar cane and hacking paths through the tropic vegetation. In battle, machetes were effective weapons, and a Spanish soldier could quickly lose an arm from a single blow.

Half-armed, ragged, ill-fed, but burning with revolutionary zeal, the patriot forces defeated the Spaniards at Yara, Baire, and Jiguaní, the last victory being accomplished by troops under the command of General Donato Mármol. On October 15, they laid siege to Bayamo, a city of ten thousand people, and on the nineteenth, they captured it. Céspedes established the government of the Republic of Cuba in the captured city.

With each new victory, more and more recruits were added to the rebel forces. At the same time, the revolutionaries received aid which proved to be very opportune, in view of their lack of military experience. A group of Dominican exiles, led by Máximo Gómez, Luis Marcano, and Modesto Díaz, utilizing the experience they had gained in the Dominican wars against Spain, became instructors of military strategy and tactics. The military experience of these men was to prove invaluable for the revolutionary cause. None contributed more to this cause than Gómez.

Máximo Gómez was born in Bani, Santo Domingo, the child of a prosperous family which furnished him with a good education. He fought the Haitians and lost all of his property in the Civil War of 1866 in Santo Domingo. He became a farmer in Bayamo, and, when the Ten Years' War broke out, he enlisted as sergeant, rapidly rising to the highest ranks in the revolutionary army. A master of guerrilla and "scorched earth" warfare, Gómez explained years later why he had joined the revolutionary cause in a country that was not his own:

> When I arrived in this land and saw the plight of the poor workers, I felt wounded with sadness. There was this poor wretch working beside magnificent grandeur; beside all that beautiful richness was so much misery and so much low morality. When I saw the wife and children of the poor worker covered with rags

and living in a battered hut, I was touched with the enormity of the contrast. When I asked for the school and was told that there had never been one, and when I entered innumerable towns and saw no culture, no morality, no clean people, no acceptable living accommodations and was received by the mayor and the priest, then I felt indignant and profoundly disposed against the elevated classes of the country.[10]

With reinforcements and guidance from the Dominicans, the rebels defeated Spanish detachments, cut railway lines, and gained dominance over vast sections of the eastern portion of the island. On October 28, Holguín rose in arms; by November 8, the patriots had advanced within a mile of Santiago de Cuba, the capital of Oriente. On November 4, a group of Cubans in the province of Camagüey, led by Ignacio Agramonte y Loynaz, raised the flag of revolt. Agramonte was aided by the arrival of a well supplied expeditionary force under the command of General Manuel de Quesada, who had won his rank in the Mexican Army. This force also included Manuel and Julio Sanguilly and a group of Havana youths. On February 9, 1869, Las Villas district rose in arms under the direction of General Federico Cavada, a colonel in the U.S. Volunteer Service during the Civil War.

As the number of skirmishes multiplied, as the Cuban victories mounted, and as the damage to Spanish forces increased, the Spanish provisional government of General Prim began a full-scale military buildup. Thousands of youths and men were mustered in Spanish villages and hamlets and loaded on ships at Cadiz and Vigo to fight and die in Cuba. From November 1868 to December 1869, Spain sent its finest officers to the Cuban war to command 35,000 veteran soldiers and thousands of others who were not too well trained. In addition, it sent fourteen warships and a train of artillery equipped with the latest model Krupp cannons.

On the sea, of course, Spain held complete sway; the revolutionaries had no navy at all, and by the end of 1869 Spain had a powerful fleet based on Cuba—about fifty vessels of 400 guns, including the iron-clads *Victoria* and *Zaragoza.* This was no small advantage, for it often enabled Spain to keep outside aid, in the forms of arms and men, from reaching the rebels. In spite of Spain's vigilance, considerable material did reach the Cubans. In June 1869 the Revolutionary *Junta* in the United States claimed that seven or eight expeditions had reached Cuba from American waters. The *Junta* was made up of revolutionaries residing in the United States and some American sympathizers. It had, by then, succeeded in delivering more than 20,000 small arms, twenty-two small cannon, and a large number of men, most of whom were Cubans and other veterans of the Civil War. General Thomas Jordan, a well-known Confederate officer, landed in Cuba in May 1869, and was soon made Cuban chief-of-staff.[11]

With these supplies of arms and ammunition, the Liberating Army was able, for several months, to offer strong resistance to the powerful Spanish forces and to win important victories. But by the late summer of 1869 the United States government stopped the flow of arms and ammunition. Although supplies continued to come from Latin America and Jamaica, it was a mere trickle compared with the needs of the insurgents.

Faced with a great inferiority in numbers and materials, the insurgents were forced to adopt the only logical military strategy—guerrilla warfare. They could not sustain the heavy losses caused by frequent large-scale battles under traditional warfare. The main policy of the *insurrectos* was attrition, to discourage and tire the Spanish armies and the Spanish government; the great hope in this strategy lay in making the war economically disastrous for Spain, and thereby forcing the Spaniards to sue for peace. This required that the rebel fighting units create the greatest possible economic dislocation by cutting railway and telegraph lines, destroying sugar mills and other valuable property, preventing any profitable production, and generally paralyzing commercial and economic activity on the island.

The type of strategy employed by the rebels involved innumerable small skirmishes and few large battles. Occasionally they were unwittingly drawn into large-scale combat, and at rare intervals they entered into it for prestige and morale purposes. But the *insurrectos* usually avoided large battles unless they believed they held a decided edge, and on the terrain in which they preferred to operate.

Armed with machetes, with a variety of firearms, and with scanty supplies of ammunition, the guerrillas roved the weeds and poured out of ambuscades. They cut railway lines and aqueducts, destroyed communications, and burned the plantations and estates of those not in sympathy with their cause. Often, after the Spaniards had removed roadblocks and rebuilt burned bridges, the roads were cut again in their rear. The Spaniards held possession of every seaport and most of the towns on the island; the guerrilla bands often controlled the mountain bridges and forests less than a mile away. Their aim was to confine the Spanish army to the cities, and then, by cutting the roads, to isolate the units and force them to surrender. When enemy troops were sent out, the guerrillas hid in the depths of the interior where they dared not follow. The Spaniards shelled, strafed, and fired at the unseen enemy, and returned to boast of having "cleaned up" the rebels. But no sooner had the report been made than the resistance burst forth again. Thus the pattern continued throughout the long war.

What the Cuban army lacked in numbers, experience, warfare training, and arms and equipment was often compensated for by their thorough knowledge of the country, effective use of guerrilla tactics, greater immunity to cholera and other diseases that flourished on the island, and above all, patriotic devotion. The most important asset of guerrilla warfare is an ideal; the rebels were fighting for the liberation of their country, and this gave them the popular support without which a guerrilla movement cannot be effective. "Every tree and flower and grass had a use or virtue with which they seemed acquainted," reported James J. O'Kelly, the Irish journalist. The *guajiro* and the *campesino,* the slave and the free black, not only moved steadily into the ranks of the Liberating Army, but aided and shielded the patriotic fighters, even though they risked their own lives by so doing.

The guerrilla warfare carried on by the rebels over a period of years was commanded by Máximo Gómez, Calixto García, and Ignacio Agramonte. (Agramonte was the only one of the three who did not survive the war. He was killed in 1873 in a skirmish at Jimaguayu.) All three were masters of guerrilla strategy, but General Gómez developed this type of fighting to perfection. It was according to his plan that the *insurrectos* were divided into highly mobile small units, operating continually on the move. The army, however, retained effective overall command and organization, which permitted a concentration of troops at any given time.[12]

It was inevitable, in this new type of warfare, that the older leaders, accustomed to traditional military strategy, would lose prestige and that new and younger men would gain in standing. It was in this respect that Maceo was to prove himself one of the great guerrilla fighters of all time. In skirmish after skirmish, particularly in those of El Cristo and El Cobre at the very outset of the war, Maceo showed such exceptional courage, initiative, and leadership that he was quickly promoted, first to the rank of sergeant and then to captain.[13]

It was during the campaign of Bayamo that Maceo first won real distinction. The easy and rapid victory of the rebel army and the occupation of this important town made them optimistic that the war might soon be over. To dispel this illusion, the Spanish captain general of the island, Francisco Lersundi, dispatched a powerful military column, under the command of the Count of Valmaseda, to drive the Cuban troops and government from Bayamo. In the face of this imminent danger, Céspedes ordered Generals Díaz and Mármol to engage Valmaseda at the Caute River in order to halt his advance. Captain Maceo was operating in Mármol's forces, under the immediate command of Colonel Pio Rosado.[14] As the Spanish column approached the advanced Cuban position, Colonel Rosado left Maceo in charge of his unit while he hurried to General Mármol to announce that the enemy column could not be stopped. Meanwhile, Maceo fell upon the vanguard of the Spanish forces with such determination and fury that he forced their retreat and temporarily halted the entire column. Having achieved what Rosado had declared was impossible, Maceo reported his success to General Mármol, who praised him enthusiastically. Maceo's courage, initiative, and ability, in contrast to Rosado's defeatism, greatly enhanced his prestige in the eyes of the revolutionary leaders.[15]

Maceo's victory was only the first round in the larger battle for Bayamo. The more experienced General Valmaseda completely outmaneuvered Mármol, and suprised the main body of the Cuban forces at El Saladillo on January 7, 1869, completely routing them. This defeat was not due solely to Mármol's inexperience and faulty strategy. The Cuban division was composed of 4,000 untried exslave troops, armed only with machetes, and 500 black and white troops, armed with an assortment of rifles and various types of firearms. More than 2,000 Cubans, most of them the recently freed slaves, died in this encounter. On the next day, remnants of the defeated division and other Cuban units continued the battle on the plain of La Caridad, and two days later, after clashing with Díaz's forces, Valmaseda crossed the Caute River and found an open route to Bayamo.

Maceo's unit was one of the few that maintained discipline after the bitter defeat of El Saladillo. Under his command, it constantly harassed and inflicted damage on the rear guard of the Spanish column. On January 15, Valmaseda entered

Bayamo, but found it a smoldering ruin. The Cuban defenders of the city had burned it to the ground when they realized they could not keep it out of Spanish hands.[16]

On January 16, 1869, in recognition of his meritorious conduct during the Bayamo campaign, Antonio Maceo was promoted to the rank of commander. A further reward was indicated in the decision to allow the intrepid black to operate with independent forces, although he was still under the organizational jurisdiction of General Mármol.[17]

With greater freedom to formulate his own tactics, young Maceo began to operate brilliantly in guerrilla actions near Mayari and Guantánamo, and as early as January 26, he received a promotion to lieutenant colonel of the Liberating Army.[18] Too often among Cuban military leaders, intrigues and personal aspirations interfered with necessary effective military operations. But in Maceo's encampment, there were only two objectives—winning military victories and securing the goals of the revolution. Maceo instilled in his men the concepts of discipline, duty, and the aims of the revolution, and the soldiers, in turn, showed him not only respect, but love.[19] He set a high example for them, for he never seemed to rest. The majority of his troops relaxed after a combat, but Maceo, together with his escort, immediately roved the area, preparing the next ambush. Like an experienced officer, matured in the career of arms, he took advantage of the terrain with care and certainty. Gómez, under whose instructions Maceo was to fully develop the art of guerrilla warfare, noted that from the first month of the war the black commander displayed an uncanny ability to prepare all the details before entering into combat; that he took all the necessary precautions to keep his troops covered in case of a surprise; and that his retreats were well planned and took place in successive stages.[20]

On many occasions, Spanish officers were completely fooled by Maceo's whirlwind attacks against their superior forces.

When the initial attack was repulsed and the seemingly desperate retreat was followed up by the Spaniards, they found themselves suddenly trapped in a well prepared ambush on unfavorable terrain. Maceo delighted in outsmarting the Spanish generals; again and again, he decoyed them into situations that were disastrous to them.[21]

When he was not fighting, Maceo took advantage of the old *palenques,* the abandoned shelters constructed by fugitive slaves in the depths of the forest or in the most inaccessible mountain retreats. In these natural sanctuaries, he established crude hospitals, workshops, living quarters for the families of the troops, and food stores which were operated by his mother and wife—Mariana Grajales and María Cabrales. Of these two remarkable women, General Enrique Loynez del Castillo wrote:

> María Cabrales de Maceo is an honorable model of the Cuban woman. She appeared in the encampment among the hurrahs of those valiant Orientales. They knew her virtues from the time when she was a child, and her virtues were even more admired than her impeccable beauty. With her companions she conquered the wild and difficult mountains, and none was more agile in climbing to the summit, nor more solicitous in caring for the sick. Only Mariana Grajales, the mother of the Maceos—who can only be compared to Cornelia of the Gracchi—only she could match her as a majestic character in the grand epic.

Whenever conditions permitted it, Maceo used the sloops of the network of illicit traffic operating in the Caribbean to import, in small lots, medicines, salt, ammunition, and other indispensable necessities from Jamaica, Santo Domingo, or Haiti. The other main source of war materials, and therefore a constant objective in all military engagements, was the taking of enemy booty. Through these two sources, Maceo managed to see to it that neither food, clothing, nor munitions were lacking. The 200 men who comprised his forces were relatively well fed, well dressed, and well armed.[22]

Maceo's military successes continued unchecked. In the period from February to May 1869 he defeated the Spaniards in several bitter clashes. In one of these, on May 14, 1869, his father, Marcos Maceo, was killed at his side. By now, Mariana Grajales had lost a son and a husband. "Her unhappiness," wrote Emeterio S. Santovenia, "urged her in direct ratio to her pain to continue in the work of destroying the chains which kept Cuba bound, and Mariana Grajales, living incarnation of Cuban patriotism, cried out to the youngest of her sons, still a little boy: 'And *you,* stand up tall; it is already time that you should fight for your country.' "[23]

Notwithstanding the mourning caused by the death of his father, just about a week earlier, Maceo attacked the strongly defended sugar mill, "Armonia," capturing the garrison and reducing the mill to ashes. In the final phase of this action, young Maceo received the first of his innumerable wounds.[24] He was carried back to one of his hidden rest camps, where his wife and mother nursed him back to health. A few weeks later, Maceo and his wife suffered the death of their two small children, victims of the hazards of war. Then in July came the news of the death of his godfather, Don Ascencio, a millionaire in Havana, and his friend and boyhood companion, Exuperancio Alvarez.[25]

During the period when he was not fighting, and during the forced rests resulting from his frequent wounds, Maceo sought to improve his education. Dr. Félix Figueredo, a man of broad culture, spent hours lecturing to Maceo on history, politics, and political science, and supplied him with books to read.[26]

In his attack on the fort of the sugar plantation "Arroyito" in Santa Cruz de Villalón, Maceo captured the fort, the soldiers guarding it, and all the arms. In each of his incursions into the zones rich in sugar cane, Maceo fulfilled one of his basic reasons for fighting: he freed the slaves of the sugar mills and explained to them that one of the major purposes of the war was to wipe out slavery in Cuba. And the slaves, now free men, "swelled the ranks of the Liberating Army."[27]

While the various rebel units were concentrating on winning military victories, the revolution was passing through a series of crises.

The men who raised the banner of revolt at Yara, though great patriots, were still men of wealth and spokesmen for the interests of the Cuban landowners in the eastern provinces. They wanted a revolution that would eliminate Spanish domination, but they also wanted to make sure that it was their class—the *hacendado* class—that controlled the revolution and would dominate once Cuba was liberated.

But from the first day of the war, the essentially conservative character of the insurrectional movement, headed by Céspedes, came into conflict with the aspirations of the popular classes. The Cuban lower classes, black and white, who made up the bulk of the revolutionary army, were fighting not only for the liberation of their country from Spanish tyranny, but also for social reforms—especially for greater political power in the hands of the common people and the abolition of slavery. A conflict inevitably emerged between these two aspirations.

A split occurred over the monopoly of powers vested in Céspedes—commander-in-chief of the army and head of the government. A more fundamental cleavage, however, grew within the revolutionary ranks over the issue of slavery. In his first manifesto as chief of the Revolutionary *Junta,* on October 10, 1868, Céspedes said that "we desire the gradual indemnified emancipation of slaves." Under his plan, even this narrow objective was to be put into operationly only *after* the revolution emerged victorious. For Céspedes, to act on this question before victory was achieved would mean forfeiting the support of the *hacendado* class, particularly the rich Western planters (perhaps 1,500 in number), whom he considered essential for the triumph over Spain. In his concern for the protection of the *hacendados* and their property, including slaves, Céspedes, on November 12, 1868, issued an important decree. It ordered the summary execution by firing squad of "soldiers and officers of the Republican forces who, faithless to their sacred mission, shall burn, rob or defraud the peaceful citizens, *and those who introduce themselves into the farms whether to stir up or remove their work crews.*"[28] Thus, the top leadership of the revolutionary movement assured the slaveowners that they would be able to enjoy the fruits of their work crews in peace.

There were many in the revolutionary ranks who felt that the policy of appeasing the propertied classes, in the hope of winning them over, was not only futile but disastrous to the revolution's success. In fact, soon after the outbreak of the war hopes of receiving support from the *hacendado* class were demonstrated to be illusory. With few exceptions, the *hacendados* of the West, the richest part of Cuba, not only refused to give any help to the revolutionary cause, but placed themselves on the side of the Spanish government. The same was true even in Oriente; the *hacendados* of the sugar zone of Santiago de Cuba quickly pledged their support to Spain and even turned over 10,000 pesos to the Spanish authorities for the purpose of "exterminating the revolution."[29]

It soon became obvious that to cling to a policy of appeasing the *hacendados* would avail nothing. The slaveowners, convinced that their investment in slavery was best protected by the Spanish authorities, had already largely cast their lot with Spain. The appeasement policy seriously weakened the revolution's appeal to the Cuban masses and caused many blacks already in the rebel army to question the antislavery aims of a struggle for which they were ready to give their lives. Finally, it held back thousands of blacks who were prepared to join the revolutionary ranks. Although slaves incorporated into the revolutionary army had been declared free, no formal decree abolishing slavery had been issued. Without such a decree, the status of the black in the Liberating Army was uncertain.

It did not take long for this conflict to come to a head. Céspedes, it will be recalled, had established the capital of the rebel government in Bayamo, the first major town taken by the Liberating Army. On October 28, 1868, ten days after the city was captured, the Revolutionary Municipal Council of Bayamo—two of whose members were blacks—petitioned Céspedes to proclaim the immediate abolition of slavery. The petitions pointed out that it was naive to expect the slave-owners to support the revolution, while failure to proclaim immediate abolition seriously weakened the fighting capacity of the Liberating Army and hampered its ability to attract support from abroad.

Exercising his dictatorial powers, Céspedes rejected the petition. Recognizing the growing opposition to his timid policy on slavery, he decreed on December 27, 1868, a cautious abolitionary measure designed to impress the outside world while not really antagonizing the propertied classes of Cuba. Céspedes recognized publicly "that a free Cuba was incompatible with a slavist Cuba." But he promptly added that abolition of slavery was contingent upon the final success of the revolution. Meanwhile, the Republic would respect slavery, and fugitive slaves belonging to rebel owners would not be admitted into the revolutionary ranks without the consent of their proprietors. Slaves of those who had been convicted of being enemies of the revolution would be confiscated and declared free without payment of an indemnity.[30]

Céspedes' proclamation hardly constituted an advance toward emancipation. It meant that Cuban slaveowners who aided the revolution could, if they wished, continue to enjoy the fruits of slave labor. Nor did Céspedes recognize the liberty of the slaves who joined the revolution. The slave could not enroll in the Liberating Army *unless his master authorized it,* and those who handed over their slaves to the revolutionary service without liberating them were able to keep them as property.[31]

The Revolutionary Assembly of the Central Department, an outgrowth of the Revolutionary Committee of Camagüey, criticized the inadequacies of Céspedes' decree. It called for a more decisive policy for the immediate abolition of slavery, and, on February 26, 1869, issued a declaration which began: "The institution of slavery, introduced into Cuba by Spanish Dominion, must be extinguished along with it." The assembly then announced that slavery was abolished throughout the Central District; that the slaveowners would be indemnified in due time; and that all those who were liberated by the decree would, if suited for it, be welcomed into the Liberating Army, "enjoying the same compensation and the same consideration as other soldiers of the Liberating Army."[32]

Although the decree had no effect in the areas of greatest slave concentration (according to the Census of 1869, the Occidental District had 300,989 slaves and the Central and Oriental Districts, 62,297), and although the rebel forces did not yet control enough territory to give it necessary backing, it was an important statement of aims, for it revealed the rising opposition to Céspedes' conservative policies. Recognizing this opposition, Céspedes conceded that the time had come to end his dictatorial régime and to begin operating on democratic principles. He issued a call for a constitutional convention to be held at Güaímaro, a town thirty-five miles from Puerto Príncipe. It was to draw up a fundamental document for a free Cuba and establish a functioning democratic republic.

The Constitutional Convention met at Güaímaro on April 10, 1869, with delegates present from Villaclara, Sancti Spíritus, Jiguaní, Holguín, and Camagüey. A constitution was adopted providing for a republican form of government to consist of executive, legislative, and judicial departments. The legislative power was vested in a House of Representatives in which there was to be equal representation from each of the four states into which the island of Cuba was divided—Oriente, Camagüey, Las Villas, and Occidente. Céspedes was elected president and Manuel Quesada commander-in-chief.

Article 24 of the first Constitution of Free Cuba, drawn up by the Camagüeyan delegates, declared that "all the inhabitants of the Republic are absolutely free." This certainly represented a victory for the popular forces. So, too, did the replacement of absolute rule by a representative form of government, and the provision in the Constitution that the House of Representatives "shall not abridge the Freedom of Religion, nor of the Press, nor of Public Meetings, nor of Education, nor of Petition, nor any inalienable right of the People."[33]

But the conservative elements were not to be defeated so easily. They scored important victories at Güaímaro. The convention declared that the rebels were fighting for annexation to the United States as well as independence. The Congress of the Cuban Republic, established by the new Constitution, followed this up by asking the United States government to admit Cuba into the Union. During the discussion, it was freely admitted that annexation was the safest way to guarantee that the more radical elements in the revolutionary movement would not emerge triumphant following independence.[34]

The conservatives' victory was particularly evident in the convention's failure to put into effect the constitutional provision abolishing slavery. On July 6, 1869, the House of Representatives rejected the Constitution and instituted instead the *Reglamento de Libertos* (Rule of the Freed), which continued slavery in the Republic, although in a more discreet form. The slave, who was now called *liberto,* was compelled to continue to work for his master, but the latter was not obligated to feed, clothe, or even pay him wages. This system, which remained in force until December 25, 1870, was simply "forced labor." In short, the top leaders of the revolutionary movement, still concerned about antagonizing the *hacendados,* especially of the Occidental District, refused to make all the inhabitants of the Republic "entirely free."[35]

In the Occidental District, where the Liberating Army had not penetrated, the provision in the Constitution abolishing slavery had little practical effect. It did serve, nevertheless, to stimulate the exodus of fugitive slaves who tried to escape to the regions where the rebels exercised control. But when the news reached the slaves in Occidente that they were exchanging slavery for "forced labor," the exodus slowed to a trickle. This permitted the sugar planters to continue production without interference and contributed to Spain's ability to conduct the war. The nullification of the abolition clause of the Güaímaro Constitution also had a dampening effect on the morale of the revolutionary soldiers, many of whom, especially the blacks, felt that the real objectives of the war of liberation were being sabotaged by the conservatives.[36]

Fortunately, the revolutionary spirit of the Liberating Army survived this betrayal. Many of the guerrilla units, like the one led by Maceo, continued to liberate the slaves when they captured sugar plantations and mills, and either recruited the freedmen into the rebel army or set them to work for wages on land confiscated from loyalist planters. The more revolutionary commanders sent emissaries to urge slaves in the Occidental District to escape to Las Villas and Camagüey, where they would be under the protection of the Liberating Army, and where "their masters may lose all hope of recovering them."[37]

Under the pressure of the popular forces, Céspedes made a sharp turn in a more revolutionary direction. In October 1869, he decreed the "destruction of all the cane fields of the island." "Better for the cause of human liberty," the decree declared, "better for the cause of human rights, better for the children of our children, that Cuba should be free, even if we have to burn every vestige of civilization from the tip of Maisí to the tip of San Antonio, so that the Spanish authority shall be eliminated."[38] (Maisí was the eastern tip and San Antonio the western tip of the island.) A month later, Céspedes formally approved the revolutionary practice of urging the uprising of slaves on the plantations.

By the end of 1869, even though "forced labor" was in operation, the revolution, under the pressure of the popular forces, was becoming more and more abolitionist in character. While this had a tremendous effect on the fighting ability of the *mambises* in general, nowhere was it more evident than in the new exploits of Antonio Maceo. For now it seemed clear that a Cuban victory would bring with it the breaking of the chains that bound so many of Maceo's own people to slavery.[39]

3

The Ten Years' War: Part 2

On March 12, 1870, the Dominican Luis Marcano was treacherously assassinated, and on June 26, Donato Mármol was killed. In the reorganization of the Liberating Army that followed, General Máximo Gómez was placed in command of Maceo's area.[1] Gómez and Maceo were to become, from that time on, the dominant military figures in Cuba's drive for independence.

Already an excellent guerrilla warrior, the young Maceo grew even more effective under Gómez's tutelage. Maceo himself acknowledged that he learned more about the strategy of guerrilla war from Gómez than from any other source. As for the Dominican, a man noted for strict discipline and exacting standards, he viewed young Maceo as the embodiment of what a military officer should be. He was, as Gómez informed the Secretary of War, a soldier's soldier.[2]

On July 20, Gómez reorganized his forces. General Calixto García was designated as second in command, while Lieutenant Colonel Antonio Maceo was put in charge of the third battalion. Heading a battalion of only 187 men, Maceo took part in numerous attacks under Gómez's command. On October 2, after repulsing a Spanish attack on his camp in Majaguabo, Maceo received another severe battle wound. By the twentieth, however, he was again active, taking part in the highly successful assault on the town of Ti-Arriba, which resulted in the destruction of the town and the capture of a large quantity of booty.[3] Writing to the Secretary of War, Gómez revealed both his own high regard for the Maceo's fighting ability and also the concern the black warrior was already arousing among the Spaniards:

> Notwithstanding the fact that Valmaseda [commanding general of the eastern district for the Spaniards] had concentrated his operations in this district, bringing in considerable reinforcements, he has had little success, and I do not believe he will ever be able to defeat my division. In desperation he is using every means at his command to fulfill his promised, guaranteed, and never realized pacification of this Department. Thus it has occurred that . . . Antonio Maceo was offered a thousand ounces of gold and passage by boat to the outside world for his family from whatever port he chose if he should surrender himself and his unit. This proposition was rejected with the energy and noble sentiments which characterize this leader, and the Cuban parliamentarian who relayed the proposal was hanged in accordance with the verdict of a council of war.[4]

Gómez's policy was to avoid combat with stronger enemy columns—a policy that Maceo found difficult to accept because he hated to avoid any conflict with the enemy. When Maceo fought numerically superior enemy forces, he depended upon surprise, swiftness, and the confusion and terror that his troops aroused as they fell suddenly upon the enemy: their gleaming machete blades brandished on high and fierce war whoops piercing the air. And always at the head of these famous charges was Antonio Maceo himself. It is little wonder that he was wounded so often. During the attack on the fortress of Baraguá on December 4, he suffered still another wound. His suffering was made more severe by the death of his younger brother, Julio, in the same battle.[5]

Maceo was, by now, building a legendary reputation in the

entire revolutionary army. Even while his wounds were healing, he was able to defend against any Spanish troops that ventured near his camp. When he was fully recovered, he gained great distinction in several savage battles during the Guantánamo campaign.

By July 1871, having accumulated sufficient war materiel to take the offensive, Gómez decided to invade the Guantánamo zone, which was strongly defended by Spanish elite units. In this venture, Gómez was seeking not only to defeat the enemy, but to test the officers' corps he had been training, and he relied heavily upon Maceo and Calixto García. His confidence was not misplaced. At the beginning of the campaign, Maceo clashed with the famous rifle battalion of San Quintín, one of Spain's most aggressive and best disciplined units. The battle was fiercely fought, lasting five hours and ending in a bloody hand-to-hand victory for Maceo. During the bitter battle, Maceo's aide, Manuel Amábile, sacrificed his life in order to save that of his leader.[6] It was not the last example of the love Maceo's soldiers had for him.

One of the most savage conflicts of the Guantánamo campaign was the assault on the coffee plantation, "La Indiana," which was exceptionally well fortified. After two successive attacks had failed and the Cubans had suffered heavy losses, General Gómez ordered a retreat. However, José Maceo lay wounded in front of the enemy trenches, and Antonio refused to retreat without another effort to save his brother. With grim determination, the young officer led a charge through a veritable shower of bullets until the fortifications were breached and the buildings set on fire. The defenders, just as determined as the rebels, fought to the death with only one man escaping from the attack. The severely wounded José Maceo was rescued and, after a long period of illness, his life was saved.[7]

Maceo's actions played a decisive part in Gómez's victory in the Guantánamo campaign. The rebels proved that the Spanish troops were unable to protect the sugar plantations and mills. Property owners in the area were by now completely panic-stricken.[8]

In order to restore confidence in the Guantánamo zone and in other districts of Oriente, the captain general of the island, Francisco Lersundi, sent General Arsenio Martínez de Campos on a special mission in the region. During the last week of August, the forces of Gómez and Martínez Campos engaged in a series of almost continuous battles, with heavy losses suffered on both sides. Although Maceo won a victory over Colonel Sestrada, one of Martínez Campos' commanders, the overall outcome of the battle was a series of stalemates. The Spaniards remained in control, but they were still unable to pacify the area or prevent the destruction of property by the rebels.[9] On October 15, General Gómez left Maceo in charge while he held conferences with the government on the strategy of the war.[10] Even though it was only temporary, it was the first area command to be entrusted to Maceo and was an indication of the confidence he commanded.

The reason for the conferences was the bleak picture confronting the rebels. They had been pushed back steadily from the western districts, and by the fall of 1871; were offering successful resistance only in Oriente. In his diary, Gómez wrote frankly:

> The state of the Revolution [in October 1871] was hardly encouraging, since the only portion which sustained itself with apparent advantage over the enemy was the one I commanded . . . especially the occupation of the rich territory of Guantánamo. . . . Everything else held out only the prospects of ruin and decadence for the Republic. Bayamo was lost and disorganized; the Venezuelan General Manuel Garrido who commanded it had been disgraced; Camagüey was sustained only by a spearhead of valiant men led by the audacious and noble Agramonte and with the rest [of the province] in the power of the

> Spaniards; Las Villas was totally abandoned with the remnants of the army drifting from Camagüey to Oriente. That was the state of things in those memorable and bitter days.[11]

At his meeting with President Céspedes, Gómez insisted that only one policy could remedy this dangerous situation—an invasion of the western provinces. Fortunately for Spain, up to this point, the Matanzas, Havana, and Pinar del Río provinces—the richest part of Cuba—had never been invaded. Indeed, commerce there had actually increased during the revolt and sugar production had been maintained at a fairly constant level.[12]

The principal strategy of the rebellion, as we have seen, was to make the revolution an unbearable economic burden for Spain. But as long as fighting and destruction were confined to Oriente, this strategy could not really be effective. Either the strategy would be applied to the whole of the island, or the rebellion would remain limited and gradually lose its impetus. It was essential, Gómez argued, to invade the western provinces, paralyze production, and create a chaotic situation in these areas. The advancing Liberating Army, carrying the banner of emancipation, could hit the economic life of the Occidente at its most vital point. Once the slaves fled in large numbers to join the revolutionary movement, production would be completely disrupted. Spain would be deprived of the means and resources for waging war, and the wealthy oligarchy that ruled Cuba and dictated policies to Spain would be compelled to call for the abandonment of the war effort. To continue to leave slavery and economic production in the western provinces untouched was to fight the Spaniards with one hand tied behind one's back:

> While liberty is not given to the thousands of the slaves who are groaning today in the jurisdiction of Occidente, the most populated and richest of the island; while exportation by the enemy of the production of the great sugar plantations established there is

> not impeded . . . the revolution is destined to last even much longer, Cuban resources will be drained, and lakes of blood will flow unfruitfully in the fields of the island.[13]

Gómez's plan was much like that used by the Union army in the American Civil War, once the Lincoln Administration realized that the emancipation of the slaves (and the consequent disruption of the Confederate economy) was the key to victory. As long as the slaves continued to work for the Confederacy, the Union forces were seriously handicapped. It was not until the Emancipation Proclamation was carried into the South by the Union Army that the slaves were induced to run away from the plantations, and the productive forces of the Confederacy were disrupted. Then, and only then, did the Union cause begin to make rapid headway.[14]

General Federico Cavada of the Liberating Army, who had fought with the Union forces in the Civil War, urged the revolutionary government to apply the lessons of that conflict. He cited the example of General Benjamin F. Butler,[15] of the Union army, who had invaded the South, and freed slaves in Virginia on the grounds that they were "contraband of war," and urged a policy of emancipation of the slaves as a means of defeating the Confederacy. Cavada repeatedly called for an invasion of the West and the liberation of the slaves in that area by the revolutionary army.[16]

Cavada's proposal met with fierce opposition from the conservative representatives of the *hacendado* class in the revolutionary government, and was rejected. Gómez's plan for the invasion of the Occidental District fared no better. Céspedes agreed that there was an urgent need to destroy the industrial capacity of the great sugar-producing district. But he refused to countenance Gómez's plan, arguing that it was a hopeless venture and that the rebel army must wait for more supplies. The Liberating Army, he pointed out, had hardly 7,000 men in Oriente and Camagüey provinces. Moreover, the rebel army had no artillery and suffered from a constant lack of ammunition. Gómez replied that the rebel army in Oriente had proved its ability by winning victories against overwhelmingly superior forces, and that it could duplicate this feat in the West. But Céspedes remained adamant.[17]

A month after the discussion with Gómez, Céspedes did approve the sending of a military expeditionary force to the rich province of Las Villas. If successful, it would open the door to a broader invasion of the West. But there was such great opposition to the proposal by the opponents of a western invasion that the plan was dropped. The decision brought relief to the conservative forces in the revolutionary government, to the *hacendados,* and to the wealthy emigrés who were opposed to military action against the plantations they had left behind.[18]

Gómez withdraw dejectedly to the zone of Guantánamo, noting the "suspicion that Antonio Maceo would be fighting all of Spain."[19] Maceo, who had won tribute after tribute for his courage and success, was indeed opposing more than his share of Spanish troops. On January 27, 1872, Gómez informed the Secretary of War: "The conduct observed by the chief of operations of the jurisdiction of Guantánamo, citizen José Antonio Maceo, is very worthy of the post which he occupies, as is evident in his valor, skill and activity."[20] Martínez Campos, the Spanish general, after failing to defeat Maceo with 1,000 men, declared: "It is impossible to end the war by means of arms." On April 16, 1872, a month after he had promoted Maceo to the rank of full colonel, President Céspedes wrote him:

> A few days ago I received the news that the operations of the enemy in Guantánamo had been completely paralyzed. This fact, which can be due to various causes, is primarily due to the brilliant operations and heroic efforts of the Cubans who fight against the Spaniards in that district. Those have been operations and efforts which have obtained the sort of glory that is justly

associated with your name and which is admitted and recognized by all.[21]

How well deserved this praise was became evident when Martínez Campos sent for additional troops from Camagüey in an effort to contain the situation in Maceo's area. Informed of the Spaniard's plan, Maceo decided to intercept the reinforcements before they could unite with the regulars of the area, and to humiliate them at the very outset. On March 8, in a series of flank and rear guard attacks, Maceo inflicted a number of harassing wounds on the advancing Spanish column. On the eighteenth, however, the Spanish column received additional support and engaged the rebel leader in six hours of continuous combat, forcing him to retreat. Nine days later, Maceo hit back and inflicted a tactical defeat upon the same column at Loma del Burro. Colonel Calleja, commander of the Spanish forces, renewed combat a few days later at Santo Domingo. Fighting in a torrential rainstorm, Maceo was finally victorious when the Spanish commander had to break off contact and seek refuge in the sugar mill, "Sabanilla," to await additional reinforcements.[22]

While Maceo was fighting the enemy in the field, his commanding general was holding conferences with the government and worrying about the dissension and defeatism that continued to surface inside government circles. After one of these conferences, General Gómez had all the troops under his command in the zone of Guantánamo parade before the members of the government in formal review. It was on this occasion that President Céspedes met Maceo in person for the first time. A short time later, the president wrote to his wife: "Gómez presented me to General José Antonio Maceo. He is a young mulatto, tall, heavy-set, of agreeable appearance, and of much personal valor."[23]

In the meeting, which lasted from May 26 to June 7, Gómez renewed his pressure for his plan to strike out to the West, arguing that although the Cuban victories in Guantánamo were important, the revolution could only make real headway if it moved westward. Gómez realized that his plan would not be approved, so he proposed a modified version. Under this plan the main forces of the Liberating Army would concentrate at Holguín, continuing operations until a junction was effected with Agramonte's forces in Camagüey province, which had been virtually isolated for months.

Gómez finally succeeded in persuading the government to accept this plan. But before it could be put into operation, he was ordered to divert men from the expedition to protect the members of the government. When he refused to obey the command, Céspedes removed him as commander of the province of Oriente for disobedience. Once again, Gómez's plan was abandoned. The entire episode so disgusted him that he declared:

> I believe that the men who compose the present government of Cuba are not competent to direct the revolution. With them the insurrection will never triumph. They seriously affect the spirit of the army; and they lack any ability to deal even with small matters.[24]

Having already made clear his high regard for Maceo, Céspedes made it further evident by offering him Gómez's command on a temporary basis. Maceo, at first, refused. As he expressed himself to Gómez, he was reluctant to be part of the act of his commander's removal. In spite of this feeling, however, he finally yielded to Céspedes' insistance and accepted the post.[25]

On June 20, General Calixto García, who had been second in command in Oriente, took over Gómez's position as commander of the province. Maceo, who had been named brigadier general on June 8, took charge of the Second Division of the First Corps of the Liberating Army. By July 1, the whole army of Oriente was united under Calixto García to wage offensive warfare. During the next four months, the rebels won victory after victory in the Guantánamo district, and in many of these triumphs Maceo and his unit played a leading role. This period of unbroken successes for the Cubans was initiated in the battle of Rejondon de Bagnanes, led by General Manuel de Jesús Calvar. Maceo received principal credit for a brilliant victory over more than 400 Spanish soldiers conducting a convoy from Holguín to Baraguá. "First when it seemed that the Spanish battalion might break through the Cuban ambush," wrote Fernando Figueredo, a witness of the battle, "there was heard at the vanguard a discharge which made the earth tremble. It was Maceo who . . . had hastened to our aid, and majestically arranging an ambush, received the Spaniards. . . . The enemy was completely demoralized. There was no longer any hope of resistance."

More than a hundred Spanish soldiers died in this encounter, and the rest fled, leaving their wounded and equipment behind. The Cubans seized 146 rifles, 14,000 cartridges, many bags of clothing, and the battalion's records. This victory over a numerically superior enemy had a stimulating effect on the rebel soldiers. "The army of Oriente," Fernando Figueredo noted, "was inspired by the victory and marched from that moment from one triumph to another."[26]

The brilliant victory was also significant for the progress of Maceo's career, since it was witnessed by President Céspedes and the members of the revolutionary government. In his personal report, Céspedes gave Maceo principal credit for the victory.[27]

The campaign in Oriente continued. From July 10 to November 19, Maceo, returning to Guantánamo, kept the countryside in a constant turmoil with fighting, destruction, looting, and repeated forays. In late November, he rejoined General García to help in the capture of Holguín, a plan originally conceived by Gómez. Exactly one month later, the town was captured. Maceo won new fame with this victory. The Spaniards repeatedly condemned him to death as a bandit, but could do nothing to carry their decrees into effect.[28]

The resignation of Captain General Valmaseda late in 1872 was a direct result of the successes of the Cuban campaigns. In order to check the new impetus of the rebels, General Cándido Pieltán, the new captain general of the island, placed 54,000 men, 42 artillery pieces, and 2,000 horses in the field, not counting the thousands of guerrillas and volunteers who were not part of the Spanish army and were employed primarily in guarding the towns, garrisons, plantations, and mills. The Liberating Army, on the other hand, had hardly 7,000 men in Oriente and Camagüey provinces. Moreover, the rebel army had no artillery and suffered from a constant lack of ammunition.[29]

In the latter part of September, Maceo took part in operations under General García and was largely responsible for their successes.[30] Unfortunately, just at this very promising point in the war, the internal dissensions in the government leadership, which had been brewing all the while, came to a head. The successful march of military operations had to be temporarily suspended while the conflict within the government was resolved.

The adoption of the Constitution at Güaímaro had temporarily stemmed the rising opposition to Céspedes' absolute rule—but not for long. Harassed continually by the Spanish columns, the members of the House of Representatives of the Cuban Republic were rarely able to meet, and by 1873, many of them had either been killed or died. In this situation, Céspedes has assumed all civil powers, assigning a secondary role to members of his cabinet. In a manifesto on October 24, he asked for even greater authority.

At the beginning of the war, Céspedes had the support of the conservatives, who regarded him as an effective spokesman for for the wealthy propertied classes and as a defender of their interests. His early stand against the immediate abolition of slavery and against the policy of stirring up slave revolts had won him their support. But as Céspedes began to see the need for a forthright abolitionist position and for "the policy of the incendiary torch," he began to lose the support of the conservatives. His action in assuming complete authority and interfering in military matters—especially his removal of Gómez from command—prevented the revolutionaries, who approved of his policy on slavery, from rallying to his support. In short, Céspedes was isolated in the revolutionary movement. Through his radical policy toward slavery and of the incendiary torch, he lost the support of the conservatives without winning any solid following among the popular forces. When to this was added the personal jealousies (there was a widespread feeling that Céspedes showed too much favoritism toward members of his family) and political opportunism, it is not difficult to understand why a political crisis arose.

Matters came to a head on October 27, 1873, when several members of the practically defunct House of Representatives called a meeting of that body in Bijagual without inviting President Céspedes. All the principal military leaders of Guantánamo, Santiago de Cuba, Holguín, Jiguaní, Bayamo, and Las Tunas attended, and were accompanied by more than 2,000 soldiers. The main business of the assembly was the removal of Céspedes. His isolation became clear when none of the groups—conservative or revolutionary—came to his defense. Since Vice President Francisco Vicente Aguilera was on a mission abroad, the president of the House of Representatives, Salvador Cisneros Betancourt, was proclaimed president of the Republic. A message was sent to Céspedes, informing him of his removal.[31]

With this decision taken, those present swore allegiance to the Constitution. Cisneros then named his cabinet, and the officers and soldiers returned to their respective camps. With a new government, Gómez revived his campaign for an invasion of the West. He proposed that the invasion move into Las Villas and carry the revolution to Havana itself. He pointed out once again that as long as the Occidental District kept on grinding its sugar, exploiting the slaves, and nourishing the Spanish treasury with the necessary funds for exterminating the revolution, the Cuban Republic, regardless of whether Céspedes or Cisneros was president, could not survive. The only hope for a definite victory lay in applying the torch to the mills and other centers of production in the western provinces and liberating the *libertos*. "Five hundred men . . . under the command of the then Brigadier General Antonio Maceo was the only force which I asked of the Government," Gómez wrote in his diary, again revealing his great respect for Maceo.[32]

The new administration reacted coldly to Gómez's appeal, demonstrating that the conservative spokesmen for the *hacendados* still exercised great influence. The reason given was that the situation in Oriente was too dangerous to spare troops for an invasion of the West. In addition, President Cisneros had his attention fixed on the arrival of new filibustering expeditions, which left secretly in violation of American laws, of arms and men from the United States. One of them, the *Virginius*, was captured by the Spanish and fifty-three of its crew, including its American captain, Joseph Fry, were summarily executed.[33]

Maceo, in the meantime, was busy fighting under the command of General García, and his victories helped turn the tide in favor of a Western invasion. In describing Maceo's audacious assault, organized by García, on the well-defended town of Manzanillo, Félix Figueredo noted that he had "the most difficult part of the operation. Maceo, who was always a model in the matter of obedience, asked only that to accomplish the part of the mission assigned to him, he be given the permission to choose the officers and soldiers who would accompany him, since the delicacy of his task required picked personnel."[34] Although this operation was only partially successful, since the assault had been discovered and the alarm given before it could be launched, there were other battles that ended in total victory.[35] In January 1874, for example, García and Maceo won an important victory at Junurún-Nelones against three Spanish battalions and a guerrilla unit under the command of the famous Colonel Federico Esponda. The Spaniards were completely routed, leaving behind 150 dead, including 5 officers, and taking with them more than 200 wounded.[36]

With this victory, the situation in Oriente improved to a point where the government was unable to postpone any longer Gómez's long-delayed plan for a western invasion. At the beginning of February 1874 a meeting was held of the highest ranking generals of the Liberating Army, the president, his cabinet, and the House of Representatives. At the meeting, Gómez delivered a lengthy presentation of his plan, demonstrating that the western invasion was not only necessary but feasible. Supported by all of the rebel generals, except Secretary of War Vicente García, Gómez succeeded in persuading the government to grant him permission to put his plan into effect. There was some opposition to Gómez's proposal to make Maceo second in command, on the ground that he was needed in Oriente. But Gómez insisted that Maceo was essential for the success of the invasion, and he had his way.[37]

On February 4, 1874, Gómez formed a force of 500 soldiers from Oriente and Las Villas (300 infantry and 200 cavalry). The long-awaited invasion of the West was about to begin.

"The news," wrote a contemporary, "caused a kind of invigorating dizziness. Nothing else was thought about in Oriente. Everything appeared small, insignificant, when compared with the prospect of invading the fields of Occidente. . . . Nothing else was talked about except the invasion, and everyone wanted the march to begin right away."[38] Pieces of paper were passed from one Cuban patriot to another. On them were written the words of the hastily-prepared "The Hymn of Las Villas." Quickly put to music, it became one of the most popular songs of the war. Although it is impossible to convey the beauty of the Spanish verse in a literal translation, the following gives some idea of the spirit of the song:

There are green valleys, brothers
  Where the golden sugar cane grows.
There the greedy despots
  Are enjoying our wealth.

Do you not see the lucky tyrants
  Who are sustained with the sweat
Of the African's miseries?
  A gross insult to their sorrows.

Corrupt air of bacchanalias
  Is breathed alone by youth.
Lubricious pleasures and immoral,
  Rob them there of virtue.

We must save the Cubans
  From such a system of corruption.
And it is a noble enterprise, brothers,
  To bring redemption to these people.

The generous peoples of Oriente
  Call up the flower of their warriors,
And with you march the valiant
  Battling Camagüeyans.

Raise up a hymn that rises to the sky
  And which, plowing rapidly across the sea,
Teaches the world that Cuba knows how
  To overthrow its tyrants.

And that in the breast of the Cubans
  Heaven has placed all the vigor
Of American torrents
  And the volcanoes of Ecuador.

Hurrah! To Las Villas! Because the voice
  Of the people which weeps there calls to us
On the shores of the Agabama
  And on the banks of the Damjjí.[39]

On February 10, the invading Cuban army of 500 soldiers defeated 2,000 artillery-equipped veteran Spanish troops, under

General Manuel Portillo. The victory was due largely to the skillful maneuvers organized by General Gómez; but Maceo inspired the tremendous efforts of the rebels. Colonel Manuel Sanguilly, a participant in the battle, described Maceo's actions in these words:

> The Spaniards had been driven to the right, and around four hundred had sheltered behind a parapet. . . . The Orientales reached it under a tremendous fire from their opponents. We do not know if the troops from Oriente hesitated or not, but it is certain that General Maceo, like a colossus, was seen seizing the soldiers nearest him by the collars and belts and propelling them against the Spanish positions like projectiles.[40]

Maceo did not stop fighting after the Spanish retreat. He attacked their rear guard furiously.

Another Cuban victory followed on February 16, in the battle of Las Guásimas, against overwhelmingly superior Spanish forces. Once again, the victory was the result of the combination of Gómez's brilliant strategy and Maceo's skillful and courageous leadership in action. Given the responsibility of superior command by Gómez, Maceo marched with 200 cavalry and 50 infantry against the Spanish column of 2,000 men sent from the city of Camagüey with cavalry, infantry, and artillery. In all, the Spaniards poured 6,000 men and six pieces of artillery into the battle. Battered constantly by Maceo and his soldiers, they had to retreat. Maceo's troops pursued the fleeing enemy, attacking their flanks and rear guard and causing further casualties, until their ammunition was expended. The Spaniards lost 1,037 dead and wounded, and the Cubans 174. Maceo was one of the Cuban casualties, for he was wounded once again at the end of the victorious battle.[41]

Another and more serious casualty was suffered shortly thereafter by another member of the Maceo clan. On April 18, Antonio's brother, Miguel, died in his arms from wounds received in the attack on the Spanish garrison at Cascorro. An observer described the scene in the following words:

> Before the body of Miguel, his brother, killed by a rifle shot, Brigadier General Antonio Maceo stood in mute contemplation. He remained in that position for the time necessary to collect the last impression of that manly figure whom he loved as a patriotic and heroic companion of arms and with the just and natural passion of a blood relative.[42]

The death of any member of the intrepid Maceo family was naturally a cause for rejoicing among the Spaniards. But it was Antonio's death they now sought most avidly. Three years earlier, General Valmaseda had condemned Maceo to death as a bandit, and this decree was issued again on August 6, 1873. Later, on April 16, 1874, Captain General José Gutiérrez de la Concha signed an additional decree, proclaiming the death penalty and ordering the confiscation of all Maceo's possessions for the crime of sedition.[43]

The Cuban victory at Las Guásimas, inspiring as it was to the rebel cause, had its drawbacks. So much ammunition and other war materials had been consumed in the five-day battle, to say nothing of the dead and wounded, that the invasion of the West had to be called off for the time being. The decision to fight such a large-scale battle was not in keeping with Gómez's basic strategy—namely, to rely on guerrilla attacks and invasions of the production units in the areas, and to avoid major battles against numerically superior Spanish forces. Although the Cubans might win such battles and would suffer fewer losses than the Spaniards, they could hardly afford such victories with the small number of fighting men and limited resources available to them.

Gómez announced the postponement of the western invasion; yet he fully expected to obtain government aid in carrying through his plan later. But when he proposed a revival of the project in May and June, 1874, he came up against a series of obstacles, some old and some new.[44]

The invasion of the West had always been opposed by the conservative representatives of the *hacendado* class in the revolutionary government. They had repeatedly emphasized that the revolution, if it was to get the support of the *hacendados* of the Occidente, had to protect their property—both mills and slaves—from the "horrors of the insurrection." They argued further that "the policy of the incendiary torch" was bound to antagonize the emigrés who looked forward to the day when they could return to their Cuban plantations. Without their support, how could expeditions be organized from outside the island to bring much-needed supplies to the rebel fighters?

The conservative pressure on the government intensified when Gómez and Maceo were leading their small army westward. But now another argument was added: the danger of black domination of Cuba. The conservatives had watched Maceo's emergence to a position of importance and leadership in the Liberating Army with growing concern. If, led by Maceo, the Liberating Army should move through the West, freeing slaves as it went, would not the liberated black population seek to dominate Cuba and make Maceo, their champion, the foremost figure on the island? "Do we," the conservatives asked, "liberate ourselves only to share the fate of Haiti and Santo Domingo?"[45]

During the invasion of the West in February 1874, the conservatives launched an all-out slander campaign against Maceo, particularly among the troops of Las Villas, charging him with seeking to use the invasion to build the foundation for a black-dominated Republic. The campaign produced results. When Gómez proposed a revival of the invasion of the West, the troops of Las Villas refused to accept Maceo as their commander. While it was not unusual during the Ten Years' War for units of one area to refuse to accept a commander from another region,[46] the opposition to Maceo, in this instance, stemmed primarily from the effects of racial prejudice and the propaganda about "black domination"—a fear created by the conservative opposition to the invasion.[47]

Since the troops of Las Villas were to occupy a prominent

place in the campaign through that province, Gómez was forced to capitulate, and Maceo was recalled to Oriente. However, Gómez realized that the reason given by the Las Villas forces for not accepting Maceo as their chief—that "he was not from Las Villas"—was only an excuse to cover their objection to him because he was a black. Gómez therefore designated Lieutenant Colonel Cecilio González, "a man as black as ebony," as the leader of the campaign. "Of this one they cannot say he is not from Las Villas, because he was born in Cienfuegos," Gómez declared in announcing González's appointment. "And the white racists of Las Villas had to accept the black González as their chief," notes the Cuban historian Emilio Roig de Leuchsenring.[48]

After staying with Gómez for a short time, participating in the activities at Camagüey, Maceo was recalled to Oriente to fill the position of Calixto García, who had been captured by the Spaniards and made a prisoner on September 4, 1874. Maceo assumed command of the Second Division, with responsibility for his old territory of Santiago de Cuba and Guantánamo. With this post went the obligation to coordinate the activities of the Second Division with those of the First Division of Bayamo, Holguín, and Jiguaní, under the leadership of Calvar.

The final irony of the racist campaign against Maceo was that even when he was out of the way, the government refused to approve Gómez's request for the revival of the invasion plan. José Morales Lemus, the spokesman for the wealthy emigrés and a long-time opponent of a western invasion, warned the government that such an invasion, and the application in the Occidente District of the "policy of the incendiary torch," would jeopardize any possibility of securing aid from the government of the United States, which, he predicted, would shortly recognize Cuban belligerency. The Spaniards, he emphasized, were spreading propaganda in the United States that an invasion of the West, if successful, would bring about the "black domination of the island," and that Cuba "would be converted into a second Haiti." This, he maintained, was hurting the Cuban cause.[49]

The revolution was thus restricted to the least important economic section of the island, and the most vital districts continued to provide Spain with the resources to carry on the war.

4

The Ten Years' War: Part 3

The first few months of 1876 found the rebels in their most promising position since the start of the war. They held a strong grip on Oriente and Camagüey provinces, they moved at will in the countryside, and the Spaniards controlled only the towns and the strongly garrisoned areas. "We could almost call ourselves masters in Oriente and Camagüey," General Enrique Collazo recalled. "The government of the Republic exercised its functions in these provinces with entire and complete liberty."[1]

In addition, General Máximo Gómez, disregarding official objections to the plan, had finally succeeded in the first phase of his cherished dream of invading Las Villas province. On January 6, 1875, Gómez crossed the *trocha*,[2] the long fortified line that the Spaniards erected to prevent the penetration of the West. Immediately, Gómez, *el hombre de la tea* (the man of the torch), unleashed a devastating campaign. "The objective," he told his men, "is the destruction of the plantations which sustain the enemy, principally the mills from which the *hacendados* derive their wealth and with which they support Spain's war effort." These flames, he wrote, "will snatch the slave from the domination of his master."[3] In a little over a month, he burned eighty-three mills.

Gómez's success created panic among the Spanish bureaucrats and slaveowners. The alarm was even felt in Havana, where, for over six years, those who sympathized with Spain lived in peace, confident that the rebels would never succeed in penetrating the *trocha.* There followed a series of rapid changes in the post of captain general of the island, ending in the selection, for the third time in the war, of Valmaseda.

Encouraged by Gómez's success in Las Villas, the *mambises* redoubled their efforts in other provinces. There was common talk that 1875 would see an end both to the war and to Spanish despotism in Cuba. There was even a decline in the divisionist tendencies in the revolutionary government. "There was greater unity than at any other time," Collazo recalled, "and a general will to give priority to military measures for winning the war." President Cisneros bestowed official blessings on Gómez's plan and issued an order to the various generals to select soldiers to send him "to carry the war to Matanzas and Havana."[4]

"Fortune was smiling on us," wrote Collazo, "and the future looked happy and agreeable."[5] But the great hope for victory was soon to be destroyed. Once again, dissension reared its head in the revolutionary movement.

It will be recalled that a year earlier, Vicente García had been the only general to openly oppose Gómez's plan for an invasion of the West. Although he was an excellent general and occupied the post of Secretary of War, García constantly fought the Cisneros administration. He claimed, on the one hand, that it was not sufficiently revolutionary, and, on the other, that it should not countenance Gómez's policy of the "incendiary torch." García attracted both the radical elements who wanted governmental reforms and the conservatives who opposed Gómez's revolutionary methods. Ironically, García was also supported by the relatives and associates of former president Céspedes, despite the fact that he was one of the first to demand Céspedes' removal from office.

García, renouncing his allegiance to the revolutionary government, called an assembly at Lagunas de Varona, on April 27, 1875, of all elements dissatisfied with the progress of the revolution. The announced purpose of the meeting was to demand substantial reforms in the government. All the troops in the Las Tunas zone, where García had a substantial following, attended the meeting, and many in Oriente province left the battlefield to attend.

García's move resulted in disrupting the whole revolutionary movement. Even when this was pointed out to them by Cisneros, García and his followers were unmoved. Finally, Cisneros offered to resign. The offer was not accepted, and the government was paralyzed. Gómez withdrew his forces from Las Villas, forcing military activity on almost every front to a halt.[6]

Maceo, who was furious at García's sabotage of the war effort, continued to operate against the enemy. He had refused to attend the meeting and, instead, had worked actively both to hold the front against the Spaniards in Oriente and to reinforce Gómez's army. In an effort to prevent any future dissension in the ranks, he sent the following message to President Cisneros on June 29, 1875:

> To the end of avoiding the demoralization which began to appear, I felt it my duty to convoke a meeting of officers and officials on the eighteenth of the present month at a point named Alcalá in the jurisdiction of Holguín. At this meeting we agreed to send a statement to the House of Representatives requesting the harmonization of the interests of the country so far as possible.[7]

During the confrontation at Alcalá, Maceo told García personally that he thought his actions sabotaged the revolution. He explained that while he was in favor of worthwhile progressive reforms of the government, he was firmly opposed to anything and anyone that tended to create divisions and interruptions in the war effort. In conclusion, he bluntly informed García that he did not regard him with favor and would not serve under his command.[8]

After the meeting, Maceo returned to fighting the Spaniards. The House of Representatives had, meanwhile, accepted Cisneros' resignation and it named Juan B. Spoterno, president of the House, as interim president of the Republic; on March 20, 1876, it elected Tomás Estrada Palma president. Estrada Palma made some efforts to reinvigorate the military operations that had been dormant for so long. He met with Gómez and discussed a revival of the invasion of the West. Gómez, eager as ever to put his plan into full operation, moved once again into Las Villas. Thus, after a year of relative inactivity, there was new hope of united efforts against Spain. But once again these hopes were to be frustrated.

In his interview with Gómez, Estrada Palma, who had close links with the Cuban exiles, assured the Dominican general that military supplies were on their way from the United States, and that the chances of recognition of Cuban belligerency by the North American republic were brighter than ever.[9] The new president turned out to be unrealistic on both points.

Military supplies in support of the revolution were not coming through. The wealthy Cubans in the United States, on whom Estrada Palma depended for funds, were refusing to contribute. Whatever money was raised came from the tobacco workers in Key West, Tampa, and other cities. Throughout the long years of conflict, these Cuban workers had contributed, from their meager wages, monthly quotas to the revolutionary cause. But the rich Cuban exiles, who had millions deposited in New York banks, safe from taxation and confiscation by Spain, refused to help Gómez's army.[10] Gómez himself acknowedged this: "The poor Cubans responded well, and if Miguel Aldama and men like him had responded immediately to what was asked of them, who knows how far we could have gone?"[11]

Estrada Palma's assurance to Gómez of the imminence of U.S. recognition of Cuban belligerency, bringing with it the right to purchase arms for the rebel army, was also inaccurate. It is true that President Ulysses S. Grant occasionally referred to the need to recognize the Cuban Republic and that public demand for such a step had been rising since 1868. From the outbreak of the Ten Years' War, however, Secretary of State Hamilton Fish had shown that he would exert every effort to prevent recognition of Cuban belligerency, and he was the one who determined the Grant administration's policy on Cuba. The aristocratic New Yorker frequently expressed support for "people . . . struggling for more liberal government," but he did not include the Cubans in this category. "He placed a low estimate upon the intelligence and moral qualities of much of the [Cuban] population," writes Allan Nevins, Fish's biographer. "He doubted the aptitude of the conglomerate of Indian, Negro, and Spanish blood for self-government and thought . . . that evolution under Spanish tutelage might be better than revolution. Moreover, he felt a certain friendliness to Spain."[12] In addition, Fish believed that once the island was devastated by war, Spain would be willing to sell it to the United States. Until that time, however, he was convinced that it would best suit United States interests to have the island remain under Spain's control.[13]

To stave off adoption by Congress of resolutions favoring the recognition of either belligerency or Cuban independence, Fish announced in November 1875 that he was seeking to achieve action by the European powers, led by England, to restore peace on the island. Such a peace would include neither the abolition of slavery nor the independence of Cuba, but nothing came of this maneuver. It did, however, enable President Grant to urge Congress in his annual message of December 1875 to do nothing about the Cuban situation by intimating that negotiations to end the war were under way. The message achieved Fish's objective, and he wrote jubilantly that it "was all that could be desired, and left the Administration master of the question without apprehension of resolutions of recognition, etc."[14]

Dissension within the revolutionary movement was meanwhile increasing. One clear sign of this was the renewal of a vicious campaign against Maceo. As before, he was accused of seeking a Cuban Republic dominated by blacks. Ugly rumors circulated that Maceo was waiting for an opportunity to lead the black soldiers against the whites for the seizure of power. He was accused of refusing to obey the government's decision and of favoring black officers over whites. These slanders represented the feelings of important elements in the revolutionary camp. After he became a prisoner of war, Colonel Ricardo Céspedes told the Spaniards that he and other officers of the Liberating Army "saw ruin coming in the support given to the colored element." Naturally, the Spaniards spread this statement widely throughout Cuba.[15]

Maceo had ignored the slanders for months. Instead, he conducted himself in such a way as to prove that they were lies spread by foes of the revolution in order to sow confusion, alarm, and dissension in the revolutionary ranks. He told his officers and men that there were no black and white soldiers—that all were Cuban warriors and all were entitled to equality of treatment. There should, he insisted, be no domination of one race over the other in the future Republic.[16]

By May 1876, however, Maceo realized that his failure to respond publicly only encouraged the racists to intensify their slanderous campaign. On May 16, from his camp in Baraguá, he dispatched a protest and rebuttal of the slanders to the president of the Republic that merits being quoted in full:

> Antonio Maceo y Grajales, native of the city of [Santiago de] Cuba, Brigadier General of the Liberating Army, and at present Chief of the Second Division of the First Corp, respectfully states:
>
> That for some time I have tolerated acts and conversations which actually I discredited because I believed they only came from the enemy, who, as everybody knows, has used all weapons

to disunite us to see if by this means he can defeat us. But later, seeing that the issue was growing, I tried to see where it came from, and at last I am convinced that it does not come only from enemy sources, but, painful for me to say, it comes from our own brothers who, forgetting the republican and democratic principles which should guide them, have followed personal political ends.

Therefore, in view of this development, I believe that it is my duty to appeal to the Government which you represent, so that when you understand the reasons which I shall present at a later point, you will proceed with justice and resolution, taking the necessary measures to clear all doubt as to my conduct and to remove the slightest smear from my name. The desire all my life has been, is, and will be to serve my country, defending its proclaimed principles. This I have done many times. The cause must triumph and sacrosanct principles of liberty and independence must remain safe.

I have known for some time, Mr. President, through a person of good reputation and prestige, that a small circle exists which has manifested to the Government that it "did not wish to serve under my orders because I belong to the colored race." And later, through different channels, I have learned that they are now accusing me of "showing favoritism to the colored over the white officers in my command." In doing so they are serving their own particular political interests; by this method they hope to destroy me as they have not been able to do so by other means. They are trying to do this to a man who entered the revolution for no other reason than to shed his blood to see the slaves and his country free. After learning what was occurring, I spoke to one of the men who belongs to this circle and I became more convinced than ever of their evil goals. In planting these seeds of distrust and dissension, they do not seem to realize that it is the country that will suffer the consequences.

And since I belong to the colored race, without considering myself worth more or less than other men, I cannot and must not consent to the continued growth of this ugly rumor. Since I form a not inappreciable part of this democratic republic, which has for its base the fundamental principles of liberty, equality, and fraternity, I must protest energetically with all my strength that neither now nor at any other time am I to be regarded as an advocate of a Negro Republic or anything of that sort. This concept is a deadly thing to this democratic Republic which is founded on the basis of liberty and fraternity. I do not recognize any hierarchy.

Those who are to mold the future nation must prove themselves now. The men who act in the manner which I have described can never form a part of that nation if it is to be the sort of country for which we are fighting. They are as much the enemies of the revolution as those who are fighting openly and directly against me, and they must be treated as such.

If for some unbelievable reason I should be denied my just demands, I shall be forced to leave the cause in which I had so much hope; if politics is to have the upper hand, then I must ask for my passport to some civilized land. This does not mean that I am looking for an excuse to quit the war; the country needs its good sons as never before, and I am not the kind who tires so easily, in spite of the eleven wounds which I proudly carry in my body. I shall never tire of fighting so long as I believe the goal to be worthy of the effort.

I am addressing this letter to you because I want to see the truth prevail and because I expect the guilty to be discovered and punished.[17]

Maceo did not dispatch this letter to the government immediately. Aware of the seriousness of the issue and wanting to be sure that he would be acting in the best interests of the revolution, he sent the letter to his close friend and adviser, Colonel Félix Figueredo. He asked Figueredo "to make all the observations that you believe to be prudent in the matter and to send them to me in writing by the same messenger who brings this letter." Figueredo urged that the letter be sent to the government.[18]

Unfortunately, the government did nothing in response to Maceo's demand; while the slanders continued, the Spaniards continued to raise the specter of a black Republic. Maceo did not carry out his threat to resign his post and leave the country.

On the contrary, he continued to oppose all those who tried to use the racial issue to destroy the revolution, just as he opposed men like García, who tried to use the need for reforms to destroy the revolutionary government.[19]

"Unity to fight the common enemy." This was the keynote of Maceo's message to the Cuban people and the revolutionary commanders. He admitted that there were justified criticisms of the revolutionary government's conduct, but he insisted that only the Spaniards would benefit if these criticisms were permitted to create dissension and thereby render the military campaigns futile. His advice was fortified by his own conduct. His single mindedness of purpose—victory over Spain—and his readiness to sacrifice personal ambition stood in sharp contrast to the actions of many of the officers and officials who showed themselves to be more interested in political intrigue than in unity for the cause of the revolution.

On May 11, 1877, in Santa Rita, Camagüey, García issued a new manifesto similar to the one issued at Lagunas de Varona, demanding reforms in the revolutionary government and calling upon the Cuban people to follow his lead in withdrawing recognition from it. He also dispatched representatives to all the principal rebel camps to persuade them to join the revolt.[20]

When this new revolt within the ranks occurred, Maceo was in the extreme eastern part of Oriente, where he had gone to initiate a new military campaign. (By now, he was a major general, having been promoted to the rank by majority vote in a secret session of the House of Representatives.)[21] Consequently, he did not learn of García's action until July 3, when three of García's representatives entered his camp at San Augustín, on the banks of the Caute River. They related the latest course of events and presented a letter from García. They then told Maceo of their intention to proceed through his territory, to inform the people of that province of García's break with the revolutionary government, and to urge them to follow suit. Maceo's reply was brief but brusque: "You will not pass through my territory, and I am giving you twenty-four hours to get out of the area under my jurisdiction. If you fail to do so, I will subject you to a council of war on the charge of sedition."[22]

In his letter to Maceo, García had insisted that the Cuban position was desperate, and that an entirely new course was required. He invited Maceo to join his movement. In reply, Maceo declared that if the situation was indeed desperate, "the blame belongs to the attitude which you, the forces of Las Tunas, and those of the western border of Holguín have adopted." Conceding that some reforms were needed and that he was in favor of them, he added: "I will never support rebellion and disorder to make use of my rights." And he went on:

> Certainly you have not taken the best route to unite the patriots. If dissensions exist, they do not require the reprehensible means which you have chosen to employ. To satisfy the aspirations of the people it is not necessary to authorize disobedience to the constituted government and laws as you did at Lagunas de Varona and are doing now. Thus, far from achieving unity to fight the common enemy, your actions have resulted in the common indignation of those who obey the legitimate government and its laws against you and your followers.

Maceo pleaded with García to submit his objections and proposals for reforms through legal channels and not to attempt to succeed by splitting the armed forces. Although the harm already done was great, he maintained that García could still remedy the situation by placing his complaints before a democratic assembly. However, if he persisted, it would be clear that he was guided solely by personal ambition. The result of such a course, Maceo warned, would be that history would view García as an enemy of the Cuban people. After refusing García's request for an interview, Maceo concluded: "I advise you to abandon the bad advisers who . . . are ruining your reputation."[23]

Maceo failed to get García and the other rebel chiefs to forget their personal differences and unite for the success of the revolution. There is no doubt that racism played an important part in this failure. Colonel Céspedes told the Spaniards that he and other officers resented Maceo's rapid rise to influence and leadership in the Liberating Army.[24]

With each passing month, dissension in the revolutionary ranks increased. Gómez was removed fron command of the forces of Las Villas because the other officers would not function under him. Discouraged and disheartened, he first retired to his plantation, *La Reforma,* but soon left to become Secretary of War and Commanding General in Oriente under President Estrada Palma. However, his removal from command in Las Villas doomed the whole plan for offensive action in the West.[25]

As long as most of the activity of the Spanish army in Cuba was defensive, this internal dissension was not fatal to the Cuban cause. But in the spring of 1877 the situation changed. During the previous fall, General Arsenio Martínez Campos had arrived in Cuba at the head of 25,000 additional reinforcements for the Spanish army. His plan was to abandon defensive warfare, invade the rebel territory near Las Villas, and from there move east to Oriente.

With special authority as the commander of the entire Spanish field army, Martínez Campos opened a vigorous offensive in the months of March and April 1877. He decreed that any rebel caught with arms would be executed. He also developed a shrewd policy to take advantage of the divisions within the revolutionary camp. He made a concentrated effort to get in touch with all the dissident elements; he sent prisoners of war back into the revolutionary ranks to create greater dissension; he offered money to those who seemed likely to lay down their arms; and he circulated the complaints, accusations, rumors, and heated remarks of one rebel group against another, playing up, for example, the menace of a black Republic if the rebels won. Along with these tactics, Martínez Campos made peace overtures and requested interviews with the legal government of the revolutionists. On May 5, 1877, he issued a proclamation rescinding all orders of banishment "for political motives," and lifted the penalities imposed on insurgents (except for the leaders of the insurrection) who presented themselves for pardon before the end of the war.[26]

Martínez Campos' military offensive resulted in heavy loses by the insurgents. The revolutionary cause was further weakened by the desertions of rebel officers and soldiers in Las Villas, and the rebellion of the soldiers of Holguín, led by the black officer Limbano Sánchez, known as the "Lion of Holguín."

Maceo learned that Sánchez had joined García's rebellion and he set out to find him and persuade him to abandon his antigovernment stand. When Sánchez was informed that Maceo was seeking him, he tried to avoid the encounter, but Maceo finally located his camp. He ordered his men to remain behind in the outskirts of Sánchez's refuge while he entered the camp. Maceo apparently wished to avoid any bloodshed. Two men—Fernando Figueredo and Félix Figueredo—followed Maceo at a distance. It was Fernando Figueredo who described the following scene:

> "Who goes?" echoed on the mountainside, interrupting the silence which surrounded the scene, and before we could collect our wits the quick reply came from the General—"General Maceo, Chief of the Division."—"Hands up, Chief of the Division!" replied the sentinel. The Chief answered serenely:
>
> "In the territory under my command none has the right to detail me!" The zealous sentinel gave the voice of alarm with words that fairly ran together in their rapidity, as he called for the officer of the guard and for Colonel Sánchez. The notes of a trumpet were heard coming from the camp followed by voices crying, "Viva the reforms! Viva General Vicente García!" The sounds became lost in the immensity of the mountainous sur-

roundings. Then the abrupt voice of Lieutenant Colonel Sánchez, clear and penetrating, exclaimed, "Hands up, General Maceo! If you don't raise your hands"—pointing with his modern and magnificent revolver at the head of General Maceo—"I will fire!" Figueredo and I ran toward the group. Meanwhile the trumpets in the interior of the camp played "Call to colors," and voices cried again insistently, "Viva the reforms! Viva Vicente García!" and the echoes repeated the sounds, gradually disappearing in space.

"Fire, coward!" exclaimed the General. "If you want to kill a man, shoot!" he said with his arms crossed. And since Limbano hesitated, like a bird, fascinated by the eyes of the boa, Maceo ordered him to "holster that sidearm!"

And the arm which nearly gave the death blow to the country, and which almost committed murder, fell as though dominated by its own weight, at the order of the General. Maceo embraced Limbano Sánchez. In that moment Figueredo and I drew nearer to the scene.

"Have no fear!" said the Chief to his subordinate—"I have come over to save you from the ruin that threatens you; turn your troops over to me and return to obedience!"

Sánchez was placed under technical arrest, but was given freedom of the camp on his word of honor not to escape, which he promptly ignored; at the first opportunity, Sánchez fled with those troops still loyal to him.[27]

Maceo had failed once again in his efforts to convince García, Sánchez, and their followers to lay aside all differences in the face of the need for unity. Rebel morale was sinking rapidly, and some revolutionary leaders talked of peace without independence, in spite of their oath not to do so. On August 7, 1877, Hamilton Fish, who had left the office of Secretary of State, wrote with great delight: "The end of the Cuban trouble is approaching."[28]

On August 4 and 5 Maceo and Gómez conceived a plan for solving the internal crisis and raising the morale of the troops by launching a new infiltration campaign against the Spanish army. On the following day, they attacked a strong Spanish column. One of the Spanish officers in the skirmish, Colonel Ramón Domingo de Ibarra, described Maceo's action in the following dramatic manner:

> With complete serenity and pronounced arrogance, an enemy cavalryman advanced at the head of the first squadron, some thirty paces in front of his soldiers, whom we then recognized as being Maceo, on his spirited horse Guajamón. Wearing a wide felt hat and a striking coat, he gesticulated with a revolver in his right hand which he fired at intervals, and he frequently turned his men as if to encourage them.[29]

As on so many other occasions, Maceo recklessly placed himself in a dangerous position. This time his luck failed him, and he received a very serious wound. For a time it was feared that he would die. "This development," Gómez wrote sadly in his diary, "leaves me in a very grave situation since there is no leader who can command the same influence as Maceo. Meanwhile, the Spaniards are increasing their operations."[30] At the end of September 1877, however, Gómez was able to add the following entry: "General Maceo was seriously wounded, but that man, with his indomitable spirit and iron constitution, is already active again."[31]

Antonio Maceo not only lived, but he accomplished another of his seemingly impossible deeds. He was protected by a small bodyguard of eight men, commanded by his brother, José Maceo, and treated by Dr. Félix Figueredo. "The robust and privileged physique of Maceo," wrote Estrada Palma, "aided by the efficient medical assistance of Félix, put the hero of a hundred battles, the defender of law, order, and authority, and the model of civil and military citizens—put him, and soon, I repeat—in condition to assume the command of his troops and to face the enemy again."[32]

An informer had advised General Martínez Campos of the seriousness of Maceo's wounds, of the small size of his escort, and of the exact place where he could be found. Martínez

Campos immediately dispatched a column of 3,000 men who completely surrounded the area. On September 27, 1877, less than two months after he had received his seemingly fatal wounds, Maceo got off his litter, mounted his horse, and galloped away in a cloud of dust and gun smoke. In his report of the affair to Madrid, Martínez Campos wrote:

> I thought I was dealing with a stupid mulatto, a rude muleteer; but I found him transformed not only into a real general, capable of directing his movement with judgment and precision, but also into an athlete who, finding himself indisposed on a litter, assaulted by my troops, abandoned his bed, leaped upon a horse and outdistanced those pursuing him.[33]

During the period of forced rest that followed, Maceo again used the time to broaden his knowledge. In addition to nursing him back to health, Félix Figueredo, a man of broad culture, spent hours lecturing Maceo on history, politics, political science, and literature. Although we do not know the books Maceo read during this period, we do know that on February 21, 1878, General Rafael Rodríguez wrote Figueredo that he had sent "*Les Miserables* of V. Hugo so that you may save it for Maceo."[34]

Soon Maceo was again leading the rebels in Oriente. He completely defeated a Spanish army in the battle of Pilote. With Maceo once more sound, the outlook in Oriente seemed promising.

But in Camagüey and Las Villas, the situation was deteriorating rapidly. In desperation, the House of Representatives removed Estrada Palma from command of the army. It then asked Gómez to take over, hoping that he could revive the spirit within the insurgent ranks and confront Martínez Campos' offensive with a unified revolutionary army. Unfortunately, Gómez allowed this opportunity to slip by. He had become increasingly dismayed by the constant political intrigues, and refused to accept the command. Gómez explained that he was declining the post "so long as the political situation of the country was abnormal."[35] This was precisely the situation that called for a man of Gómez's experience and leadership, and his refusal only prolonged and intensified the "abnormal" condition.

While it is not difficult to understand Gómez's disgust with the constant internal bickering and repeated sabotage of his plan to invade the West, his decision was a serious blow to the cause to which he had already devoted almost a decade. In the eyes of many revolutionaries, it was the final blow to the Ten Years' War.

5

The Protest of Baraguá

In November 1877 Estrada Palma was captured and imprisoned by the Spaniards, and General Vicente García was named president of the Republic. After a long struggle against the authorities of the revolutionary movement, García finally took the helm—but the ship was sinking. Many of the rebels were thinking of some kind of peace overture. A number had concluded that if the war continued, it would end in a triumph for the people of color. Colonel Antonio Bello, chief of the regiment Luz de Yara, wrote to General Juan J. Rus of Bayamo:

> What will become of the Republic with the capture of President T. Estrada Palma? . . . A dictatorship by one of these two Generals, Maceo or Gómez, is imminent. You do not know the tendencies of Maceo. You told me that the day would not be far distant in which he, at the head of the blacks, would take off our heads. Have you forgotten?

Ignacio Mora, a representative of the landowners of Camagüey, a man who viewed Maceo as a "badly educated and ambitious mulatto," warned that peace must be signed quickly because "the revolution was falling into the hands of the common people." In general, men like Mora believed that if the war was "prolonged," Cuba would become another Haiti, with "horrors that will terrify the civilized world."[1]

While Gómez rejected such fantasies, even he was wavering. His advice to the government was that an uncompromising truce should be obtained so that the rebels could decide whether they wished to have peace or to continue fighting. Should they decide to continue, he urged that they elect a government by democratic vote and form a united front. If that happened, valuable time for reorganization would have been obtained through the truce period.[2]

While Gómez was offering his solution, rebel officers were already making separate peace agreements. By the middle of December 1877 the government was ready to discuss terms with Martínez Campos and asked for the neutralization of a part of Camagüey province, in which a conference could be held. On February 5, 1878, a conference was held between the most important leaders of the government and the Spanish generals. At the conference, President García declared that continuance of the war would destroy the country, and he asked for peace. Martínez Campos answered that while his acts would havc to be approved by the Cortés in Madrid, he would consider terms proposed by the Cubans. The conference ended without accomplishing much. But at this point, the government, including President García and the House of Representatives, resigned. A *Comité del Centro* (Committee of the Central Department) was then formed to complete the negotiations. General Gómez was asked to join the *Comité*, but he refused to take part in the negotiations or the acts of the government on the ground that he was a foreigner.

On February 9, the *Comité del Centro* asked Martínez Campos for terms on which the Spanish would cease their fighting. The terms proposed by Martínez Campos were essentially "a general pardon" for the revolutionary leaders and soldiers; political equality of Cuba with Puerto Rico; liberation of slaves and Asians in the insurrectionary forces; and liberty for all leaders who desired to leave the island. These terms were taken back to the insurgent leaders. They rejected the implication of guilt in "a general pardon," and suggested a "general amnesty" instead. They also asked for a "status" for Cuba equal to that of the provinces of Spain.

Martínez Campos opposed the granting of a "general amnesty" on the ground that this would imply too sweeping a recognition of belligerent rights. The phrase finally agreed upon was "forgetting the past." As for the demand that Cuba be given the same status as the provinces, Martínez Campos, after consulting his associate in command, pointed out that the province of Puerto Rico and the provinces of Spain possessed "substantially the same status." On this basis, the insurgents accepted.[3]

On February 11, 1878, the commissioners of the Cuban Republic met with Martínez Campos at Zanjón, in Camagüey province, where the conditions of the capitulation embodied in the *Pacto del Zanjón* (Treaty of Zanjón) were accepted. The final peace terms included eight articles: (1) the establishment in Cuba of the political and administrative laws enjoyed by Puerto Rico; (2) no action to be taken against anyone for political offenses committed from 1868 to the date of the treaty, freedom for those who were under indictment or serving sentences within or outside the island, and amnesty for all deserters from the Spanish army; (3) freedom for slaves and Asians who were in the insurgent ranks; (4) no one who submitted to Spanish authority should be compelled to render any military service before peace was established over the whole territory; (5) any individual who wished to leave the island should be free to do so; (6) the capitulation of each force was to take place in uninhabited areas; (7) the insurgents of the other departments were to be offered free transportation within the Central Department; and (8) the pact with the *Comité del Centro* was deemed to have been made with all the departments of the island which might accept its conditions.[4]

The *Comité del Centro* specified February 28 as the date on which the capitulation would be effected in Puerto Príncipe. Commissioners were dispatched to the different departments with instructions to join in the capitulation. An emissary was sent to New York to give the Cuban emigrés an account of the capitulation.

The majority of the generals of the Cuban revolution accepted the Treaty of Zanjón and laid down their arms, and the news of this was greeted with satisfaction in Spain. On hearing of the capitulation, the Cortés voted a resolution of congratulations to the king and General Martínez Campos for their success. In Cuba, all those who had been loyal to Spain rejoiced, and a *Te Deum* was sung in the churches of Havana.

"The peace was a necessity imposed by necessity," wrote General Collazo. "Prolongation of the conflict would have meant ruination of the country without hope of success. The conditions of the Spanish government were very bad . . . but our state was even worse." There were, nevertheless, many patriots who were grief-stricken and shocked by the capitulation. They did not minimize the war-weariness of the Cuban people, the hostility of the *hacendados,* nor the refusal of the wealthy emigrés to provide support. These patriotic Cubans protested against the surrender of the two key demands of the revolution: independence for Cuba and emancipation of all its slaves.[5]

More than any other Cuban patriot, Antonio Maceo rescued the revolution from the setback it sustained at Zanjón. While the leaders of the Republic were negotiating the terms of surrender, Maceo continued fighting in Oriente. There was little activity elsewhere to draw off the pressure upon him, and, as a result, he had to face a particularly strong concentration of Spanish forces. Eugenio Antonio Flores, who accompanied Martínez Campos in the campaign of 1877–1878, and who knew every Cuban leader personally, commented on Maceo's activity: "General Polavieja [a famous and respected general]

. . . fought daily clashes with the forces of Maceo, who was then the only general who dared move in the Sierra Maestra mountain range which Polavieja continually penetrated."[6] Maceo did much more than just move. On January 29, 1878, he set a very successful ambush for an unusually large column of enemy troops, capturing rich war booty and forcing the Spaniards to retreat with a large number of dead and wounded.[7] By February 1, Maceo was camped at the mouth of the Caobas River, referred to under the picturesque name of *Llanada de Juan el Mulato* (Plain of John the Mulato). On February 4, he ordered Commander Ramón Gonzáles to take nearly the entire force to reconnoiter Pueblo Nuevo, some four leagues away. Maceo was left with thirty-eight rebels—the officers armed only with pistols and machetes—and fourteen soldiers equipped with rifles, and sufficient ammunition.[8]

Four hours later the Spanish *Cazdores de Madrid* battalion overran the camp sentries and completely surrounded the rebels. Reportedly outnumbered more than eight-to-one, Maceo's tiny unit executed an almost unbelievable turnabout of events. After three hours of brutal combat, the Cubans completely routed their enemy. Following this victory, Maceo ordered his aide, Lieutenant Colonel Lacret, to write to the Spanish commanding general of the district, advising him of the bravery of his troops and inviting him to pick up the prisoners.

On February 7, 8, and 9, in the region of San Ulpiano, Maceo achieved a brilliant victory over the famous San Quentín battalion, although he used a much larger force than in the earlier battle of Llanada de Juan el Mulato. The Spanish battalion was almost completely destroyed, although it fought bravely and repeatedly refused to surrender. Its utter destruction was avoided only by a last-minute rescue by two battalions of infantry and two squadrons of cavalry.[9]

Maceo learned through letters from Gómez that at the very moment he was winning victories for the revolution, a peace treaty was being signed at Zanjón. His immediate reaction, as reported by Félix Figueredo, who was with him, showed his keen grasp of the reasons for the Spaniards' eagerness to end the war:

> Don't you understand, friend Figueredo, that when General Martínez Campos proposes or accepts a transaction, an agreement, it is because, with his experience of what this war is, he is convinced that they will never defeat us by means of arms? And this I say and maintain; doesn't General Gómez know it a thousand times better than we do?[10]

On February 18, agents of the *Comité del Centro* gave Maceo a complete account of all the events leading up to the Treaty of Zanjón. They asked Maceo to join in the surrender ceremonies scheduled for February 29 at Puerto Príncipe. After hearing the report, he announced that he did not agree with the treaty since it did not provide for either independence or the abolition of slavery. Moreover, he said that he would not speak for the revolutionary movement in Oriente. Instead, he would call a rebel assembly and abide by their democratic decision.[11]

Soon after, Maceo wrote to Martínez Campos asking for a truce and requesting an immediate meeting.[12] Maceo received a letter from General Enrique Bargés y Pombo, thanking him for the return of the Spanish prisoners, but warning him that if he tried to continue fighting alone he would have to face much stronger opposition. Maceo's answer was: "I warn you that the men under my leadership will not weaken no matter how difficult the decision of time; the future, like the past, will be the best judge."[13]

On February 24, 1878, Martínez Campos replied to Maceo, rejecting a truce and postponing the requested meeting until the middle of March. Martínez Campos was not particularly desirous of meeting with a black at close quarters, but he realized that he could not say that he had ended the war until Maceo was forced to capitulate. *"This Negro Maceo is the key to a real peace,"* he wrote on February 26.[14]

While preparing for his interview with Martínez Campos, Maceo sought to save the sagging revolution. He invited all the leaders who had not yet agreed to capitulate to a meeting at the Sabana de San Juan, near the Cauto River. He explained:

> Oriente will decide its future soon; if it inclines toward peace, it can obtain it honorably and advantageously; and if not, it will be in a state to continue to fight in which, favored by a thousand circumstances, it can win victory or make the fight interminable.[15]

Although everything was operating to discourage Maceo, he seemed confident of indefinitely continuing a hit-and-run type of guerrilla struggle while living off the countryside and causing ever increasing damage. However, after an exhaustive reevaluation of the situation with his friend and adviser, Fernando Figueredo, he concluded that in order to succeed, the revolution had to be expanded beyond the scope of narrow guerrilla warfare.[16]

During this same period Maceo learned of a plot by some rebels to ambush and assassinate the Spanish general along the route to the meeting. Maceo immediately wrote to them insisting that any such plans be abandoned or suppressed. The letter was intercepted and turned over to Martínez Campos. He thus became aware before they met that Maceo had made a vigorous effort to block an assassination attempt.[17]

News of the assassination plot led Martínez Campos to have companions accompany him to his meeting with Maceo. He received a great number of requests from Spanish officers, for there was a great deal of curiosity about this fabled black about whom so much had been heard. Because he stilled feared an assassination attempt, the Spanish commander limited those who could go to only single men.[18]

The meeting was set for March 15 at Baraguá, near Santiago de Cuba. On March 8 Maceo camped at Baraguá. To present the strongest front possible, Maceo invited the other rebel leaders who had not yet surrendered to gather with their units at Baraguá. Suppressing his resentment against President García, he appealed to him to participate.

Not all of those who were invited attended the gathering: the forces of Bayamo, under Generals Modesto Díaz, Francisco Javier de Céspedes, and Luis Figueredo, had already surrendered. In addition, García, who had encamped near Baraguá with his forces from Las Villas, explained that even though he had participated in the peace negotiations, he now refused to accept the Treaty of Zanjón. However, he now had his own idea about how to carry on the fight, which he was not prepared to reveal. He urged Maceo not to go through with the interview with Martínez Campos.

Maceo rejected this advice, and was supported by the rebels who had come to Baraguá—1,500 officers and soldiers. In a speech to these rebels, Maceo explained the process that had culminated in the Treaty of Zanjón. He denounced the internal dissensions that had weakened the revolutionary struggle, criticized both the wealthy Cuban exiles for having failed to provide funds for military supplies and the *hacendados* for having sabotaged an effective invasion of the West. He did not excuse these forces for dealing with the enemy and signing a peace treaty on a dishonorable basis. They had degraded the Cuban people by requiring that the rest of the armed forces of the Republic accept the shameful pact. As for himself, he was determined "to save the Cuban Revolution from the claws of the intriguers and traitors, facing resolutely the Spanish monarch and its representatives." But he could not speak for those who were at the meeting. He asked if they stood with him in this resolve.

The 1,500 officers and soldiers of Oriente unanimously endorsed Maceo's stand and resolved to follow him to the bitter end to achieve Cuba's independence![19]

On the morning of March 15, 1878, General Martínez Campos and the other representatives of Spain met with a small gathering of black and white Cuban officers, led by General Maceo. Despite the fact that they had fought against each other on several occasions, Martínez Campos did not know Maceo by sight. Upon entering the camp, he asked, "Which of you is Señor Antonio Maceo?" Throughout the meeting, Martínez Campos addressed Maceo only by the title, "señor."

The Spanish general began the meeting with a lengthy discourse emphasizing that there had been enough war, that it was time to make peace, and that it was time for Cuba "to unite with Spain in a march towards progress and civilization." He then requested General Polavieja to read the terms of the Treaty of Zanjón. At this point, Maceo began talking. With measured words, instilling each phrase with the "dignified and expressive revolutionary firmness of a leader of a slave people," he told Martínez Campos that neither he nor his companions from Oriente were ready to accept the pact which had been signed without consulting them. They still hoped that Cuba and its people would achieve peace and happiness, but they were convinced that this would be impossible without liberty. He could not believe in the sincerity of the reforms promised unless they were preceded by the immediate abolition of slavery.

"Gentlemen," Martínez Campos said after Maceo had finished, "I believe that you came to speak of peace. If you are not in agreement with any of the terms of the treaty, what is it that you want?" "What we want is independence," Dr. Félix Figueredo answered quickly. Martínez Campos replied that he would never have come to the meeting if he had thought the rebels would settle for nothing less than independence, since it was beyond his power to promise that. Insofar as slavery was concerned, while he personally would like to see it abolished, there were opposing interests involved; therefore, the matter would have to be debated in the Spanish legislature. He could not compromise the Spanish government by an agreement in the field. What he could do, however, was promise that the slaves who had fought in the revolutionary ranks would remain free.

General Calvar replied for the Cubans: "We cannot accept a peace without the indispensable provisions of independence and the abolition of slavery. Nor can we accept the pact because it is dishonorable." Martínez Campos then asked Maceo directly: "That is to say, we are not in agreement?" Not being contradicted, he asked further: "Then hostilities will again break out?" "Hostilities will again break out," Maceo replied emphatically. Martínez Campos then asked how much time the Cubans would need before the outbreak of hostilities. "For my part," answered Maceo, " I do not find it inconvenient that they break out right now." Finally, an eight day truce was agreed upon and Maceo terminated the meeting with the words: "On March 23, hostilities will break out."[20]

Thus ended the historic and dramatic meeting. After eight days the fighting was renewed. Maceo issued a proclamation to the inhabitants of Oriente asking for their support as he continued the war for immediate abolition of slavery and complete independence from Spain:

To the Inhabitants of the Eastern Department:

Since the time of the unfortunate and base design which brought this Department a new policy in harmony with the total neglect of the Centers by the New York *Junta*, whose policy has been to separate us completely from the President and the Camagüey *Junta*, we have agreed with the leaders Flor Crombet, Belisario Grave de Peralta, Pedro Martínez Freire, Vicente García, José Maceo, Guillermo Moncada, and others, not to enter into the peace agreement that the Central Department has made. We have had ten years of suffering and hardships without number; our army is strong, hardy, and experienced. . . . Our policy is to free the slaves, because the era of the whip and of Spanish cynicism has come to an end, and we ought to form a new Republic assimilated with our sisters Santo Domingo and Haiti.

The great spirit of Washington, Lafayette and Bolívar, liberators of oppressed peoples, accompanies us, and is one with us, and we believe that we will accomplish our work of regeneration. Inhabitants of the Eastern Department, your Major General Maceo is counting on your cooperation.[21]

The "Protest of Baraguá," as it was immediately called, symbolized the best that was in the Cuban Revolution. It was a great protest against those who had surrendered without achieving the revolution's main goals—independence and abolition of slavery—and a formal rejection of the Treaty of Zanjón. It stirred the Cuban masses, black and white, who looked with renewed hope to the resistance movement led by Maceo. Juan Arnao put it well when he wrote: "General Maceo had saved the honor of the Cubans." The Spanish viewpoint was expressed by a leading general who declared: "The 'Protest of Baraguá' is the most arrogant act of the whole campaign since the *Grito de Yara*."[22]

The "Protest of Baraguá" aroused international attention. On April 6, 1878, New York's *La Verdad* paid tribute to Maceo's action: "The hero of the day is Maceo, and it appears it is up to him to raise Cuba again to the pinnacle of its glory." A month later, the same paper published a message sent to Maceo by S. R. Scottron, the black Secretary of the American and Foreign Anti-Slavery Society and also Chairman of the Cuban Anti-Slavery Committee. He wrote:

> My Society has read with infinite pleasure your honorable and just demands in the recent conference with General Martínez Campos. You have demanded the immediate abolition of slavery as a price for your allegiance. Few men in the history of the world have had the good fortune of finding themselves in such an honorable position as that which you now occupy. And none have occupied one more noble. . . . The friends of liberty in America as in Europe have their eyes anxiously fixed on you, hoping that perhaps you will save that noble Cuban army which successfully sustains the flag of liberty.

The Anti-Slavery Society of London cited the "Protest of Baraguá" in an appeal to the British government to apply pressure upon Spain for the fulfillment of its promise to emancipate all the slaves of Cuba, "a promise so many times repeated and so often violated."[23]

To give meaning to the "Protest of Baraguá" it was necessary to reorganize the entire resistance movement. At Maceo's request, all officers with the rank of colonel and above who adhered to the "Protest" met, drew up a new constitution, formed a new government, and assigned new military commands. Maceo did not seek a position in the top leadership of the government and he became neither president nor commander-in-chief of the army. Instead, Manuel de Jesús Calvar was named president, and Vicente García, who had not even participated in the "Protest of Baraguá," was made commanding general of the Liberating Army. Maceo accepted the post of second in command of the army and commander-in-chief of the Military Department of Oriente. His decision was motivated by his desire to establish the strongest unity in the resistance movement. "To realize the formation of the new government," he wrote to General Julio Sanguilly in New York, "I proposed that all the leaders of this department should make friends with General García and that we should give him what he so much wanted to achieve by political means in order that all united they should help me to save our principles and the honor of our arms."[24]

The revolutionaries faced almost insuperable odds. The long years of suffering and the resulting weariness had created demoralization and a lack of will to fight. In addition, rebel commanders continued to surrender with their forces. Martínez Campos' tactics of infiltrating the rebel ranks and persuading or bribing some of them to accept peace was producing results. With Maceo, however, the Spaniards failed completely. He ordered the arrest of the Cuban emissaries who were sent to persuade him to make peace. On one occasion, the Spanish military commander of Barrancas de Cauto sent a messenger to Maceo with a letter offering large sums of money if he would leave the island. After reading the letter, Maceo asked the messenger brusquely: "Commander, do you know the contents of that document?" "No," replied the official, "I am only a messenger of my superior officer and am in absolute ignorance of its contents." "I am glad," said Maceo, "because it prevents me from having the pain of hanging you on that tree." With the approval of the provisional government, Maceo sent his answer by the same messenger. It characterized the author of the attempted bribe-letter as an "infamous coward."

On another occasion, on March 18, 1878, when Maceo was offered a considerable sum of money if he would accept the Zanjón pact, he replied:

> Do you think that a man who is fighting for a principle and has a high regard for his honor and reputation can sell himself while there is still at least a chance of saving his principles by dying or trying to enforce them before he denigrates himself? Men like me fight only in the cause of liberty and will smash their guns rather than submit. I believe that the sentiments of General Martínez Campos are very noble, but we don't need anything else but the things for which we have to go on living. So on this account, it would be impossible for me to receive you with open arms after you have offended me so much.[25]

The rebels, led by Maceo, initiated an intense campaign of military action. At first, the Spaniards confronted these actions with passive resistance. General Martínez Campos instructed his soldiers not to fight and to answer all assaults with shouts of: *"Viva Cuba! Viva la Paz! no hagáis fuego, pues somos hermanos!"* (Long live Cuba! Long live peace! Don't shoot, since we are brothers!) This strategy did not continue for long, for the Spanish soon hurled all their soldiers against the rebels. Day by day, the rebel ranks were thinned by death and wounding, by constant Spanish pressure, and by a steady stream of desertions.

With all of Spain's forces concentrated against him and his followers, Maceo faced a hopeless situation unless he could obtain immediate aid and widen the scope of the battle. At this moment, he received news that the revolutionary officials in the United States had quit their posts. In the face of this, Cuban tobacco workers in Key West and Tampa had organized clubs and contributed funds for military supplies, and a support demonstration had been held at the Masonic Hall in New York. But General Sanguilly had met with a cold response from the wealthy Cuban emigrants, and his expected supply expedition had failed to materialize.

The difficult situation confronting the new revolutionary movement was clearly described by Dr. Félix Figueredo:

> The persecution directed by General Martínez Campos was so active that the provisional government and Maceo could not keep a fixed camp and could not rest except during the night hours. . . . Meanwhile, not a day passed without the arrival of unfavorable news for the revolution. The Cuban forces of Manzanillo and Bayamo, and those of the western border of Holguín, which Colonel Belisario G. de Peralta commanded, were dispersing amidst the most profound disorganization. What had already happened in Camagüey and western Las Villas was occurring in eastern Las Villas. . . . To complete this picture of dissolution, many *insurrectos* of clear intelligence, upon returning to their families and seeing themselves respected and well treated by the Spanish military chieftains, cooperated with the peace move by sending letters to their companions still in arms.[26]

On May 1, Figueredo noted in his diary that a return to peace was inevitable, and on May 3, he wrote of a plan offered to the government designed to save Maceo from the certain death that awaited him, and to prevent a forced and humiliating surrender. This plan proposed that Maceo be sent abroad to secure supplies and reinforcements for the insurrection.

At first the idea received a negative response; the attitude was that all should go down or all be saved. Finally the government decided that Maceo should be spared the dishonor of a compromise. If sufficient aid could not be obtained, he could then lead a new movement at some future date. General Mármol, another member of the government, argued that the revolution would almost certainly die without Maceo, but he added that there was no other choice but to send him for aid since it seemed likely to fail even if Maceo remained.

When Maceo was informed of this decision, he replied:

> I will obey whatever order the government gives on condition that it promises, in the event that it has to leave the battlefield, not to capitulate until my return or until I have made a report on this situation among the emigrants and on whatever hope they offer for the continuance of the fight.

Arrangements were made with the Spaniards for Maceo's departure. Meeting with Martínez Campos, Maceo thanked him for his kind consideration for himself and his family, but added that he did not consider himself bound or restricted in his future conduct and that he would try again. "As I am not compromised," he concluded, "I will do what I can to come back and then undertake my work anew."[27]

On May 10, 1878, a Spanish cruiser left Santiago de Cuba for Jamaica with Antonio Maceo aboard. On the following day, Henry C. Hall, the American Consul in Havana, wrote to the State Department:

> The surrender of the "Chief" Maceo is without doubt the most important event that has occurred since the capitulation of Máximo Gómez and others in February ultimo. . . . His force, according to the *Diario* [*de la Marina*] of today, comprised 400 men and upwards, and was admitted to be a very efficient corps, as was also Maceo himself considered a very efficient and energetic chief, frequently, and even recently it is said, successful in his encounters with the Spanish forces. His surrender is the more

important as regards the pacification of the Island, as his force still remained a nucleus to which the many discontented spirits of the insurrection could rally.[28]

Hall was not entirely correct, for Maceo had not surrendered. Indeed, he left behind in Cuba a great symbol for the future, for it was his "Protest of Baraguá" that enabled all patriotic Cubans to say that the revolutionaries had never surrendered, and had never been defeated—that there had only been a temporary truce declared.

6

The Little War

Maceo's mission to Jamaica was a total failure. In spite of his twenty-one wounds and the fame he had earned through the "Protest of Baraguá," he was regarded with suspicion for having left Cuba on a Spanish cruiser. As a result, he was able to raise exactly five shillings and seven volunteers in Kingston.[1] After sending a discouraging report to the revolutionary government in Cuba, he departed for New York on the steamship *Atlas*. His arrival there on May 23, 1878, went unnoticed in the *New York Times*, but then it must be remembered that the *Times* had not mentioned Maceo once in the course of a lengthy review of the Ten Years' War on March 4, 1878. Other papers, however, were excited about Maceo's presence.

Maceo immediately met with the Cuban exiles and leading black Americans, including the distinguished minister Henry Highland Garnet, president of the American and Foreign Anti-Slavery Society and a long-time champion of Cuban independence. Editors sought interviews with Maceo, convinced that their readers were interested in learning more about the man of color who had risen from being a relatively unknown soldier to a position of high rank in the rebel army and had exhibited such extraordinary military skill. Maceo, however, was reluctant to meet reporters, partly because he wished to keep details of the planned struggle in Cuba secret, but also because he tended to be reticent in conversation, and, unlike the bold, imaginative, and aggressive qualities he displayed in battle, he was rather shy in public discussions. Rumors circulated by Spanish agents were spreading to the effect that Maceo had made a deal with the Spanish authorities, and it was this that had enabled him to leave Cuba on a Spanish vessel. *La Verdad,* a Cuban revolutionary paper published in New York put the matter directly when it noted on June 8 that

> in honor of Maceo, we must say his leaving was not with the agreement of the Spanish chief. Nor did he sell out, as a Madrid newspaper charges, but he was fulfilling an order of our government, and that's that. Does General Maceo deserve our confidence? Yes, he does deserve it, because his conduct stands as guarantee for his word, and as a valiant proof that he is serving our cause with the purity of a patriot, with the abnegation of the valiant soldier who puts above all the honor and glory of his flag.[2]

Finally, Maceo consented to an interview with *Las Novedades.* It was published on June 12, 1878, and in it he was described as "a man about thirty-five years old, tall, well-built, very thick beard, reserved about certain answers and certain others he left out completely." When the reporter asked Maceo to comment on the "capitulation carried out with General Martínez Campos," he replied:

> I should tell you that I have not capitulated. At the beginning of April I asked for a meeting with that General which took place. But we could not reach an agreement. Nevertheless, hostilities did not continue, but the truce lasted eight days, and when this was over, my forces had several encounters with the Spanish troops. On June 7 I received an order [which he showed] from the leader of the government, [Manuel de Jesús] Calvar, in which he gave me instructions to abandon the ranks, to go abroad as the general agent of the government and return to Cuba with results of the trip. I must tell you that General Martínez Campos knew

the object of my trip, for when I said goodbye to him I told him that I was going abroad to work for Cuba to which he answered that he already knew it.

Reporter: And how do you explain that General Martínez Campos, knowing the object of your leaving the island, against the interests of Spain, not only permitted you to leave, but let you do so in a Spanish warship?

Maceo: I don't know how to tell you. I believe that it was Señor Calvar who arranged all this business.

Reporter: So you are trying to work here in favor of the insurrection?

Maceo: Si, Señor. I have here a proclamation of Calvar to the Cuban emigrés. Tonight I am going to present it to them at a club and urge them to support me in my work and help me in the getting together of the means to continue the war.

The account ended on a touching personal note:

We were not alone with Maceo since there were with us several more individuals from the American press, so we did not wish to prolong the interview. Furthermore, he seemed not to be feeling very well. The humid weather made him feel his wounds. There were twenty-one of them of which seventeen were shots and the rest are *arma blanca* [bayonets], which last circumstance we can attest to because his hands had evident signs of wounds and mutilations on the fingers.[3]

According to a black American who spent time in Maceo's company in New York, the latter used the opportunity to improve his military knowledge. Writing years later in the *AME Church Review,* Frank J. Webb described how Maceo went to the U.S. Military Academy at West Point incognito, and in order to study cavalry tactics, accepted work as a hostler. "Daily he noted every point, watched and learned every strategic movement, ignored no detail concerning the drill and movements of large bodies of men," wrote Webb. And no student, he went on, was more attentive than Maceo:

> The ready, willing, dark-skinned hostler gave his whole time to the study of war. He devoured every book the students gave him. Poor in pocket he did many an errand for the cadets and received his pay in old books on military tactics. No one dreamed that the hostler with the burning eyes and determined face was the hero of the Ten Years War.
>
> With his wages he bought every book treating of war he could; and no movement was ever wasted during his stay at our Military College. The students, it is a matter of record, all liked this modest man; had they known who he was, they, with the enthusiasm and the natural veneration of youth for daring deeds, would have worshipped him.[4]

Since there is no other account in any work dealing with Maceo's career that mentions this anonymous stay at West Point,[5] it is likely that the story is apocryphal. Still, it was very much in keeping with Maceo that he should ever be seeking to improve his knowledge of military tactics by reading whatever he could on the subject—all with the aim of more effectively waging the struggle for Cuban independence.

Maceo's reception by the Cuban emigrant groups in New York was better than in Jamaica, but the results were still unsatisfactory. He had just begun a report to President Calvar on the divisions existing among the revolutionary organizations in New York when he learned that the rebel government had accepted the Spanish peace terms on May 21. Realizing that the government hc represented no longer existed, and that there was no fighting force left in Cuba, Maceo soon after departed for Jamaica.[6] There he devoted himself to farming and to correspondence with other rebels concerning the possibilities for a new revolution in Cuba.

Maceo and other Cuban patriots regarded the Zanjón treaty as only a truce, not a surrender. In their view, the Cubans had not stopped fighting because they were defeated, but because they needed to pause to renew their strength and secure better weapons. At first these views were not too popular in a country that was weary of so many years of bloodshed, but each passing month brought new converts to the idea. Life soon demonstrated that the Treaty of Zanjón was a cruel joke. The key provision—the promise of the same political concessions to Cuba as were then enjoyed by Puerto Rico—proved a hoax. Puerto Rico was under a state of siege. In 1874 the concessions made as a result of the "Glorious Revolution" of 1868 had been suspended, and Puerto Rico enjoyed no other political right than representation in the Cortés. Martínez Campos repeatedly wrote to his government, asking for the fulfillment of the treaty as he understood it, but the Spanish government refused to budge. Supported by the most reactionary elements in Cuba and by statesmen in Spain, who considered all Cubans except the most reactionary groups on the island as disloyal, the government in Madrid continued to undermine the hopes that had surged with the capitulation at Zanjón. Under these circumstances, it is not surprising that there were elements who again spoke of liberating the island from the Spanish yoke.[7]

This movement for a new rebellion was launched by veterans of the Ten Years' War who had settled in New York after the Treaty of Zanjón. The highest ranking officer in this group was Major General Calixto García. In 1874, after holding off the enemy for one hundred days, García had shot himself under the chin so as not to be taken alive. The bullet was deflected and his life saved, but he remained a prisoner until Zanjón, when he was released. He came to New York with his reputation intact, for he was one of the few leaders of the revolution who had not signed the pact. He immediately reorganized the *Comité Revolucionario Cubano* (Cuban Revolutionary Committee) under his presidency. In October 1878 he issued a manifesto inviting all Cubans to unite in the fight against Spanish despotism, and urged all separatists on the island to organize into secret groups "to work by all means conducive to the achievement of independence, contriving and collecting financial resources and material for war."[8]

The response to this appeal was surprising. An underground movement was organized in Cuba. Beginning in Oriente, it spread like wildfire to other parts of the island. The conspiracy even began to attract supporters in Havana.[9] Many recruits came from the black population; they were eager to resume the battle for independence and for the complete abolition of slavery, and they were encouraged to do so by some of the more radical leaders of the revolutionary movement. "Take your machetes in hand, and burn the cane," *La Independencia*, organ of the Revolutionary Committee, urged the slaves on November 23, 1878.

One of the chief lessons learned from the Ten Years' War was that a regional movement alone could not successfully combat the overwhelming Spanish superiority in men and supplies. To be truly effective, a rebellion had to take place simultaneously throughout the island. With this in mind, Colonel Pedro Martínez Freire prepared a detailed plan which called for a spontaneous uprising throughout the island. This revolt was planned to coincide with the seizure of the Spanish arsenals in Santiago de Cuba. Under Freire's plan, immediately after the outbreak of the rebellion, García and Maceo were to arrive on the island and assume supreme command.[10]

Freire's plan received enthusiastic support from Calixto García, who began to mobilize the revolutionary movement in the western part of the island from his base in New York. In Oriente province, José Maceo and Guillermo Moncada were making preparations for an uprising; in Las Villas, Emilio Núñez and Serafín Sánchez were preparing to join them; and in Havana and in other provinces, the revolutionary clubs were maintaining contact with these preparations.[11]

But it was impossible for the movement to continue for long on so smooth a course. Spanish spies among the revolutionaries easily learned of the project and sought to arouse the old divisive tendencies in the rebel ranks. They pointed to the fact that Antonio Maceo was scheduled to lead the insurrection in Oriente, and that other blacks—José Maceo, Guillermo Moncada, Flor Crombet, Jesús Rabí, Cecilio Gonzalez, and Serafín Sánchez—were among the most active conspirators. They then asserted that these men, under Maceo's leadership, were plotting to take over the newly-projected revolution as the first step in the establishment of a black Republic.

The Spanish propaganda campaign was abetted by those Cubans who were still tied financially to the institution of slavery, and by those who clung to reformism and wished to crush the budding revolutionary movement. These Cubans spread the charge far and wide that the new revolution was being planned solely by "4,000 Negroes who proclaim not only the flag of separatism but also a war of the races." From Cuba, the Revolutionary Committee in New York received letters that emphasized: "A belief is circulating and being hotly discussed that the movement in Cuba is made up of people of color only, and is simply a prelude to a war of races."[12]

A number of Cuban exiles who occupied influencial places in the Revolutionary Committee and were influenced by a white-supremicist ideology, reacted to these reports by seeking to limit the role of blacks in the revolution, and especially to prevent Maceo from assuming a commanding role. They accused him of trying to operate independently of the Revolutionary Committee—a charge that had some substance—but they were motivated primarily by racism. They also wrote to Calixto García urging him not to place Maceo in a position of command in the new expedition.

Maceo became so disgusted that he did something that only added to the hostility toward him. He impulsively turned over 400,000 rounds of ammunition in his possession to Leoncio Prado, a Peruvian who wished to use this material in the war between Peru and Chile, and who assured Maceo that it would be returned when the Cuban revolutionaries again had need of it.[13] Maceo did this when he believed he would no longer play a role in a new expedition, but it was a foolish act and served to further infuriate those who were suspicious of him.[14]

Maceo soon became involved in the new revolutionary movement. Calixto García and his followers discovered that no one commanded greater respect in Oriente than Maceo, and Oriente, after all, was the seat of the genuine rebellious spirit in Cuba. On August 5, 1879, at a conference in Kingston, Jamaica, Maceo and García reached an understanding on the projected uprising.[15] In the meeting, Maceo was led to believe that he would be the commander of the Oriente district, as well as the leader of an expedition to the island. He immediately sent letters from Kingston to friends in Oriente, advising them to make preparations for the approaching conflict: "The moment for returning to the field of battle has arrived. We must conquer what rightly belongs to us by armed might."[16]

A few days later, Maceo heard that the revolt had broken out in Cuba. What has historically come to be called *La Guerra Chiquita* (The Little War) began prematurely on August 26, 1879, in Santiago de Cuba. As in the case of the Ten Years' War, the Spanish spy system forced the rebel leaders to begin fighting before the fixed date to avoid being seized and imprisoned. When José and Rafael Maceo, Antonio's brothers, together with Guillermo Moncada and Quintín Banderas, raised the standard of revolt in Santiago de Cuba, other similar declarations followed in Oriente and the central part of the island. Las Villas responded under Brigadier Ramos, Emilio Núñez, Serafín Sánchez, and Francisco Carrillo. These rebel leaders, black and white, were followed by hundreds of men, including large numbers of runaway slaves.[17]

Calixto García and Antonio Maceo waited for the right moment to land in Cuba and assume leadership of the movement. With his two brothers and many friends and followers already in the struggle, Maceo was eager to depart for the island. He made what financial arrangements he could for the care of his mother and wife and sent a manifesto from Kingston to Santiago de Cuba, calling upon all Cubans to fight for liberty, and urging the slaves to join the Liberating Army:

> Slaves! The tyrant has denied you liberty, and has condemned you to martyrdom. The black man is as free as the white; the wickedness of your oppressor has you suffering under the cruelty of your masters. You endure the whip that still strikes your shoulders because you are deceived.
>
> You must remember at all times that your comrades who fought in the last war achieved their liberty because they embraced the Cuban flag which belongs to all Cubans alike. Get together again under the same flag, and you shall obtain freedom and your civil rights, and after that, you shall be able to make common cause with those that today want to redeem you from the degraded situation in which you find yourselves now.[18]

The Revolutionary Committee in New York decided not to let Maceo head the expedition. Instead, it placed Brigadier General Gregorio Benítez in charge. When Maceo asked why Benítez, who possessed neither his following nor prestige, had been chosen, he was told that it was because of racial prejudice. Calixto García put it to Maceo bluntly: "Comrade, I have decided upon the departure of Benítez ahead of you, because the Spaniards have said that this is a race war and the Cuban whites fear that this may be true. In order not to create the impression that this propaganda has validity, I thought it best you should not go first." The Spaniards were loudly proclaiming that Maceo wished to achieve black domination of the island, he said, and many Cubans were swallowing the Spanish propaganda. "However," García added, "you know that I am not capable of believing such a thing." Nevertheless, in order to give the lie to Spanish propaganda, Maceo would have to wait. He was assured, however, that it was only a matter of time before he would be given notice to leave.[19]

Although García was telling the truth when he said that he himself did not believe the Spanish propaganda, it is unfortunate that he yielded to the pressure of those elements in the Revolutionary Committee who either did believe it or who used it to foster their own ambitions. García should have foreseen that the exclusion of Maceo from the leadership of the revolution would disillusion many on the island. Many blacks now felt that the Cuban rebels did not really have their interests at heart and were only using them to advance their own purposes. How much faith could they now have that the Republic they were fighting for would abolish slavery and grant them equal rights?

Although justifiably bitter, Maceo refused to sever his connections with the revolutionary movement. In 1876, he had decided, after some hesitation, not to allow the racists in the revolutionary ranks to prevent him from fighting for Cuban independence and for the liberation of his people from slavery. Now in 1879, his decision was the same, even though he was far from happy over the turn of events.

Maceo's gloom over this racism was temporarily lifted during a visit to the black Republic of Haiti in his quest for support for the Cuban revolution. There, he was among members of his own race, and in Port-au-Prince people came in droves to see and speak to him. The ruling Liberal Party, led by Boyer Bazelais, welcomed Maceo warmly.[20] Gaston Revest, a Frenchman who lived in Port-au-Prince, wrote of the thirty-four-year-old rebel leader:

> Maceo was tall and reminded one of a statue that moved. He was dressed elegantly. His deep black sidewhiskers caused the splendid shine of his onyx pupils to be even more noticeable. At first there were receptions and celebrations everywhere for the hero, so recently arrived from the fields of battle. He was a gracious and courteous gentleman of exquisitely masculine manners.[21]

Maceo addressed a lengthy letter to General Joseph Lamothe,

the Liberal Party leader, requesting his continued support for the Cuban cause. With great emotion, Maceo spoke of the slavery issue that still had to be resolved in Cuba and called upon Lamothe, as a representative of a nation ruled by the sons of former slaves, to extend his aid whenever possible. It is one of Maceo's finest letters:

> I believe it is useless to relate the history of Cuba. You know it, as Cuban history is Haitian history or the history of any colony.
>
> The sons of the conquerors who are born on the island are not able to enjoy the liberties that their parents enjoy in Spain. The majority of the population, composed of men of our race, are deprived of all political and social rights and are subject to the most unreasonable prejudices. Finally, 350,000 men exist in the most severe servitude, and are born, live and die under the iron yoke of slavery. The Spaniards, in spite of the world's disapproval, in spite of the advice and example of other nations and all the efforts of the abolitionists, have been able to maintain slavery in their colonies. Cuba, the most beautiful land in the world, has been changed into a bulwark of this infamous institution. The slaves soak the soil with their sweat, without ever seeing the product of their efforts. This includes not only the Negroes brought from the African coasts and their descendants, but many others carried from other Spanish colonies or even from Haiti by their owners. . . . I will not dally in describing the horrors of slavery. . . . You, along with all men of color, have been interested in studying them, and you know them well. It suffices to say that there are in Cuba around one half million men, who are the exclusive property of some others who exercise over them the right of life and death, and can buy and sell them, who make them work day and night without any pay, who order them whipped for the slightest mistake, regarding them completely as beasts, and who deny them even the right to have a family.
>
> Those slaves, General, worn out from the whip and chains, are too weak to break their own bonds, and looking around they see us, men of color who have had the good fortune of not being born into slavery, or of having freed ourselves from it, and they seek our help. Our duty is to concede to them, to deny it would be a

> crime. . . . So the Cuban people, tired of suffering such evils, and taking pity on the cries of their brothers, have launched a revolution and will die to achieve their liberty. . . . I am not, General, the Ambassador of a government which comes to propose a new alliance with some clear advantage. . . . I am the emissary of an enslaved people who struggle to gain their independence near another people of the same origin who enjoy an independent existence, and who are too generous not to continue to extend a protective hand to their brothers.
>
> Pardon me, General, if I dare to write you today, but my brothers are fighting on the battlefields and duty obliges me to rejoin them as soon as possible, and today inaction on my part would be an unpardonable fault.[22]

Unfortunately, while Maceo was visiting the Cuban immigrants in Jacmel, Jérémie, Aux Cayes, and Cap Haitien, the Liberal Party lost power. The new government, under the presidency of General Lysius Salomón, was anything but friendly to the heroic visitor. The new president had established close ties with Spain during his service as Haitian representative in Madrid, and he continued to depend on its favors.[23]

Spanish officials, working with Salomón's agents in the press, spread rumors that the Cuban revolutionary cause was basically a racial movement against blacks, that Maceo had been eliminated from leadership because he was a black, and that by continuing to support the revolutionary cause under these circumstances, he was a traitor to his own race. The irony was that it was the Spaniards who had originally initiated the propaganda charge that the revolutionary movement was a plot on the part of blacks, under Maceo's leadership, to create another "Haiti." But in Haiti itself, they spread the propaganda that the Cuban movement was insufficiently represented by blacks in its leadership, and was racist from top to bottom.[24]

On the heels of these journalistic attacks on Maceo's credibility as a leader of the black people came the first of several plots against his life. On December 14, 1889, two would-be assassins—Dominican generals Quintín Díaz and Antonio

Pérez—approached Maceo with a proposition concerning weapons and ammunition for the Cuban cause. The two men planned to lure him to a secluded spot on the coast and either kill him or turn him over to the crew of a Spanish war vessel to perform the deadly work. Maceo was warned by a friend inside the office of the Spanish consul enabling him to elude the trap. It soon became known that the plot had been planned and paid for by the captain general of Cuba, Ramón Blanco, acting through the Spanish consul in Port-au-Prince. To make matters worse, the conspiracy had the endorsement of President Salomón![25]

This was not Maceo's only narrow escape in Haiti. Acting on the advice of friends to flee the country, he set out on horseback to cross the border into Santo Domingo. He was attacked by a group of riders but, by expert horsemanship, he managed to escape and returned to Port-au-Prince, where a Cuban friend, Santiago Pérez, harbored him at his home.[26]

Meanwhile, a rumor spread throughout the Haitian capital that Maceo was dead. Many Cubans and Haitians began a demonstration against the government; the police, fearing a rebellion, began to arrest Maceo's friends and suspected acquaintances.[27] To prevent further persecution of his friends, Maceo resolved once more to leave the country. Finally, on January 7, 1880, in the company of his brother, Marcos, he boarded the French steamer *Deserade* for St. Thomas in the Danish Virgin Islands. Commenting later on his visit to Haiti, Maceo made a distinction between official ill-treatment and the courteous welcome accorded him by intellectuals and common people:

> I have received innumerable kindnesses from various persons and from distinguished families who loaded me with favors and made me the object of a treatment so exquisite and obliging that I can't find sentences capable of describing it. Neither do I believe it possible to find words to express with exactitude the memory that such treatment leaves in my heart.[28]

In St. Thomas Maceo ran into new difficulties. The press accused him of stirring up trouble in Haiti and sneered at his reputation as a fighter against racism. If he were really interested in the welfare of Cuban blacks, the newspapers charged, he would oppose the rebels and join the side of Spain, for it was the Spaniards, not the revolutionists, who were defending the interests of the black Cuban population. The press cited as proof the racial prejudices against Maceo himself among his fellow rebels, and the fact that the proposals for the gradual abolition of slavery, just debated in the Spanish Cortés, had been opposed only by the Cuban representatives.[29]

Maceo persistently defended the revolutionary movement,[30] although he knew only too well that the charge of racism in its ranks was more than justified. He still sought aid for the new rebellion, but not only was he turned down in St. Thomas, but the Spanish authorities succeeded in making it difficult for him to obtain passage from the island. So dangerous had association with Maceo become that Cuban revolutionists in various parts of the Caribbean made it clear that they preferred that Maceo not visit them. The president of a revolutionary club in Santo Domingo wrote to the Cuban Revolutionary Committee in New York:

> By now you must have news of what happened to Maceo in Haiti; today he is in St. Thomas trying to come here, but we have written him not to do it. His coming would bring great inconvenience and might even cause a conflict with Spain. . . . It would be wise for you to cable Maceo in St. Thomas advising him to join General Calixto García. Otherwise he may be captured at sea. The Spanish ships are guarding this coast closely.[31]

Maceo had been strongly advised by Fernando Figueredo against proceeding to Santo Domingo, and had even been warned by others that he might be killed by the Spaniards if he did come to that country.[32] He sailed nonetheless, his vessel being followed closely by the Spanish war ship *El Leon.* In Santo Domingo, contrary to all expectations, so many Cubans and Dominicans alike came to pay their respects that Maceo had to move from his hotel to larger quarters in the *La Republicana* theater.[33] The great Puerto Rican revolutionary, Don Eugenio Mariá de Hostos, was a frequent visitor to these sessions.[34] Pablo Ramarol, Dominican poet and secretary of the government, not only attended but wrote a poem in *El de la Opinion* entitled "To my Good Friend General Maceo."[35] Other Dominican officials, especially General Ulisses Heureaux, treated Maceo with the utmost respect, courtcsy, and friendliness.[36] It was indeed a welcome change from Haiti and St. Thomas. Maceo was grateful that despite constant Spanish pressure, Heureaux had refused to interfere with the Cuban's activities, and he had even been able to leave without difficulty. "He put at my disposal," Maceo wrote later, "all the means for my personal defense, and showed the most exquisite care for my person within the bounds of his office."[37]

In Cuba, however, things were going from bad to worse for the revolutionary cause. The Spanish government arrested all who were under the slightest suspicion of being in sympathy with the rebellion, especially blacks. In Santiago de Cuba alone, 350 blacks were arrested, shipped to Havana, and thrown into the Morro Castle dungeon, there to await the arrival of ships that would transport them to the Ceuta penitentiary, an island off the coast of Spain. In Havana province, the revolutionary movement was crushed; the rebels were arrested, deported to Spain, or shipped off to Ceuta; others were sent to the Isle of Pines; while still others succeeded in escaping to New York. In Oriente, where the movement had initially made the greatest progress, the situation had deteriorated seriously. Harassed by the vigorous efforts of a powerful Spanish army, and constantly in need of provisions and support, General José Maceo, Brigadier Rafael Maceo, Guillermo Moncada, and other leaders surrendered on June 1, 1880. The surrender was arranged through the efforts of the consuls of France and England in

Guantánamo, on the condition that the rebels be given safe passage from the island. But once they were on the high seas, a Spanish warship seized them and took them to Spanish prisons in Africa.[38]

The revolution had suffered grievous blows, but many still looked to García to lead the fighting and hoped that Maceo would land with an expeditionary force. They were bitterly disappointed on both scores.

The courageous García, relentlessly pursued by the Spaniards from the day he landed, never made contact with the scattered bands of *insurrectos.* With his forces decimated by pursuit, hunger, and weariness, and he himself sick with fever, García wandered through the hills with only six ragged, barefoot companions. On August 3, 1880, García was forced to surrender and soon was on the way to Spain to suffer again the discomforts of prison.

When Maceo learned of the setbacks, he decided to depart for Cuba, even though he had few men and scarcely any resources. In a final effort to dispel the suspicions that he was leading a race war, he wrote a letter to *El Yara,* the Cuban paper published in Florida:

> I have never been affiliated with any political party. I have always been a soldier of the national freedom which I desire for Cuba, and I reject nothing with as much indignation as the pretentious ideas of a race war. Always, as in the past, I will be on the side of the sacred interests of the people, totally and indivisibly above the mechanization of parties, and never will I stain my sword with internal war, which might prove traitorous to the internal unity of Cuba. When Spain ceases to administer Cuba, we should not think of a situation emerging where one sector of the society dominates the rest; on the contrary, the goal in mind is to make our people master of their destiny, and for that purpose we have to be united. . . . There is no place for reflective thought in a mind that is full of prejudice because such thought arises in a

serene conscience under the guidance of reason. . . . I love all things and all men, because I see more of the essences than the accidents of life; for that reason I have above the interests of race, whatever that may be, the interest of Humanity.[39]

Maceo left Santo Domingo on June 28, 1880, with thirty-four companions and a cargo of arms, ostensibly bound for New York. The Spanish intelligence service had learned about the expedition through a member who was one of its spies. When the ship dropped anchor at Cap Haitien, Haiti, Maceo and his men were denounced to the Haitian authorities, who confiscated the money that Maceo had sent ashore to be used for the purchase of arms and ammunition and also prevented the delivery of military supplies that friends had collected. Maceo was forced to depart, empty-handed, for Turks Island, a British possession.[40]

Spanish sailors there prevented the transfer of arms from shore. With his plans completely disrupted, Maceo and his companions remained in the English colony. As before, a spy in his group informed the Spaniards of his every move, and on July 6, 1880, a third attempt was made to assassinate him. Although it too failed, the incident, together with Spanish pressure and the support of ardent abolitionists on the island for Maceo, caused the English officials to order him and his companions to leave. Maceo refused, and in order to prevent a further deterioration of the situation, the governor of all the Bahamas finally dispatched a warship from Jamaica with orders to take Maceo and his fellow conspirators to Kingston.[41] Although some forty citizens, principally abolitionists, sent a note to Maceo urging him not to leave, he finally decided that his presence was causing too much difficulty. Before he departed he addressed a note of thanks to the inhabitants of Turks Island:

I want to acknowledge in some way the manifestation made by the people in favor of the principles which I defend . . . with the

> assertion that the Cuban people better than I will know how to thank you for such beneficent service, while such as I thank you for the efforts you have made because men of the black and white race suffer in Cuba the horrors of tyranny. . . . May the 300,000 Negroes who suffer from the cruelest oppression soon be freed from this horrible tyranny![42]

While en route to Jamaica, Maceo learned of Calixto García's surrender and of the almost total destruction of the revolutionary force. Juan Bellido de Luna, director of the Cuban revolutionary paper in New York, *La Independencia,* wrote to Maceo on August 24, 1880, urging him to give up any idea of invading Cuba: "I fear that you may sacrifice yourself for a sterile cause. What has happened to Calixto is proof of the general demoralization of the Cuban people."[43]

Shortly thereafter, Bellido advised Maceo that the valiant young Emilio Núñez, the last rebel chieftain left fighting, had surrendered, and that the defeat of Cuba was complete.[44] Convinced that any effort now was useless, Maceo disbanded his expedition. His feelings as he did so are revealed in a letter he wrote to Bellido:

> That Calixto García has fallen prisoner for the second time is to be lamented for the great loss it brings to our cause. But the situation of that general is more enviable than my own; he had the good fortune of reaching the battlefields of Cuba while my fate was to remain in foreign areas when he most needed me. It was not my fault. Everyone knows what efforts I made to get there before him. But the constant setbacks which I have suffered and the lack of sufficient resources to carry the thirty men in my company to those beaches prevented me from being among the fortunate ones. Indeed, Calixto has the good luck of having fulfilled his aspirations, while I find disgrace hanging over me with all of my most important comrades able to reach Cuban soil.

In concluding his letter, Maceo once more revealed that he put personal considerations in the background when the struggle for Cuban independence was involved. He observed that should he assume leadership of the struggle, "some of the Cubans would have to put aside some of their social concerns, because that is the only inconvenience which I see for those for whom the fatherland is not before everything else." (By "social concerns," Maceo meant, of course, the racial question.) He went on:

> I would be happy if there were another person, who, under every concept, would fulfill the aspirations of the Cuban people, if only this could be the way to lead us for the independence of our country because it is the only thing which . . .[45]

The letter remained unfinished, but the meaning was clear.

7

Interlude

Many Cuban revolutionaries were thoroughly disheartened by the repeated failures. Morale among those in exile was so low after the debacles of the Little War that all active plotting came to an end for several years. Antonio Maceo, too, despaired of any immediate prospects for a new revolution. He now had to devote more attention to his personal affairs. The most pressing problem was that of providing adequately for his family. This included not only his wife, María Cabrales, but also several mistresses. While Maceo never liked tobacco and detested alcoholic drinks,[1] he definitely loved women. They were attracted to him—women of all colors and nationalities—and Maceo reciprocated their attention. While in Puerto Plata, Dominican Republic, he had a love affair with María Filomena Martínez, a striking, passionate woman, part Indian, black, and Spanish. Maceo visited her so often that she became known as "La Generala." So devoted was she to Maceo that when the Spanish consul of Puerto Plata, through an intermediary, offered her ten ounces of gold to lure the "Cuban *caudillo*" into a trap to capture and ship him to Cuba, "La Generala" pretended to accept the proposition but instead revealed the plot to her lover.[2]

This occurred while Maceo worked for the Little War, moving from island to island and place to place, engaged in revolutionary intrigue. With all his activities, he still had time for love affairs. When the ill-fated war was over and he returned to Jamaica, and Maceo had an affair with Amelia Marryatta, a white woman. It is known that their relationship produced a son—Maceo's only surviving child—for whom he always provided. When Amelia became pregnant, the financially embarrassed Maceo had to sell many of his personal possessions to bear the extra expenses.[3]

All this is not meant to imply that Maceo's life with María Cabrales was unhappy. At the time it was not considered unusual for a man like Maceo to have a happy marriage and at the same time support one or more mistresses. Such conduct aroused no unfavorable comment among other men. In fact, Máximo Gómez had an illegitimate son by his mistress, Lola Romero.[4]

On December 10, 1881, Gómez stopped in Kingston while en route to Honduras. The Cuban physician, Eusebio Hernández, arranged a discussion group that included Gómez, Maceo, Carlos Roloff, and José María Aguirre de Valdés, a veteran of the Ten Years' War. Citing the Little War, Gómez warned against a hasty, ill-prepared revolution. Others in the group agreed, and they also agreed to make no concrete plans but rather to maintain communication with each other wile awaiting a more propitious time for action. Maceo insisted that when that time came, General Gómez would be the one man behind whom all Cubans could unite.[5]

While Maceo kept in touch with Cuban emigrés throughout the Caribbean islands, Key West, and New York,[6] his main concern now was to find some employment to take care of his mounting expenses. María had become seriously ill, and her illness persisted until May 1881, preventing Maceo from accepting Gómez's invitation to follow him immediately to Honduras. But in June, he did follow Gómez and received an appointment in the Honduran army.[7] The appointment was heralded in the Honduran press, which praised Maceo for valor and the "great qualities which he possesses for the art of war," that had led to his elevation "to the high post which he exercised in that heroic campaign of our sister in the Antilles."[8]

Maceo's life in Honduras was a happy one. For one thing, he was given additional employment: first, on May 31, 1882, as *juez suplente* (deputy judge) of the Supreme Tribunal of War, and again, on July 31, as commander of the ports of Puerto Cortés and Omoa, with residence at the former. He used these posts to reform both the civil and military administrations. He replaced the official military text required in training programs—the *Táctica* of Captain General the Marquis of Duero—with tactics and stragegy outlined by Prussian militarists in translations acquired in Tegucigalpa.[9] He also experimented with the latest techniques in military training.

Another reason for Maceo's happiness in Honduras was that it afforded him an opportunity to study the problems of Central America and liberal democratic reforms. While he was commander of the military district of Tegucigalpa, he had many conversations with Ramón Rosa, the man responsible for the reform program instituted in Honduras under President Marco Aurelio Soto, and he learned much about the operations of a liberal government.[10] This knowledge was supplemented by his own study. He received private lessons in French, history, geography, military tactics, and public administration, both in Tegucigalpa and Puerto Cortés.[11] The time that remained after he completed all these activities was devoted to romance. But he did not forget his family in Jamaica. On October 9, 1882, he wrote to José F. Pérez, asking him to turn over the check for twenty pounds sterling accompanying the letter to "Miss Amelia Marryatta the mother of my little boy in Kingston." In the same letter, Maceo requested Pérez to aid his wife in preparing for her planned trip to Puerto Cortés.[12]

When María Cabrales arrived in Puerto Cortés in January 1883, Maceo's happiness was complete. That same month,

General Gómez called on Maceo with a business proposition—a project with the firm of Debrot, Duarte, Cabus, and Kraff concerning a proposed railroad to link the Atlantic and Pacific coasts of Honduras. In connection with this development scheme, Gómez envisaged the establishment of an agricultural colony of Cuban emigrants. He invited Maceo to participate in this project, and Maceo, who had become friendly with the Honduran president and his chief minister, agreed to approach them in behalf of the project. Both Gómez and Maceo were pleased when the project was approved by General Luis Bográn, a member of the Honduran Council of Ministers.

The prospects for the commercial venture were soon complicated by political developments. A controversy swirled in Guatemala, Honduras, and El Salvador over the idea of forming one unified state comprising the three countries. Presidents Justo Rufino Barrios of Guatemala and Rafael Zaldívar of El Salvador were in favor of such a union. But President Soto of Honduras opposed the plan as it stood. However, General Bográn took a position in favor of Barrios, with whom he was in close contact. For his part, Maceo approved of the idea of a Central American Union and felt it was important for the cause of a free Cuba to form an alliance with its proponents. He adopted this attitude even though it threatened to place him in conflict with his host, President Soto.[13]

In May 1883 Soto fled Honduras, and Maceo actively supported General Bográn for the presidency. When Bográn succeeded, both Maceo and Gómez felt that their commercial project would move forward swiftly. But Maceo's deep involvement in the Honduran political struggle subjected him to considerable criticism. To make matters worse, Bográn himself, influenced by Spanish propaganda, became suspicious of Maceo's motives. Seeing his business venture going down the drain, Maceo tried to convince Bográn of the falsity of the propaganda.[14] He finally succeeded in obtaining some assurance that if he received adequate financial support, the government would approve the commercial project. Maceo then spent time trying to work out an agreement between the financiers and the Honduran president, but neither he nor Gómez could get sufficient support to enable them to obtain final approval. Before they could look for new investors, a new Cuban revolutionary movement began to absorb all their attention.

On June 13, 1884, Maceo wrote to the editor of *El Yara:*

> Cuba will be free when the redeeming sword flings her antagonists into the sea. The Spanish domination was a shame and affront to the world that suffered it. But for us it is a shame which dishonors us. Whoever tries to take power over Cuba will only get the dust of its soil drenched in blood, if he does not perish in the struggle.[15]

In July 1884 Maceo broke off all work on the commercial project, resigned his posts in Honduras, and left the country, announcing: "Our enslaved Cuba demands that its sons fight for its freedom."[16]

8

Revolutionary Activity, 1883–1887

In addition to Maceo and Gómez, others also kept alive the idea of future revolutionary action. In Key West, the large colony of Cuban tobacco workers published the newspaper *El Yara*, and the "Order of the Sun," a secret political organization established after the Ten Years' War, maintained the hope for a new revolutionary movement. In New York, the young Cuban poet and intellectual, José Martí, was devoting every moment he could spare to reviving the spirits of the Cuban exiles, reorganizing the dispersed groups, and agitating for a new revolution

Born January 28, 1853, in Havana, Martí grew up during the Ten Years' War. At thirteen, two years before the war began, he entered the Colegio de San Pablo. There he studied under the poet and journalist, Rafael Mendive, until the latter was imprisoned for his revolutionary activities. A visit to his imprisoned teacher left an ineradicable impression on Martí. Shortly thereafter, his first revolutionary poem, "Abdala," was published in *La Patria Libre*, a journal edited by Mendive and Cristobal Madan.

At sixteen, Martí was condemned to six years' imprisonment at hard labor because of a letter he and a fellow student had written to another student, who was in the Spanish service, urging him to support the Cuban cause. He was released from prison after two months because of ill health and a wound on his ankle caused by the iron chain he wore—a wound that required repeated surgery. He was then sent to the Isle of Pines and later was permitted to go to Spain to continue his studies.

Spain was then undergoing a series of significant political changes following the overthrow of Queen Isabella in 1868, and Martí was soon as much a political agitator as a student. He published a scathing denunciation of Spanish treatment of political prisoners in Cuba, and his poetic ode to the student demonstrators shot on the streets of Havana on November 27, 1871, is said to have had an electrifying effect on Spanish public opinion. After the establishment of the Spanish Republic in 1873, he again pleaded the Cuban cause in a pamphlet entitled "The Spanish Republic Confronting the Cuban Revolution."

The Spanish Republic was overthrown in 1875, and Martí, as an ardent republican as well as an advocate of the Cuban cause, was forced into exile. He went first to Mexico, where he occupied himself in writing in behalf of the development of American, rather than European, culture and institutions. He next went to Guatemala, where he lectured at the Normal School and published the *Revista Guatemalteca*.

Returning to Cuba after the Ten Years' War, he was soon imprisoned and again deported to Spain. There he escaped from prison and made his way to Paris, New York, and finally Caracas, Venezuela, where he vowed to "arouse the world" to the Cuban cause. Because of his differences with the Venezuelan government, he soon left for New York. There he spent most of the last fourteen years of his life, working constantly in support of the Cuban cause while earning his living as a journalist, office worker at Lyons & Co., translator, contributing articles to *La América,* and founding and editing the revolutionary journal, *Patria.*[1]

Martí was in New York when Maceo was excluded from

command during the Little War because of his color, and no one deplored the decision more than he. As a member of the Revolutionary Committee, and, eager to mobilize support for the insurrection and cement greater unity among the exiles, he suggested holding a public meeting. The Revolutionary Committee agreed, and on January 24, 1880, before a Cuban audience that filled Steck Hall, Martí made his first speech in the United States. To the discomfort of the wealthy aristocratic emigrés, but to the delight of the black and white tobacco workers who filled the rear of the hall, Martí dealt with the race question as it affected the revolution in Cuba.[2] He recalled the heroic contributions of blacks in the Ten Years' War, and pointed out that they were continuing to aid the cause of independence in the current insurrection. Referring to the charge that the slaves were using the insurrection to wreak vengeance on the whites, he characterized it as Spanish propaganda. He went on to declare boldly "that the sins of the slave fall wholly and exclusively on the master." Martí made efforts to destroy the fear of possible black domination of a future revolutionary movement, seeking to create an atmosphere of harmony and fraternity:

> It would not be sensible to suppose that . . . all bitterness has disappeared, and that we can inspire absolute confidence in those we have oppressed. But it would be a grave insult to consider that a large number of men of color, as sensitive and as intellectually capable as ourselves, would harbor wicked intentions.

Martí frequently pointed out that since fighting together in the Ten Years' War many whites had become aware of the basic humanity of blacks, and he reminded white Cubans that all were struggling for similar goals. He felt that the "revolutionary tradition" had to be passed on to future revolutionaries. In an address later printed in *Patria* entitled "My Race," Martí developed this theme:

> Cuban means more than white, mulatto or black men. The souls of white men and Negroes have arisen together from the battlefields where they fought and died for Cuba. Alongside every white man there was a Negro, equal in loyalty and brotherhood for the daily tasks of war. . . . Merit, the tangible culmination of cultural progress, and the inexorable play of economic forces will ultimately unite all men. There is much greatness in Cuba, in both Negroes and whites.[3]

In November 1882 Antonio Maceo received his first letter from Martí. It was dated July 20. In it, Martí said that he had never heard "of a braver soldier nor a more tenacious Cuban" than Maceo. He went on to admit that it would be insane to precipitate a new conflict without a demand for such action by the people. He called upon Maceo to be ready "when the country called." Turning to the race issue, Martí declared:

> The Cuban problem has its answer in a social rather than a political solution. And this solution can only be obtained with the love and mutual respect of one race for the other and the dignified and generous prudence which animates your high and noble heart. For me the one who promotes hatred in Cuba or who tries to take advantage of that which exists is a criminal, and he who tries to suffocate the legitimate aspirations of a good and prudent race is also a criminal. You cannot imagine the special tenderness with which I think of these evils. My remedies for them are discreet, loving, and evangelical rather than boastful and ostentatious.

Martí concluded with a recognition of the high and important place that Maceo had to occupy in the revolutionary movement.[4]

It is not difficult to imagine Maceo's feelings when he read the letter. Having only recently felt the sting of racism inflicted by men who stood high in the revolutionary ranks, he must have been warmed to learn that this young Cuban genius understood so clearly the significance of and the need for combatting these influences. In his reply, Maceo declared: "My sword and my breath are at the service of Cuba," and he outlined his opinions on the requirements for revolution in the following terms:

> Moral and political unity are indispensable for combatting the power of Spain in Cuba and of no less importance for me today is the task of collecting funds for the execution of previous plans. There must be a solid base for the principles which we announce to the world of ideas. I would like to see an organization composed of men capable of uniting the will of the Cuban people, of understanding the mission which its citizens have confided in them, and of being indifferent to the disrupting influence of partisan ideas.

In closing, Maceo again named General Gómez as the man best equipped to lead Cubans in the field of battle.[5] He had decided to do nothing until he heard from Gómez about his feeling as to the wisdom of revolutionary action.[6] Soon, however, the volume of letters from *insurrectos* to Maceo increased, and the correspondents insisted that the situation in Cuba was becoming ripe for another attempt at a revolt, in which case his presence on the island at the head of an expeditionary force would be indispensable. Typical of these was the letter from Angel Maestre, in Vera Cruz, of October 17, 1883:

> Because of widespread misery, the situation in Cuba is now favorable to our cause. The state of corruption and general lack of confidence are gradually growing worse and becoming evident even to the most indifferent. The Liberal Party has lost all hope of reforms, and we shall have many of its members with us all the way. But to take advantage of this state of affairs you must assume your proper place. You must lend your good name, merit and prestige to the cause.
>
> Your prestige is so great that the victory of the revolution depends on you alone; with your presence not a single man would vacillate. All this obliges me to write you in the hope of getting a

favorable answer which will satisfy the aspirations of your country.[7]

"My dear friend," wrote J. Luis Peñez from New York, "we all expect you, Flor [Crombet], and the other generals to take an active part in this new movement; we never cease asking, 'What is Maceo doing?' All the emigrant groups are organized, and in Cuba there are various patriotic centers and great enthusiasm."[8]

But Maceo had been burned so many times by premature enthusiasm on the part of the emigrés that he had now reached the point where he viewed all insurrectionary movements with a critical eye. As he put it in a letter to Ramón Leocadio Bonaches in October 1883:

> Generals Gómez, Crombet, Roloff, Rodríguez, Colonel Morey, Hector Hernández, and I are in unanimous agreement as to what we should do as soon as we have the positive elements necessary to guarantee the triumph of the cause for the emancipation of Cuba. I must say that these elements must not be of an illusory nature, but rather those necessary for supporting a complete revolution for national independence.
>
> The lack of sufficient fundamental materials and money required in conformity with the urgency of the case has in the past occasioned insuperable obstacles for those who have had to face men in the field of battle.[9]

Two months later, while still warning against premature action, he predicted, with a burst of his old enthusiam, that a proper organization with sufficient money "could finish the revolution in less than a year."[10]

It is possible that when he wrote this, Maceo foresaw that he would soon be joining the new revolutionary movement, for it was becoming evident that Gómez was growing impatient to lead such a movement. On April 3, 1884, he made it definite in a letter to Maceo, in which he wrote: "As you know, the cause of Cuba comprises the ideal closest to my heart. . . .

Moreover, I have given my word to be ready forever to fight for the attainment of Cuban independence." He had sent Colonel Manuel Aguilera to the United States with a message entitled, "To the Revolutionary Centers." In this document, Gómez submitted a plan of action to which any movement undertaken for the liberation of Cuba must adhere: an advance increase in revolutionary centers; creation of a governing board with which the commander-in-chief could deal; full military powers for the commander; and the raising in advance of $200,000 to finance the movement. "The first news I receive from him [Aguilera]," Gómez concluded, "will enable us to decide if we should move and to where."[11]

Maceo replied immediately, pledging his support to Gómez's leadership and expressing eagerness to join him. He began immediately to wind up his affairs in Honduras and informed his friends and sympathizers in Key West, New York, Jamaica, Santo Domingo, and other places that he was now joining a new revolutionary movement along with Máximo Gómez.[12] Colonel Aguilera returned to Honduras with the news that the various emigré centers, including the Independence Club of New York, had approved both the program and conditions that Gómez had proposed. He also reported that he had been advised that a wealthy Cuban merchant in New York, Félix Govín, was ready to advance the $200,000 for the new revolutionary movement as soon as the general placed himself at its head.

Gómez and Maceo decided to move to the United States as quickly as possible. Maceo hastened his preparations for departure,[13] and, on July 1, he wrote to his friends in Key West, announcing his impending arrival there and asking them to make certain necessary arrangements. As sailing time approached, he sent a long letter to Anselmo Valdés, setting forth the reasons for his new campaign:

> In order to accept the duties which my country has placed upon me, I have sacrificed the well-being of my family. Our enslaved

> Cuba demands that its sons fight for its freedom. . . . Our old palladin and distinguished military leader, Máximo Gómez, will direct the revolution as its supreme general. With him we can have a new order of things without the party disputes of the past, and we can suppress the jealousies and social preoccupations which have so restricted my services to the cause of Cuba. Petty ambitions and rivalries can be annulled before they start. I have no other aspiration than to see my country sovereign and free. With national sovereignty we will obtain our natural rights, calm dignity, and the representation of a free and independent people. . . . When Cuba is free and has a constituted government, I shall request that we fight for the independence of Puerto Rico also. I would not care to put up my sword leaving that portion of America in slavery.[14]

Maceo felt that with Gómez and Martí in the picture, the racist forces that had kept him out of the Little War would be unable to operate successfully this time. Under these circumstances, he was ready to forget the long series of disappointments, and he entered the new conspiracy with supreme optimism. On August 2, 1884, Gómez and Maceo set sail with their families for the United States to join the new independence movement.[15]

They arrived in New Orleans a week later, and their problems began at once. For one thing, Maceo was furious at the treatment accorded blacks in that city, with its segregation and humiliating decrees. The fact that the Gómez family were also treated as blacks only added to his anger.[16] He was further infuriated by the complete lack of revolutionary enthusiasm among the more affluent Cubans. What did it matter if the poor people were ready for a new revolution, if funds were not available? Gómez noted in his diary the caustic comment that "rich Cubans are only patriotic when their purses are being squeezed."[17]

With little success in New Orleans, the two leaders determined to go to Key West, the nerve center of the Cuban centers of emigration. Its tobacco factory workers furnished a constant impetus for the independence struggle. In contrast to New Orleans, Key West gave an enthusiastic welcome to the two military leaders. They were greeted as prominent members of the "Order of the Sun." Maceo also had the pleasure of meeting the directors of *El Yara* for the first time. He had known them since 1875 only through correspondence and through reading the newspaper. From them, he obtained the first complete account of the death of his brother, Rafael, in Africa, and of the experiences of his other brother, José.[18]

Under Gómez's direction, the revolutionists organized one public club, the *Sociedad de Beneficiencia Cubana de Cayo Hueso,* and another secret organization. The club was supposed to maintain the feeling of hostility toward Spain, while the secret organization would engage in formulating and carrying out the plans of the *insurrectos.* The membership of the secret group was made up of active revolutionaries, workers, some radical tobacco factory owners, and small property owners. After collecting the necessary money for personal and traveling expenses, Maceo and Gómez departed for New York on September 26.[19]

They arrived in New York on October 1 and immediately began to hold conferences at the small hotel of Madame Griffon on Ninth Avenue, the headquarters of the Cuban revolutionaries. During the meetings, plans were completed for the overall operation of the movement, for the purchase of arms and ammunition, and for the hiring of transportation for the proposed expedition.

But everything hinged on the availability of money. Gómez had received $3,000 from the president of Honduras to assist the struggle for the freedom of Cuba, and they had collected $5,000 in Key West. But this was only a drop in the bucket. One of the main reasons Gómez and Maceo had agreed to come to New York was the promise by Félix Govín to give it substantial financial backing.[20] Shortly after arriving, Gómez and Maceo suffered the first great blow to their hopes. When Govín was asked to make good his promise to advance $200,000, the wealthy Cuban replied that he was engaged in attempting to recover confiscated property in Cuba, that his success depended on maintaining good relations with the Spanish administration in Havana, and that he could not afford to do anything that would jeopardize these relations. Gómez wrote bitterly in his diary: "I have suffered a blow here in New York which I had not expected. . . . My deception has been very sad because only the poor Cubans are disposed to sacrifice."[21]

The second setback was the withdrawal of José Martí. In order to raise the funds they had not been able to obtain in New York, Gómez decided to send various missions to different centers where appeals could be made to Cubans for financial aid. At a conference with Maceo and Martí, Gómez designated both of them to go to Mexico to raise funds. Martí agreed to go and proceeded to tell Gómez what he would do immediately upon his arrival in Mexico. Gómez, who had ordered a bath to be drawn, interrupted and said brusquely: "Look, Martí, limit yourself to what the instructions say, and as for the rest, General Maceo will do what he thinks should be done." Thereupon, Gómez retired to his bath. Maceo tried to smooth things over, remarking: "The 'Old Man' considers the Cuban War almost as though it is his exclusive property, and he does not permit anyone to interfere."[22] But this remark only served to add to Martí's annoyance. Even before this incident, he had become increasingly alarmed over Gómez's tendency to deal with the revolutionary movement as though it was his "exclusive property," insisting that his orders be obeyed without question.

Two days after the incident—on October 20—Martí sent a letter to Gómez announcing that he was withdrawing from the movement:

> One does not found a nation, General, with commands as issued in a military camp. . . . Are you trying to suffocate thought even before seeing yourself at the front of a grateful and enthusiastic people with all the appurtenances of a victory? The nation belongs to no one, but if it did, it belongs to the one who serves it with the greatest disinterestedness and intelligence—and this only in spirit. How, General, could I utilize the friends which I have, attract new ones, undertake missions, convince eminent men, and melt frozen wills with these fears and doubts in my soul? Consequently, I resign from all the active tasks which you have begun to place on my shoulders.[23]

Although he was unusually sensitive, what ultimately decided Martí was his fear of creating a dictator before the Cuban Republic was even born. Unlike Maceo, who knew the need for strong authority in the revolutionary struggle from past experience and was inclined to overlook Gómez's dictatorial conduct, Martí saw in Gómez's behavior an evil that had to be combatted before the revolutionary movement degenerated into a personal operation, divorced from the masses of the people. Gómez, himself, attributed this feeling to Martí when he wrote in his diary, "There is no lack of those who, like José Martí, fear a dictatorship."[24]

At first many Cuban exiles criticized Martí for his sudden withdrawal from the movement, and some even accused him of deserting the revolution. But Martí soon convinced them that, while he could not work with Gómez, he was "and always would be, with the Nation." Moreover, he insisted, it was "indispensable to the health of the homeland that someone expresses without vacillation or cowardice the essential principles of thought and method which I have believed to be in peril."[25]

Following Martí's withdrawal, Maceo left for Mexico alone on the mission assigned by Gómez. While he did create a number of patriotic centers in Vera Cruz and Mérida, he did not collect substantial amounts of money, nor could he establish an understanding with the Mexican government. Learning of this, Gómez commented gloomily: "Not one circumstance favors us at this time."[26]

Soon, however, their spirits were lifted. Sufficient money came from the Cuban workers ($25,000) and industrialists ($30,000) in Key West to enable Gómez to purchase arms and ammunition and even to enlarge the scope of the invasion, so that simultaneous landings could take place in various parts of the island, to be coordinated with the general activity of revolutionary groups in Cuba. In Mexico, Maceo aided General Angel Maestre in getting the expedition ready for the invasion, and stayed in Vera Cruz until the men were armed and the boat ready.[27]

But there were new setbacks. Gómez had sent the arms and ammunition to friends in Santo Domingo to store them until the *insurrectos* were ready to set out for Cuba. These war materials were confiscated by the authorities who had replaced the government that had been friendly to the Cuban cause. Then came the news that the industrialists of Key West had withdrawn their support from the revolution. As though this was not discouraging enough, the government of President Bográn in Honduras had also been succeeded by a hostile administration. At the same time, news of still another catastrophe reached the leaders of the new revolutionary movement. Maestre's efforts to launch the expedition on which Maceo had expended so much time and energy ended in miserable failure at Isla Mujeres, Mexico. With dissatisfaction and dissension rising among the emigrants and revolutionists, Gómez decided that the groups would leave one at a time instead of all at once, as had been planned. Maceo would go first, and he would be followed by Rafael Rodríguez, and then Emilio Núñez.[28]

Maceo had been chosen to lead the first invasion force because of his large following in the Oriente province. Dr. Eusebio Hernández explained the reason for the selection: "As soon as he touches Cuban soil the brave men of Oriente will rise in arms, and the enthusiasm of the emigrants will so multiply that there will be no inconvenience in facilitating the immediate departure of other expeditions."[29] But with all the arms and ammunition confiscated in Santo Domingo, and no new money available to spend on materials of war, the outlook was indeed discouraging. Nevertheless, Maceo assured Gómez:

> I am ready for the cause of my country, and I do not believe that up to the present I have given any reasons for doubt on that score. My devotion to the principles which we are defending does not differ in any way from the conduct I have exhibited as a soldier both outside of and inside Cuba. So give the orders and it will be obeyed without question. Since putting myself actively at the service of Cuba I have determined to be a patriot above everything else—a soldier without pretensions or conditions. I am this in spite of many things which displease me or which I believe to be wrong. But who can guarantee what things will be? We all err because we do not have the Pope's infallibility; only this divine being enjoys that prerogative which the friends of obscurantism ascribe to him. . . . I am making unusual efforts to be ready on the fifteenth on the month.[30]

New money, of course, was needed, and it could come from one place—the Key West tobacco workers. In October 1885 Maceo went there to raise money for the expedition he was to lead. Dr. Hernández, who was to go on the expedition as Maceo's assistant, accompanied him to Key West, and he described the reaction of a mass meeting after he "presented General Antonio Maceo as the leader of the first expedition which we must organize with money from them":

> The effect of these words on those emigrants was immense and extraordinary. . . . They all rose to their feet demonstrating with *vivas* and applause, leaping on the stage to embrace us and emptying their pockets for the director. Women and young girls donated their rings, earrings, watches, and whatever they had. Daughters, wives and sweethearts were seen removing the pictures of their

> loved ones from their lockets. I could not continue my discourse; with music, and followed by that enormous audience we were accompanied to the lodging which they had reserved for us. This extraordinary enthusiasm lasted until midnight.
>
> The following day a committee of young girls was named at our request to raffle the collection of jewelry. General Maceo added a tie pin from his personal belongings.
>
> In a week's time we had gathered more than we had asked for, that is, $9,000 instead of $8,000. In that Patriotic Week, Americans as well as Cubans, in fact all men who loved liberty in that free place, took part in the campaign.
>
> A hundred pages would not be enough to describe the different features which adorn the rapid, simple and superbly delicate labor of the Patriotic Week. Young girls escorted Maceo and me on our trips through the tobacco factories. Some of them, with Cuban flags wound around their bodies and their faces radiant with patriotism and beauty, preceded me on the honored tribunal reserved for the reader of the factory. Maceo, the man of bronze, was deeply moved. Repeatedly he was forced to stand in acknowledgment of the delirious and overwhelming ovations produced by references to him in the vibrant speeches of some of the peasant women, admirers of the hero.[31]

On the day of Maceo's departure for New York, the factories and shops were closed so that the Cuban workers could go to the docks to see him off. He left Key West as he had arrived—to the accompaniment of cheers, flags, and music.[32]

In New York, Maceo turned over $5,711 to J. M. Párraga, treasurer of the movement, and Colonel Fernando López de Queralta was assigned the task of purchasing arms and ammunition and arranging for their transportation to Colón, Panama.[33] From Colón, Maceo planned to launch his expedition in February 1886. Meanwhile, he went to Jamaica to work out the final plans for the Cuban invasion. In Kingston, he issued a proclamation "To My Comrades and Conquerors of Oriente":

> Liberty is not begged for; it is conquered. I swore to free you or to perish with you, fighting for your rights; I am coming to fulfill that oath.
>
> Seven years have proved the Treaty of Zanjón to be dishonorable. . . . The government of despotism and barbarism declared the extermination of the Cubans, and it reduced their spirit and killed revolutionary action. Since that ominous date, with my soul lacerated by the sad and unmerciful fate assigned to you, I have been working for your salvation. I am bringing you a war of justice and reason; come with me and you will be sons worthy of Cuba.
>
> Our invasion of all the island will carry the worthy patriots to the heights of liberty. You will be in the vanguard; you will be victorious always. Glory is eternal when it is infinite and without rival. Come to the field of honor now that I am bringing you the olive tree of liberty and justice.
>
> The unconquered Major General Máximo Gómez, supreme officer of our revolution, leads the movement with Generals Rodríguez Carrillo, Borrero, Sánchez and other leaders. Give us your valuable aid and you will save life, honor, and home.[34]

A new series of difficulties, mishaps, and frustrations, coupled with bitter internal conflicts among the revolutionary leaders, turned the promising efforts to launch an armed revolution in Cuba into a fiasco. It began with the first serious breach in the long friendship between Gómez and Maceo. In a letter to Maceo on December 23, 1885, from Santo Domingo, Gómez assured his "esteemed friend" that he was very pleased that he had been so successful in raising funds. He advised Maceo, as he was advising others, that the entire invasion must be performed in the approaching months of January, February, and March. Then, apparently in reply to Maceo's comments about impatience and dissatisfaction on the part of some revolutionaries with his leadership, Gómez added:

> I cannot and must not occupy myself with answering the other matters to which you refer in your letter, encouraging me to march to the field of battle and trying to make me understand the

necessity for doing this. I am not certain that you understand what motives are behind that and much more that you say. I have never doubted the triumph of the Revolution and never for a moment have I vacillated in occupying my post when the hour for doing it arrived.[35]

These words about his "motives" stung Maceo deeply, and he immediately shot back an angry reply to the commander-in-chief in which he wrote:

The "motives" which I obeyed are the same which guided me in Honduras when I began to concern myself with the cause of Cuba. As a matter of fact, they are the same motives that have always guided my public acts, those of honor and loyalty.

I think the same thing of you now that I thought of you then; my opinion has not changed.

After pointing out that he had always insisted that Gómez should be "the leader of the revolution," and that he still thought so, Maceo, for the first time, launched into a bitter criticism:

Permit me to say that you have the great defect of always having a lack of confidence in those men who have not "approved" your manner of being.

Your character is infernal, egoistic, jealous, haughty, preoccupied (according to the hour), intractable, inconstant, and imperative.

My thoughts concerning you obey the motives of accomplishing soon our revolutionary enterprise, subject today to a thousand misfortunes.

As for the rest, if anyone should think well of me, it ought to be you; you know me and know that I would not betray my ideals. Ambition and egotism have never twisted my spirit; I am governed only by ideas of order and legality in all my acts.[36]

Three days later, on January 16, 1886, Maceo addressed another letter to Gómez in a similar though more moderate tone. He again denied having any special prejudicial interests or "spurious motives."[37]

Maceo's letters to Gómez were written at a time when he was experiencing a particularly trying ordeal. Eager to leave for Cuba, he was finding it impossible to obtain the necessary arms and ammunition. Furthermore, with the absence of Martí from the revolutionary movement, the old racist argument surfaced that Maceo was seeking, through his leadership of the expedition, to mobilize the blacks of Oriente to create a black Republic. Hence, when Gómez wrote questioning Maceo's "motives," it appeared to him that the commander-in-chief was, for the first time, succumbing to the racism that was so widespread among other revolutionary leaders.

Meanwhile, as Maceo wrote to Ernesto Bavastro from Colón on January 29, all his efforts had met with "error after error and misfortune after misfortune after misfortune. . . . Thus I am continuing in the same anguished and terrible situation as always. I am condemned to waiting."[38] His worst fears were soon to be realized. For lack of the necessary papers to claim the shipment of arms, the war materials were not allowed to land in Panama and were returned to New York. At the same time that Maceo arranged for the arms to be reshipped to Jamaica, whence the revolutionaries were scheduled to sail for Cuba, Gómez issued a proclamation postponing the invasion on the ground that the prospects for success had been adversely affected by desertions from the revolutionary movement. Maceo immediately bitterly objected to this action and demanded that Gómez rescind his order. He wrote to the emigrant centers in Key West, declaring his opposition to Gómez's proclamation and insisting that it be ignored. With Crombet already on his way to Jamaica with the cargo of war materials, Maceo declared, postponing the invasion would be both cowardly and dangerous.[39]

Under pressure from Maceo, Gómez was finally compelled to continue the movement. But now complete disaster befell the cause. On July 20, 1886, five months after Maceo was supposed to launch his expedition to Cuba, Crombet arrived in

Kingston aboard the *Morning Star* with the arms and ammunition. But the ship's captain, fearful of being arrested with his dangerous cargo, threw the entire shipment into the sea and returned to New York.[40]

For the second time, the war materials were lost. With this new loss, any hope of launching an invasion all but vanished. At a conference of all the military and civil leaders in Jamaica on August 17, the majority voted, over Maceo's objections, to make one more effort to get the revolution started. But relations among the revolutionaries had become so strained by the repeated failures and disasters that coordinated action was almost impossible. At one point in the conference, the dissension between Maceo and Crombet reached so heated a point that Maceo challenged Crombet to a duel. (After seconds had been appointed, they decided that the duel should be postponed indefinitely for the good of the cause, and were able to persuade the two combatants to accept this decision.) Then on August 31, 1886, after a dispute over finances relating to the expedition, in the course of which Maceo openly questioned Gómez's authoritarian conduct, his integrity, and his fitness as a commanding officer, Gómez broke off their friendship.[41]

Maceo regretted Gómez's decision, but he was not one to grovel for the commander-in-chief's good will. "Do you believe it would have been more honorable of me, not being in complete agreement with your latest plans, to have submitted myself unconditionally?" he wrote to Gómez. "Did you want me to beg? That is appropriate only to the reptiles who distract you by flattering your vanity." Disclaiming any desire to place himself above Gómez, Maceo went on: "Disillusion yourself, General; before you I am small, and I have no illusions, for more than you I respect all opinions." He then proceeded to defend both his motives and his past performance, and added: "If I have any merit it is that of obedience to military discipline and respect for law; but you confuse dignity, which claims its right, with the ambition of a fool." The letter ended: "You say: 'I believe everything has ended between us.' I do not understand that; but whatever it may mean, I accept it in whatever form you may determine. I ask that you do not confuse the cause with our personalities." On the following day, Maceo again wrote to Gómez, disclaiming any ulterior motives and again pointing out his long record of loyalty and dedication of purpose as he saw it.[42]

On September 3, Gómez answered Maceo's two letters with the following short, crisp note: "As I told you in my answer, 'I believe everything between us has ended.' There remains only one thing in common between us, a sacred thing, which I made mine—the cause of our country."[43] In his diary, Gómez attributed the break in their personal friendship to the fact that Maceo had become too vain, writing: "For some time now I have had the suspicion that . . . because of the ovations given to him in Key West a badly understood love of himself has grown in him. And perhaps he could convince himself that he enjoys immunities above and beyond the interests of the revolution."[44] It did not occur to him, apparently, that he, more than anyone in the movement, viewed himself as above criticism, and that the split with Maceo, coming as it did after his split with Martí, should have caused him to reflect on the nature of his own relationships with his colleagues. The experience of the Ten Years' War should have made him aware of how sensitive Maceo was to any charge that he was putting personal or racial ambitions above the revolutionary cause.

Although the August 17 conference had rejected Maceo's proposal to temporarily suspend all efforts at armed revolution in Cuba, events soon demonstrated how sound his advice had been. By now the Cuban emigrants were so thoroughly disheartened, there was no prospect of raising new funds. Moreover, the final abolition of slavery in Cuba on October 7, 1887, dealt a serious blow to the revolutionary movement, which had depended to a great extent on the support of the black people on the island. In view of their at least temporary gratitude to the Spanish authorities for the royal decree abolishing slavery, the blacks could hardly be expected to rally to the revolutionary cause.[45]

In December 1886, Gómez, convinced that "the Cubans . . . do not want to hear a word about revolution," and that there was no hope for the cause he headed, announced the end of the rebel movement. He explained that it had failed through "unfortunate happenings and obstacles generally always unforeseen, which are never lacking in this kind of undertaking."[46]

This was only partially true. The failure was also due to a serious flaw in the organization of the revolutionary movement. Its total leadership had been in the hands of military officers, with civilians confined to the task of raising funds. The movement itself had started with the military leaders, who had then called in the revolutionary emigrés. This gave it a dictatorial character from the very outset, for the civilians were expected to blindly accept the decrees of the military leaders, especially those of the supreme commander, Máximo Gómez. Inevitably, as was illustrated by Martí's withdrawal, friction would arise not only between the two tendencies in the revolutionary movement, but also among the military leaders themselves, as in the disputes between Gómez and Maceo and Crombet and Maceo. Under these circumstances, it is hardly surprising that the entire movement deteriorated.

Whatever the cause of the end of the rebel movement, it was a bitter blow to Maceo. His eight year longing to return to the field of battle for Cuban freedom had been thwarted and obstructed, and now he had received the major portion of blame for the latest fiasco. Finally, he had lost his great friendship with Gómez and had made a dangerous enemy of Crombet. With each year of absence from military combat, his prestige was diminishing.

Bitter, disillusioned, and depressed as he was over this latest failure to lead an invading expedition to Cuba, Maceo still faced the necessity of caring for the long-neglected needs of his family. His wife had returned to Kingston after a stay in Key West, and in thanking the Fiqueredo Socarrás family with whom she had lived, he wrote: "You have cured the wounds received in this campaign with the balm that my wife has brought me."[47]

Hearing that there were opportunities with the Panama Canal project begun in 1879 by Ferdinand de Lesseps, he followed his brother José to Colón. He immediately found work in the Canal Zone and was able to send money to his wife within two weeks after his arrival. In January 1887, Maceo obtained a concession to build a large number of wooden houses in the community of Bas Obispo, and soon his status had improved considerably.[48]

Busy as he was with his new occupation, Maceo could not completely forget the revolutionary cause. He discussed politics and rebellion with the Cubans he recruited to help him in his construction work. His active participation in Masonic work, in Inter-Oceanic Lodge 44, also kept him abreast of activities in the revolutionary camp.[49] Soon enough, he was to become fully involved once more in the struggle to achieve Cuban independence.

9

The Peace of Manganese

In spite of repeated failures and unfavorable conditions, revolutionary planning continued. In the fall of 1887, José Martí and other Cuban advocates of independence were holding meetings in New York, discussing the bases for a future uprising. Guided by Martí, the Cuban exiles drew up a circular setting forth a program for united action. Five essential points were stressed "to inspire our words and acts":

1. To achieve a revolutionary solution which will win support in the country, it must be based on democratic procedures.
2. To proceed without delay to organize the military leaders outside the country and coordinate this work with that which is to be done within the country.
3. To unite the emigré centers in one magnificent democratic enterprise.
4. To prevent revolutionary sympathies in Cuba from being twisted and enslaved by the interests of one group, by the preponderance of one social class, or by the unlimited authority of a military or a civil group, or of one race over another.
5. To prevent annexationist propaganda from weakening the revolutionary solution.[1]

The circular was sent to Generals Máximo Gómez, Antonio Maceo, Rafael Rodríguez, and Francisco Carrillo, asking their support. Gómez replied briefly but affirmatively—he refused to address Martí directly, still rankling from the former dispute—announcing that he was always ready to occupy "my place in the line of combat for the sake of Cuban independence."[2]

When the circular reached Maceo in the Isthmus of Panama, he was ill with malaria. But he quickly replied, and declared himself in full agreement with the basic concepts of the circular. He stressed the need for unity of all Cubans as the key to successful revolutionary organization:

> Today as yesterday and always, Señor Martí . . . I believe that all Cubans, without social distinctions, must put aside their dissension. For the sake of our enslaved country, which each day becomes more unfortunate, we must purge ourselves of the seeds of discord sown in our hearts by the enemies of our noble cause. . . .
>
> The cordial, frank, and sincere union *of all the sons of Cuba* was the ideal of my spirit and the object of my efforts in our war in the fields of Cuba, during the good as well as the bad days. Could I think differently today when we find ourselves orphans from home and country, dispersed in all corners of the earth?[3]

After recovering from his illness, Maceo addressed another letter to Martí setting forth his political beliefs in greater detail. He stressed the need for the absolute authority of laws and legally constituted authority. Good or bad, the laws must be obeyed, he maintained; anarchy would be disastrous for revolutionary movements as well as for constituted governments. As to the form of government that would be desirable for the new Cuban Republic, Marceo wrote: "I believe that no form of government is more adequate, nor in closer conformity to the spirit of the epoch, than the republican or democratic form." He was confident that the republican form of government, "which is still a utopia for the most part, despite the passage of eighteen centuries, will tomorrow become a beautiful reality." Once again he emphasized that no race should be dominated by another.[4]

With his hopes for the Cuban cause revived by the activities of Martí and his colleagues in New York, Maceo set out for Peru. He hoped to retrieve the war materials loaned to Leoncio Prado in 1879, and place them at the disposal of Martí's group. The trip turned out a failure, and Maceo returned to the Canal Zone.[5] When work on the Canal project ceased because of a scandal involving the company in charge, Maceo returned to his family in Kingston.[6]

Receiving reports of increasing dissatisfaction in Cuba, Maceo suddenly decided to return home. He had, for some time, been eager to see his native land again, but until the end of 1889, any attempt to visit Cuba without armed force would have meant imprisonment. The new captain general, Manuel Salamanca, was now taking a different approach to the revolutionary problem. He felt that a more tolerant approach would destroy revolutionary influence. He allowed Flor Crombet to return, and now Maceo petitioned for permission to follow. He used as a pretext his desire to personally attend to the business of selling the properties that belonged to his mother.[7]

Remembering the Spanish attempts against his life in the past, Maceo carefully prepared for the voyage. At his request, two Cuban merchants in Jamaica went to the Spanish consul in the English colony and requested guarantees of safe conduct for Maceo. The Spanish official complied with their request and presented a passport in the name of Captain General Salamanca. While Maceo was in Haiti, en route to Cuba, this was supplemented by a note from the captain general, offering assurances and guarantees for the visit. Thus assured, Maceo left Port-au-Prince on January 29, 1890, aboard the *Manuelito y Maria*, bound for Cuba. His feelings at the embarkation were tense and troubled:

> Until that moment I suffered over the problem of committing a deed I considered dishonorable . . . such was my displeasure and repugnance at seeing myself under the Spanish flag spattered by the shrill and boastful breath of the Spanish sailor. It seemed that Captain Vaca and three young Cuban employees of the boat understood this, for they immediately tried to make my presence among them agreeable with their pleasant and friendly conversation. Nonetheless, the night was anguished and terrible for me. I was deeply troubled by the idea of returning to Cuba by a Spanish conveyance and of entering my country under the guise of peace and concord when what I wanted was war and the extermination of the colonial system in Cuba.[8]

On the following day, the Spanish ship tied up in the Santiago de Cuba harbor. Maceo remained aboard, and that night he was visited first by Flor Crombet and Antonio Colás, and shortly thereafter by Antonio Parreño, an employee of the ship company. Maceo advised them to stimulate an active propaganda program on the island in preparation for the uprising he hoped to lead in the near future. Crombet and Colás, in turn, assured him that Oriente was ready and waiting for the word to rise in arms.

As his ship sailed away, Maceo reflected with pride on "the patriotic energy which always distinguished *Orientales*." During the following day, he experienced mixed feelings as familiar places passed before his eyes along the Cuban coast, recalling to his mind the scenes of "my triumphs and setbacks." At Baracoa, Gibara, and in the port of Nuevitas in the province of Camagüey, the ship was visited by local insurgent leaders and, in each case, Maceo revealed his intentions to them, advising them of the type of work they could do in preparation for the eventual uprising. All gave their promise of wholehearted support. Moreover, Maceo was told that his presence had revived the lagging spirit of the rebellion.

On February 5, at eleven o'clock in the morning, the ship reached Havana, capital city of the island. Maceo was officially greeted in the name of the captain general by the marine inspector. While still aboard ship, he was interviewed by reporters for the Havana daily newspaper, *La Lucha.* Asked to give them his impressions as he entered the port of Havana, Maceo recalled later:

> In answer I told them, "Toward everything that I see I feel repugnance." The streets are narrow and loathsome like the attitude of the Spaniards who propose to govern Cuba without improving the condition of this unfortunate country.

Continuing his description and impressions as he moved through the streets of Havana en route to his hotel, Maceo noted the degradation of the women of the city, many of whom were forced into prostitution because of the lack of dignified occupations.[9]

At his headquarters in the Hotel Inglaterra, Maceo was visited by a steady stream of former rebel leaders and by others who advised him as to the state of the country, and exchanged opinions about future plans. His commanding figure, his immaculate dress, and his calm and dignified manner made a strong impression on all who saw and talked with him. His lapel was constantly being decorated with the flowers pinned on him by women. Even his enemies were not immune to his charm. One of the most capable Spanish officers in the Ten Years' War told Maceo that he was the worthiest military opponent he had ever faced.[10] According to one account—that of a Spanish officer who was later converted into an ardent revolutionary by Maceo—many Spanish soldiers saluted the *caudillo* as they would have a general on the streets of Havana.[11] On one occasion, the Spanish captain in charge of a group of spies placed in rooms adjacent to the visiting rebel leader informed Maceo of his mission. Thereupon, Maceo accompanied the captain to the palace, where he demanded and received the dismissal of the spies.[12]

Before coming to Cuba, Maceo had been warned that the

abolition of slavery by the Spaniards would cause a loss in support by the black population for the revolutionary cause.[13] He quickly discovered that this was not true. Fearing the loss of cheap labor, the sugar plantation owners had managed to secure a provision in the new law by which the freed slaves were placed under a "patronage" system amounting to police surveillance of poorly-paid labor. To be sure, some of the restrictions against blacks were removed, and, indeed, in 1884 José Beltrán, a black, initiated court action against a cafe owner who refused him admittance on racial grounds. After a series of legal maneuvers the courts decided in favor of Baltrán in October 1889, asserting that "it would be an injury to deny a man of color the service he solicited because of his race." In response to black protests, led by Juan Gualberto Gómez, discrimination was forbidden in theaters, cafes, and bars after 1889, and schools had to accept all pupils regardless of race after 1893. However, the laws were often not enforced, and discrimination continued in full force. In addition, the black population was faced with the problems of unemployment and exceedingly low wages when they were employed, and they were seething with discontent.[14]

Maceo spent much of his time engaged in discussions with young Cubans who were eager to participate in the revolutionary movement (he emphasized to the older revolutionists the importance of such work in spreading the revolutionary spirit), and leaders of the trade unions. In addition, he met frequently with journalists and literary figures. Julián del Casal, a prominent poet, dedicated a poem to Maceo and wrote: "In these times I have met only one person who has pleased me. Who do you suppose it can be? Maceo, a handsome man of robust comprehension, clear intelligence, and a will of iron."[15] Manuel de la Cruz, a leading journalist, thought so highly of Maceo that in his work, *Episodios de la revolución cubana,* he wrote: "Maceo was the flesh and bone of a legend founded in bronze."[16]

Another journalist with whom Maceo was often closeted was the black radical, Juan Gualberto Gómez. In the publication *La Fraternidad,* Gualberto Gómez stressed the need for racial equality, and he and Maceo were in complete agreement on this point. They disagreed, however, over Gualberto Gómez's plan for a separate organization of blacks and mulattoes within the revolutionary movement, to be set up under the guise of societies supposedly devoted to education and recreation. Maceo believed that to foster such groups devoted exclusively to the colored elements would play directly into the hands of the enemy. Apart from being unwilling to lose the support of influential whites, he was convinced that no revolution could be successful without the participation of both whites and blacks. While conceding that Maceo's position had merit, even though he did not agree with it, Gualberto Gómez summed up Maceo's opinion as follows:

> It consists of forming a great conglomeration of all the elements that constitute the Cuban people, a great arena where all interests will converge and all aspirations disappear . . . . where all previous antagonism will be erased by the double action of the will of the elements that form this society and by the passage of time.

Maceo was able to obtain Gualberto Gómez's acceptance of this position for the time being, and convinced him of the value of retaining Máximo Gómez as the commander-in-chief of the military in the revolution. In spite of his recent split with the Dominican, Maceo pointed out that the veteran general had superior military capabilities which were well suited to the type of warfare required in Cuba, and that, in addition, he was thoroughly opposed to racial discrimination.[17]

While the Spanish authorities were disturbed generally by Maceo's open revolutionary activities, they were especially upset by the fact that leading white Cubans looked up to him as the logical leader of the liberation struggle. Camilo Polavieja, the new captain general, who had taken charge of the post after the death of Salamanca, reported:

> For reasons that I do not know and that even if I did, I could not justify here, General Salamanca thought it convenient to extend an invitation to the ex-general, Antonio Maceo, to return to the island of Cuba. This veteran *insurrecto* and tenacious conspirator took advantage of this invitation and arrived in Havana a few days before the death of said General. Since the moment of his arrival, even in the presence of high authorities, he has boasted ostentatiously of his separatists ideas, and what is more important, of his revolutionary projects for which he assuredly has important means.
>
> Known revolutionaries from all over the Island went to see him publicly in Havana. This has given a rebirth of hopes hardly to the pleasure of Spain. And the very sad spectacle has occurred wherein he has been visited and accompanied by a considerable number of representatives of Creole families, some very notable for their social position. And this has happened notwithstanding the fact that Maceo belongs to the colored race, which generally is the object of profound contempt by the Creoles. It is because Maceo symbolizes the idea of hatred for Spain. The Creole youth, in particular, who fill the salons and literary and scientific centers of the capitol, have sought him out. None of the people concealed giving Maceo the *title of General.*[18]

Maceo attended a round of parties and banquets in his honor in Havana and Pinar del Río, which actually served as meetings for the establishment of new centers of rebellion. One result of all the conferences, meetings, and parties was the conclusion reached by the conspirators that the revolution could be launched soon from within Cuba. Indeed, Maceo, Manuel Sanguilly, Manuel Suárez, and José M. Aguirre agreed to set the date for the uprising in the capitol for October 10, 1891. This particular date was chosen because it was the anniversary of the *Grito de Yara*, which marked the beginning of the Ten Years' War. Maceo, who had resisted the demands of some of the more enthusiastic rebels that the revolution be begun immediately, had stipulated in agreeing to the October 10 date that $40,000 be collected by the western conspirators to finance the return to Cuba of Máximo Gómez and other exiled *insurrectos*.[19]

In accordance with these agreements, arms were brought from a Spanish munitions dealer with money furnished by two wealthy supporters. The plan for a revolt in the capitol called for a series of simultaneous attacks from within, calculated to give the rebels possession of all strategic locations. Recognizing that this was an exceptionally bold scheme involving a high degree of risk, the conspirators provided for a swift withdrawal to the countryside outside the city. If they were unable to capture the agreed-upon locations, they would dynamite as many of them as possible and start fires before retiring. In the neighboring town of Regla, Anselmo Aragón would stand ready to protect their retreat.[20]

All of these details had been worked out before the arrival of the new Captain General Polavieja. Maceo knew from experience that Polavieja would not continue the tolerant attitude of Salamanca; hence his desire to have everything ready by the time the new captian general had established himself in Havana. However, this required revealing the details of the proposed uprising to many more people—more, in fact, than Maceo would have wished. But he was risking everything on being able to move before his enemies.[21]

When he felt that he had done everything he could in the western province, Maceo decided to go to Santiago de Cuba in his native province of Oriente. He described his reception in one of his most moving statements:

> On July 25 at the break of dawn we entered Santiago de Cuba after having suffered a terrible night on rough waters and without anyone knowing of my arrival in the city. I took lodging at the Hotel Louvre, and this produced joy on the part of some and displeasure on the part of others; the former because they were anxiously awaiting the return to my native land, and the latter because they regretted it. When the news became known, my precautions were swept aside by the wave of visitors who

> gathered in my room—some to salute me and others to meet me. All demonstrated equal affection and interest, and all wished to make their complaints known to me and to inform me of their desires to solve the political problems of Cuba. My soul, sore from the many wounds I have suffered for the cause of liberty, began to feel joy and real hope of immediate triumph. With the sincere declarations of that people who had been self-denying in their suffering and in the sacrifice of their lives and interests on the altars of liberty, the expansion of my spirit was immense and increasing by leaps and bounds. I was the object of much attention during my stay in the town of my hopes and dreams. The sadness and melancholy of the fight for liberty, and the displeasures and misfortunes of my anguished political life disappeared with the enthusiastic promises of these people. And my spirits were lifted up more and more by the uniformity of the thoughts and ideas in the whole province of Oriente.
>
> The visitors who constantly came to see me from the country reminded me of the same sort of people who came from Las Villas and Occidente to see me in Havana. Ever surrounded by people from all the social classes, I hardly had time to get even the indispensable rest. The rich, the poor, the young, and the old honored me with their presence and with their ready disposition for the fight which they all believed necessary.[22]

Innumerable banquets and meetings were held to honor the national and regional hero. At one banquet, on July 29, 1890, an incident occurred that was to be long remembered in Cuba. A young man named José J. Hernández expressed the hope, in the form of a question addressed to Maceo, that Cuba would be annexed by the United States and become "one more star in the great American constellation." Maceo replied immediately: "Young man, I believe, although it seems impossible to me that this can be the only outcome, that in such a case I would be on the side of the Spaniards." He was unalterably opposed to the annexation of Cuba to the United States. He was ready to lay down his life for only one cause—the independence of Cuba. Indeed, he felt that only independence could justify an armed rebellion.[23] The British consul in Santiago, A. De Crowe, sent a dispatch to the Earl of Salisbury which revealed that he was not above playing the Spanish game:

> Santiago is in a state of excitement over the visit of Maceo, who has tremendous influence with the people of color, and is politically a separatist. . . . His real aim is a Cuba for the colored, and he would commence a war of races as soon as he could. . . . White liberals flatter him because they think he can help them, but they also fear him.[24]

Since Maceo went out of his way to emphasize he did not favor a racial conflict in Cuba, this dispatch was a clear distortion of his position. In an address to the *Casino de Santiago de Cuba,* a society of blacks, Maceo praised the cultural and educational activities of the group, expressed his hope that the youth of Oriente would support the revolution when it began, and called for unity of all Cubans regardless of race or color.[25]

In Santiago de Cuba, Maceo organized the movement for an uprising in the eastern part of the island. This called for the capture of the city, and, once taken, it would serve as a beachhead for the landing of Máximo Gómez and other exiles, who were to be informed in advance. Revolutionary groups in nearly all the towns of the province of Oriente—Manzanillo, Guantánamo, Bayamo, Baracoa, Las Tunas, Jiguaní, etc.—would then rise up, and the Spaniards would be confronted with a full-fledged rebellion throughout the entire province.

The plans should have called for a simultaneous uprising in Havana and eastern Cuba, but for reasons which are not clear, the date for the revolt in Oriente was set for September 8—more than a month earlier than that in the West. At any rate, by the third week of August 1890, the structure and organization of the revolution had been fully completed. Working with Maceo were the principal leaders in Oriente—Generals Guillermo Moncada and Flor Crombet, and other tested veterans of previous revolutionary struggles. The conspirators included intellectuals, workers, and peasants, black and white, and a large representation of Cuban youth.[26]

But the wealthy owners of the manganese mines, sugar plantations, mills, and other properties were opposed to armed warfare. They were afraid that a revolution would interfere with their profitable production, and were frightened by the prominent role to be played by Maceo and other blacks. These fears were reflected in the attitude of the leaders of the Autonomist Party, made up mainly of lawyers who represented the manganese mining and sugar interests. Thus, Captain General Polavieja was able to notify the Spanish government:

> What mainly determined the conduct of the leaders of the Autonomist Party was racial hatred. They did not want to give preponderance to the colored element which was so numerous in the province of Santiago de Cuba. And the majority of the whites were naturally fearful of the public aspirations of Maceo, of imposing a government of his race, creating a Republic similar to the Haitian government.[27]

That Maceo had never expressed such "aspirations" was beside the point. The Spanish authorities knew very well how to use the "Haiti" scare to split the ranks of the white Cubans, and they employed this weapon to influence the leaders of the Autonomist Party against joining the revolutionary movement. It worked because they were accustomed to equating black participation in any Cuban political movement with black domination. When to this was added their fear of losing profits from mining and sugar production, it was a foregone conclusion that they would reject the revolution.[28]

The revolutionaries went ahead with their plans, despite their inability to win over the wealthy interests in Oriente. Every move they made was known in advance by the Spaniards. Even before he had reached Cuba to replace Salamanca, Polavieja had received a complete report from the Spanish army and police on Maceo's plans. Much of this information came from left-wing members of the Autonomist Party, who had been taken into the confidence of the rebels, but who were actually opposed to an armed uprising. So many people knew of the conspiracy, and the movement was conducted with such openness, that it would have been a miracle if the Spanish authorities had not become fully acquainted with the plans.[29]

Captain General Polavieja arrived in Havana on August 24. Within forty-eight hours, he ordered the civil governor in Santiago de Cuba "to arrange for the immediate departure of Don Antonio Maceo and his family for Kingston or some other foreign port."[30] On the afternoon of August 29, a police detachment called upon Maceo and his wife at their hotel and notified them that they would have to leave the following day on an American ship bound for New York. The police then occupied the whole building to prevent Maceo from leaving.

News of Maceo's detention by the police quickly reached the revolutionaries. While many of them, especially the young, were ready to go through with the plans for an immediate uprising, dissension arose in their ranks. The more timid elements felt that with the Spanish government fully prepared for an uprising, the revolution was destined to fail. Their view prevailed, and the order was given to dissolve the groups that had already formed in various places and to call a halt to the movement.[31]

On August 30, Maceo and his wife rode in the coach of the civil governor, Juan Antonio Vinont, to the marine headquarters. While he was saying farewell, the civil governor put thirty ounces of gold in Maceo's hands. The latter immediately asked the source of the money. The governor replied that he was acting on the orders of the government. Maceo refused to accept anything from the Spanish government, but he thanked the governor for the courtesies shown him. Then he left on the Ward Line steamer *Cienfuegos*.[32]

Within a few days, General Flor Crombet, and Colonels

Pedro Castillo and Angel Guerra were also deported from Cuba, and a large number of others who had been implicated in the conspiracy left voluntarily for fear of being imprisoned. But there were some who were not so fortunate, and were sent to the prison of Guano, in the extreme western part of Cuba.[33]

Captain General Polavieja, informing Spain of the failure of the revolutionary conspiracy, paid tribute to the wealthy leaders of the Autonomist Party—the spokesmen for the manganese mining and sugar interests. Because of the importance of the manganese mining interests in the failure of the revolution, the entire insurrectionary movement led by Maceo in Cuba in 1890 is referred to under the title of *La Paz del Manganese* (The Peace of the Manganese). It was their opposition to Maceo that had prevented the revolution from succeeding, as Polavieja pointed out:

> It was my good fortune and no small matter that the leaders of the Autonomist Party rejected him [Maceo]. The conspiracy was revealed by many on the Island, and especially in the province of Santiago de Cuba, where business was paralyzed by the fears it inspired. After I expelled Maceo and some of his followers, some radicals of said party went to the offices of the newspaper, *El País* [organ of the Autonomist Party], and asked its directors to attack me for my action. They were refused and were told that I had just performed a good service for Cuba.[34]

Maceo's seven months of revolutionary activity inside Cuba ended in failure, just as had all the other movements of the decade. But none of these endeavors were completely in vain. From the experience of the Gómez-Maceo plan, the revolutionaries had learned the need for developing greater democracy in the organization of the revolution, and the proper places to be occupied by the civilian and military groups. From Maceo's experiences in Cuba, they learned that mass support for independence was mounting on the island, and that the Spanish tactic of splitting the Cuban ranks through race prejudice was not as effective as it had been in the past. As Herminio Portell Vilá points out: "All these symptoms revealed that neither autonomy nor annexation represented Cuban aspirations so perfectly as independence, and that this was the tendency which Spain feared."[35]

10

Maceo and the Cuban Revolutionary Party

Even though he had been once again disappointed by his discouraging experience in Cuba, Maceo was not ready to write off the cause of independence. While in New York en route to Kingston, he commented, "The country is still not ready to support an armed uprising."[1] Once in Kingston, he wrote to José Miró:

> Duties to my country and my own political convictions are superior to all human weaknesses; obedience to these duties will raise me to the pedestal of the free, or I shall die fighting for the redemption of my people. Tell [my friends] . . . not to permit anyone to rise in arms until I am again in Cuba. As to this I will advise you in due course.[2]

Until he returned to Cuba with another expedition, Maceo had to support himself and his mother and wife. His eyes were set on Costa Rica, whose government was generous in its treatment of Cuban exiles, often granting them governmental positions or commercial monopolies. Maceo hoped to establish a colony in Costa Rica composed primarily of Cubans with farming experience. With the government providing the land and advancing the basic funds for equipment, the Cuban settlers would develop the rich virgin land and natural resources and thus benefit both themselves and Costa Rica. Meanwhile, the lively group of Cuban emigré-revolutionaries in Costa Rica would be a source with whom to discuss and plan the future revolution on the island.

An agreement between Maceo and the government of President José J. Rodríguez to develop the lands of Salamanca, a district on the Atlantic or Caribbean coast, was cancelled because of Spanish pressure. Maceo then asked for a concession on the Pacific coast, and this time he was successful. On May 13, 1891, Joaquín Lizano, Secretary of the Department of Development, signed a contract with Maceo, providing 15,000 hectares in the peninsula of Nicoya on the Pacific coast. The agreement called for the establishment of a colony devoted to the cultivation of tobacco, sugar cane, cacoa, cotton, and coffee, and to the possible production and exploitation of rubber, sassafras, and timber. Five thousand hectares would become the property of Maceo as soon as fifty Cuban families arrived and established themselves in the colony. If, however, twenty-five families were not settled within eighteen months, the government would consider the entire contract invalid. The contract provided for transportation and food costs from the country of origin to the colony, at government expense. Each family established in Nicoya would immediately receive one hundred pesos—from a loan of 10,000 pesos stipulated in the contract—and would be entitled to from two to four hectares of land, a cow, a horse, three hoes, and the essential cooking utensils.[3]

As soon as the contract was signed, Maceo established the boundaries of the designated tract and invited his friends and relatives to share in the contract. By April 26, 1892, José Maceo, Flor Crombet, and ten other families had settled in the colony, and within a few weeks, they were busy preparing the land for bananas, yucca, corn, beans, cacao, coffee, and rice. Soon there were more than enough families settled in the colony to meet the terms of the contract, and Maceo, the long-time exile and permanent revolutionary, became the owner of a large plantation—"La Mansión."

As the colony progressed, Maceo built a comfortable house on his own farm, while the other settlers gradually erected homes of wood and metal on their respective tracts. With government aid, Maceo obtained the heavy machinery necessary for grinding sugar cane, and soon the colony was producing a valuable money crop. Not only was Maceo now the colony's largest planter; he was also the manager and contractor for the whole enterprise. As his responsibilities grew, he hired Antonio Zambrana Vázquez, a compatriot and lawyer, to represent his interests.[4]

Although his wife had joined him in Nicoya, Maceo continued his amorous ways. One of his companions recalled: "Antonio had phenomenal luck with the women; his tall, arrogant stature, his charming gestures, his wonderful temperament, and the natural softness of his accent overwhelmed many who came in his path."[5]

Maceo's experiences in Cuba in 1890 had demonstrated that the majority of the Cuban people sought the political and economic redemption of the island through independence. They would give their unconditional support to any revolutionary movement which could demonstrate a capacity for effective action.

In 1892, such a movement came into being—*El Partido Revolucionario Cubano* (The Cuban Revolutionary Party). Its organizer and leading spirit was José Martí, and it was organized after two full years of intensive preparation. By April 1892 the organization was nearly complete; Martí had groups in all of the emigration centers and a corps of dependable workers in Cuba. With this accomplished, he and his colleagues drew up a document outlining the basis for founding a central revolutionary party. This document was discussed by all the various clubs and rebel groups and, with their approval, the Cuban Revolutionary Party was formed.[6]

The new movement initiated by the Cuban Revolutionary Party was not the personal property of any individual or group of individuals. It was based on the organizations of Cuban exiles and would function democratically.

In organizing the Cuban Revolutionary Party, Martí had brought together "as many elements of all kinds as could be recruited." This had been no easy accomplishment. Thousands of the Cuban exiles had been sharply divided among rival factions, and they differed widely about the nature of the revolution and the republic to follow. It was Martí's great contribution that he was able to forge unity of so many conflicting interests. Moreover, he accomplished this without yielding to those who insisted that he place blacks in a subordinate position in the revolutionary movement.

When Martí addressed the Cuban colony in Tampa in 1891 to raise funds for the revolution, he exhorted the Cubans of *all* racial and social groups to join in the new struggle. The goal of his activities was to unite *all* Cubans into one organization. Perhaps his greatest accomplishment was to overcome the racism that divided the Cuban revolutionaries in exile in the United States, as well as those in Cuba. His formula for the new republic was simple: "With all, for the good of all." He called for the brotherhood of Cubans of all races, and he wrote in 1892:

> In Cuba there is no fear of a racial war. Men are more than white, more than mulatto, more than black. They died for Cuba in the fields of battle; the souls of blacks and whites have risen together up to heaven. In daily life, in defense, in loyalty, in brotherhood, in study, at the side of every white there was always a black.[7]

Contrary to previous procedures, Martí left the military leaders completely out of his plans until he had a strong revolutionary organization. He thereby supplied an approach painfully lacking in the previous movements. In fact, observing Martí's methods, General Gómez commented, "It appears that he is trying to eliminate the military element."[8] Only now, when he had built the necessary revolutionary organization, was he ready to call in the military. He turned without hesitation to the man he had once accused of dictatorial ambitions—Máximo Gómez. And, like Martí, the old general put past differences aside. "From this moment on you can count on my services," he declared. On January 3, 1893, Gómez was formally appointed military chief of all the men under arms.[9]

In February 1892 Maceo went to New York on business connected with the colony in Costa Rica. While there, he learned of the new revolutionary movement. He did not, as yet, give much thought to the movement, and on August 16, 1892, when he was asked for his views on insurrectionary questions, he replied that the time was not yet ripe. He mentioned his affairs in Nicoya, and expressed the fear that the Spanish government might again ruin his project if he made any threatening move.[10] When, however, Maceo learned that Martí had already invited Gómez to join the cause without having even contacted him, he reacted bitterly. But the cause still came first. Thus, he wrote:

> I have not seen Martí nor have I received a letter inviting me to take part in his work. But if, as they say, he is counting on me when it comes to making war, then I do not believe it will be necessary to consult my will. On such important matters, it is known to friend and foe.[11]

Martí was indeed counting on Maceo, and had every intention of enlisting his services. Shortly after visiting Gómez in Santo Domingo, he made a special point of paying a visit to Maceo's mother in Jamaica. Mariana Grajales, then eighty-five years old, stirred Martí deeply with her stories of the Ten Years'

War, in which she had lost a husband and three of her seven sons. In a letter to Maceo, Martí informed him of the visit and observed that Mariana Grajales was "one of the women who have most moved my heart."[12] He could not have chosen a more effective way of approaching Maceo.

After he had asked Gómez to head the liberation army, Martí waited nine months before he made any overt move to persuade Maceo to join. Jorge Mañach, Martí's biographer, suggests that he had to wait this long before asking for Maceo's participation in order that the Spaniards should not use it as a means of accusing the Cuban Revolutionary Party of plotting a race war.[13] But this hardly seems likely, since Martí did not hesitate to enlist Juan Gualberto Gómez, a black, as head of the party inside Cuba. Moreover, Martí saw Maceo as a "symbol of national integration," and at one of his great speeches before the *Liceo Cubano* in Tampa in November 1891, he said:

> To all Cubans, whether they come from the continent where the sun scorches the skin or from countries where the light is gentler, this will be the revolution in which all Cubans, regardless of color, will participate.[14]

It is probable that organizational details alone delayed Martí's invitation to Maceo. But on February 1, 1893, he offered Maceo a leading place in the new liberation movement, and promised to furnish and deliver the necessary war supplies. Although he was pleased at the idea of no longer having to acquire these materials himself, Maceo did not immediately reply. In a letter to Alejandro González on June 9, 1893, he wrote:

> The affairs of Cuba brought me to the brink of abandoning my enterprise. It seems that the government was somewhat displeased because they took certain measures. The truth is that I fight within myself because in taking up one duty I abandon the other.[15]

Just what Maceo meant is subject to some dispute. Some scholars have argued that since he was now a successful planter, he hesitated to sacrifice his new career by responding immediately to Martí's invitation. They maintain that he felt a moral obligation to the Costa Rican government to continue the project in that country, and that his reference to that government being "somewhat displeased" indicates his concern. On the other hand, José Luciano Franco, the leading authority on Maceo, rejects this interpretation. He points out that Maceo was not yet a successful planter, and leaving would not have represented much of a financial sacrifice. In addition, Franco insists that Maceo felt no moral obligation to the Costa Rican government; indeed, it would have viewed with pleasure any new struggle for Cuban independence. Finally, successful or not, moral obligation or no, to Maceo one thing was always uppermost: the achievement of Cuban independence. Such uncertainty as he may have felt probably stemmed from his concern over the continuous intrigues among the Cuban exiles, which he believed still hindered the launching of an effective movement.[16]

In any case, any such uncertainty disappeared at the end of June 1893 when he met Martí in San José. Martí simply did not rest until Maceo was recruited for the cause. He visited Maceo in Costa Rica, spending a week with him and his family. Maceo was impressed with Martí's organizational abilities and achievements, and was moved by his lecture at the School of Law on the meaning of the word "patriotism."[17]

Maceo finally agreed to join the movement. Martí again promised the necessary resources and advised Maceo to settle his affairs and get his men ready. The order to move would come from General Gómez. Martí commented later that Maceo had asked for very little—much less than he had expected.[18]

Maceo's determination to give up all for the new struggle

was strengthened by his mother's death on November 23, 1893, at eighty-five. He wrote to Martí:

> Only three times in my anguished life as a Cuban revolutionary have I suffered such strong and tempestuous emotions of pain and sadness as I have just had with her death in a foreign land.
>
> Ah! How terrible were these three things! My father, the Treaty of Zanjón, and my mother.[19]

Martí's grief over the death of Mariana Grajales was almost as great as that of her son. In *Patría* of December 12, 1893, he paid tribute to the mother of the "noble tribe":

> [Cuba's] entire people, rich and poor, arrogant and humble, masters and servants, followed this woman of eighty-five years to the grave in a strange land. Died in Jamaica, November 27, *Mariana Maceo.*
>
> All Cubans attended the internment, because there is no heart in Cuba that does not feel all that is owed to this beloved old woman, who would always caress your hand with such tenderness. Her mind was already going from having lived so much, but from time to time that energetic face lit up, as though a ray of sun were shining within. . . . I remember that when we were talking about the war at a time when it seemed as if we were not able to carry on the struggle, she got up brusquely, and turned aside to think, alone. And she, who was so good, looked at us as if with anger. Many times, if I had forgotten my duty as a man, I would have retained it because of the example of that woman. Her husband and sons died fighting for Cuba, and we all know that from her breasts, Antonio and José Maceo imbibed the qualities which propelled them into the vanguard of the defenders of our liberties.[20]

Martí wrote a long letter to Maceo, noting at the end: "And of your great pain now, can you not see I do not wish to speak of it. Your mother has died. In *Patria* I say what the news of her death took out of my heart." Knowing how unhappy Mariana was that she could not die in a free Cuba, he added:

> That continuous work for the idea that she loved is the best homage to her memory. I saw your old mother twice, and she caressed me and looked at me like a son, and I will remember her with love all my life.[21]

Maceo thanked him for his expression of sympathy and voiced his deep sadness that his heroic mother could not be buried in a free Cuba beside her husband and sons who had given their lives for its liberty.[22] Maceo declared that his mother was responsible for his own dedication to the cause of a free Cuba, and that her death increased his determination to achieve what she most desired.[23]

Martí revealed his feelings toward Maceo himself when he wrote:

> You are indispensable for Cuba. To me you are, and I say it sincerely, one of the most complete, magnificent, strong, and useful men of Cuba. You are too great, Maceo. I must say that I feel such a deep and intimate affection for you that, believe it or not, it is as though I were conceived in the same womb with you. Doesn't María love me like a brother? Didn't your mother caress me as she would her own son? Didn't she publicly call me her son? Rest assured that while I have a hand in the matter you will be fully recognized.[24]

This last observation was in response to Maceo's letter to Martí expressing his concern that he might again be relegated to a subordinate role in the revolution. For one thing, while Gómez had once again corresponded with his former military colleague, his letters to Maceo had been cold and abrupt. For another, meetings had been held at which the invasion had been discussed, but Maceo had not been included. It is not difficult to understand his uneasiness, and Martí, a master of diplomacy, had gone to great lengths to reassure him. His letter concluded with the reiteration of his original promise to send complete equipment for fifty men whom Maceo would lead to Cuba—the black *caudillo* had only to designate the place.

On December 12, 1893, Martí had given the order to the rebels in Cuba to be ready for action by the end of February 1894. The month passed and the invasion was still not ready. Gómez, as military commander, would not give his approval. He was not satisfied with the conditions in Camagüey province, where support for the revolution was limited.

While the long delay continued, Martí visited various emigré centers, seeking the necessary funds for supplies. From New Orleans, which he visited on May 31, 1894, Martí wrote to Gómez that "the purpose of our trip—seeking resources—has, I believe, been realized. We have been promised, without too much protest, . . . all that we have asked."[25] From New Orleans, Martí boarded the steamer *Albert Dumois* and sailed for a final conference with Maceo in Costa Rica.

Arriving in San José during the first week in June, Martí was met by Enrique Loynez del Castillo, who gave him ominous news about the situation in the revolutionary clubs in Costa Rica. Loynez informed Martí that an intense rivalry had developed between Flor Crombet and José Maceo. Crombet, who was slated to be second in command under Antonio Maceo, had drawn up a plan of invasion that called for him to head a separate invasion from Honduras, which was the center of his support. Loynez told Martí that Crombet's plan had a great deal of merit and that it had received some support from the Cuban revolutionaries in San José. Rumors were also circulating in that city that Antonio Maceo, faced with Crombet's truculence, had withdrawn his support from the revolutionary movement.[26]

Martí took immediate steps to reunite the revolutionaries of Costa Rica and to placate Maceo's pride. On June 10, in San José, Martí supervised the establishment of a new revolutionary club. This club, named "Antonio Maceo," helped Martí's cause with Maceo. Martí showed his astuteness once more when he persuaded Loynez, who was one of Crombet's chief supporters in Costa Rica, to accept its presidency.[27]

On June 11 Martí went to Puntarenas to confer directly with the Maceo brothers and Crombet. He found the leaders in a combative mood; in fact, Crombet and José Maceo had already arranged to fight a duel. The duel was forgotten when Martí, preaching harmony and action, was able to work out a compromise. It was decided that Crombet would recruit men for his own invasion from Honduras, which would remain under the nominal control of Maceo and would have to be coordinated with the latter's own invasion. Maceo was disgruntled, but Martí appealed to his higher sentiments. "Surely," he argued, "the future of our country means more than that individual pride which leads to petty squabbles between men."[28] Four days later, on June 22, while in Panama, Martí wrote to Maceo, who apparently was still not convinced: "I realize that we incur a certain risk by giving Crombet such an important position, but the consequence of not doing so would mean a permanent fracture in our ranks." Martí urged him to make every effort to maintain harmony among the Cuban revolutionaries in Costa Rica.[29]

Unquestionably, Martí once again made a strong impression on Maceo, and his plea for unity was taken to heart. When Maceo received an anti-Martí letter from Enrique Trujillo, director of the rebel paper, *El Porvenir* in New York, complaining of Martí's increasing domination of the movement, he replied by sharply rebuking the editor and demanding that this carping criticism be halted. He emphasized that there must be more unity and less division.[30]

While waiting impatiently to launch the revolt, Maceo was once more the target of an assassination plot. Although rumors spread through San José that such an attempt would be made by Spanish agents while he was attending the theater, Maceo insisted on going to see the play, "Felipe Derblay," an original comedy by Jorge Ohnet, presented by the Company Paulino at the Variedades theater. After the play, Maceo left the theater accompanied by seven Cubans for protection. A group of Spaniards attacked the party, and one of them ran close to

Maceo and shot him point-blank. Before he could fire a second time, the assassin was killed by one of the Cubans.[31]

The bullet penetrated Maceo's shoulder, but did not pass through it. When the doctor declared that it would be necessary to probe for it, Maceo exclaimed: "Don't cut! I have enough wounds already in my body; let that ball join the others that have gone there since the war." It was the twenty-second wound that he had sustained during his career![32]

During his convalescence, Maceo became more impatient than ever and kept prodding Martí for the decision to move. The latter answered his complaints by assuring him that everything was in readiness and that all that was needed was the sign from Gómez. However, the old general was still preoccupied with the situation in Camagüey province, where the sugar mill owners were pleading for time to finish the harvesting and grinding, while promising money for the invasion if their pleas were heeded. Gómez, who had little respect for wealthy and propertied groups, finally tired of the delay and ordered the movement to begin. In arriving at this decision, Gómez said: "This situation will not change; the rich people will never enter the Revolution. We must force the situation—precipitate the events."[33] On September 30, 1894, he wrote to Maceo: "After November 15 at the latest, we must all be prepared to move immediately. Nonetheless, if you are completely ready, this letter, which may very well be my last one from here, constitutes the order to move which you desire."[34]

Maceo was elated, and despite his wound, he was fully prepared to move. Martí, of course, shared his joy. "How can I paint my happiness," he wrote Maceo after learning of Gómez's decision, "which is only clouded by the news that you are still not well."[35]

In the October 6, 1893 issue of *Patria,* Martí had written a long, insightful article on Antonio Maceo. He described Maceo's life in Costa Rica, observing that he "is admired by peasants and ministers alike." Maceo, Martí noted, was a happy man indeed "because he came from a lion and lioness." His mother was old, "yet she still has the hands of a young girl for caressing anyone who talks to her about her homeland." She had spent many hours in holes in the ground during the Ten Years' War "while all around her there were sabers and machetes crossing to the hilt." But she still dreams of a free Cuba, and "accompanies to the door those who in the name of Cuba are still coming to see her." Then there was Maceo's wife, María, "an exceptionally noble lady," a "cultured matron," who had proved to be the "best untrained doctor in the war." Martí added the highest tribute: "It is easy to be heroes with such women!" His tribute to Maceo was on the same level:

> The Cuban who had no rival in defending with strength and respect, the laws of his republic now lives in Nicoya. . . . Within his formidable frame lies a great heart. Apparently that man can never, with his serene vigor, harm or offend the country which he loves so dearly, so dearly that when he talks about its realities and the fire burning within it, his eyes light up with happiness and he becomes speechless. The camp is before him, the horses galloping, and the way is clearly seen. His is the joy of a bridegroom, and it must be assumed that there is substance in what he says because Maceo's mind is as powerful as his arm. No childish enthusiasm would get the better of his wise experience. His thinking is firm and harmonious, like the lines of his skull. His words are polished, as though with constant energy, and of an artistic elegance derived from his painstaking adjustment to wise and sober ideas. He does not give himself away verbally, which is truly noteworthy, but treats the subject at hand in a roundabout way, while, like someone returning from a long voyage, he hints at all the pitfalls and difficulties. He leaves no phrases ragged, uses no impure expressions or hesitates when he seems to do so; rather, he carefully considers his subject matter or his man. He never exaggerates or drops the reins. But the sun sets one day and rises another, and through the window that looks out upon the field of Mars its first splendors shine upon that warrior who

> spends a sleepless night searching for paths for his country. His supports will be himself, never his dagger. He shall serve his troops with his ideas even more than with his courage. Strength and greatness are natural to him.

As we shall now see, Martí's words became reality on the battlefields of Cuba.

11

The Second War for Independence Begins

On Christmas Day, December 25, 1894, José Martí wrote a letter to Antonio Maceo in which he used the code expression, "I am going on a voyage with four friends." The purpose of this was to tell Maceo that he was leaving New York and that soon Máximo Gómez would land in Cuba. Gómez's landing was to signal a general uprising throughout the country. The final details were drawn up: three yachts—the *Amadis,* the *Lagonda,* and the *Baracoa*—had been chartered to take the Cubans to the island. Each ship had been assigned a full complement of arms.[1]

The three yachts had been chosen because they were faster than the boats used by the Spaniards. Their destination was ostensibly Central America with the following stops: at a certain point in Florida, to take on board Carlos Roloff and Serafín Sánchez with 800 men; in Costa Rica, for Antonio Maceo, his brother José, Flor Crombet, and 200 men; and in Santo Domingo for Martí, José María Rodríguez, and Máximo Gómez. The *Lagonda,* the yacht which would carry Maceo and his party, would sail from Fernandina, on the coast of Florida, to Costa Rica, and then to Guantánamo. Crombet's proposal that he should lead a separate invasion from Honduras had been dropped, and the *insurrectos* on the *Lagonda* would be under the command of Antonio Maceo.[2]

Last-minute delays plagued the Cuban Revolutionary Party, but by New Year's Day, 1895, all seemed ready. Martí spent most of that week in Florida, arranging the last details. He had been able to ship a great many arms, ostensibly purchased for the Tampa firm of Hall & Knight, to the tiny port town of Fernandina. Martí also had the cooperation of N. B. Borden, a resident of Fernandina, who owned a warehouse that was used to store the purchased arms. Believing that everything was ready, Martí returned to New York on January 5 to arrange for the shipment of some military stores. He was planning to return to Fernandina on the *Baracoa,* which was sailing south from Boston. In Cuba, the revolutionary leaders were informed of the impending action, although Martí did not reveal the details of the expeditions, and they were ordered to support the invasion.[3]

In Costa Rica, Maceo was awaiting further news of the vessel that would pick up his expedition. Finally the word came that the revolutionary leaders had suffered a tremendous catastrophe. López de Queralta, a member of the expedition belonging to Sánchez's group, carelessly revealed the plan to one of the captains of the three yachts who, in turn, passed the information on to the shipowners. In short order, a Spanish official heard of the plan, protested to Washington, and on January 14, 1895, the federal government detained the three yachts and confiscated the materials of war.

It was a terrible blow. Nearly three years of work, and some $58,000 had been lost. But what Martí feared even more was the loss of prestige and confidence in the revolutionary leaders. Depressed, he finally decided to travel to Santo Domingo and Costa Rica to tell Gómez and Maceo about the failure.[4]

Yet the catastrophe had exactly the opposite effect from what had been feared. Both the revolutionaries in Cuba and the exiles in the United States and other centers revealed their pleased surprise at the scope of the expedition. Who would have thought it possible that Martí could have organized such a detailed undertaking with the limited resources at his command, and carried it out (until the last fatal moment) with such efficiency and secrecy? Enthusiasm for Martí's leadership grew both in Cuba and abroad. "Those who had hitherto thought him a poet and a dreamer," recalled Horatio Rubens, Cuban lawyer for the revolutionary groups, "were now more impressed by the magnitude and promise of his plan than by its temporary frustration."[5]

After Fernandina, Martí and the expeditionary leaders agreed that each of the leaders would have to shoulder most of the responsibility for getting their groups to Cuba. Gómez persuaded Ulisses Heureaux, the president of the Dominican Republic, to lend him 2,000 pesos to finance his departure. Martí, however, could only offer Maceo $2,000. Although Maceo felt this was inadequate, Flor Crombet insisted that he could manage on that sum. Crombet went over Maceo's head directly to Martí, insisting that he, not Maceo, should lead the expedition, since Maceo simply did not know how to handle funds promptly. This resulted in a series of letters between Crombet and Martí of which Maceo knew nothing.[6]

Juan Gualberto Gómez, in Cuba, was given the responsibility of setting a new date for the uprising, subject to the final approval of a military committee composed of the principal military leaders abroad. Two basic criteria were adopted to guide them in fixing a date: first, no less than four provinces must be ready for and favorable to the revolution; and second, one province in addition to Oriente must be prepared for the landing of military officers.

After consulting with local leaders, Gómez decided that these two conditions had been satisfied, and the date of February 24, 1895, was agreed upon.

The insurrection began in Cuba on the day scheduled. On February 24, the *grito*, or "cry" was sounded at Baire, a village about fifty miles from Santiago de Cuba. Unfortunately, on that same day, the uprising in the West was defeated by the

Spanish authorities. Having learned of the plans, they captured General Julio Sanguilly and Don Aguirre de Valdés, the supreme and assistant commanders of the whole Western Department, as they were leaving the city of Havana to lead the uprising in the west. Without leadership, the revolution collapsed in the western provinces on the very day it was supposed to begin.[7]

When the *Grito de Baire* was sounded, the supreme military figures had not yet appeared in Cuba. Gómez was still in Santo Domingo and Maceo in Costa Rica. It was imperative that they leave for Cuba as soon as possible. On February 27, Gómez wrote Maceo: "The smoke of gunfire is visible in Cuba, and the blood of our comrades is being shed on its soil. We have no choice but to leave from wherever and however we can."[8] Maceo agreed. "I do not think we can afford to wait any longer," he wrote. "We are running a great danger. Once in Cuba, we can depend on the machete to open the breach."[9]

It was just at that point that Maceo was surprised and shocked by the contents of a message from Martí. He informed Maceo that, since Crombet could organize the expedition with the amount offered, the entire responsibility for getting Maceo's group to Cuba had been entrusted to Crombet. On March 8, Frank Agramonte, Martí's agent, arrived in San José with the party's $2,000 and with orders to turn it over only to Crombet. It is not difficult to imagine Maceo's feelings. Not only was the decision a blow to his prestige, but he was even more hurt by the knowledge that these arrangements had been made behind his back.[10] Never again would he view Martí with the same respect and affection he had felt up to that time.

Still, when Martí appealed to Maceo's patriotism, the plea was effective. "Cuba is at war, General," he wrote. "When that is said, the picture is changed."[11] Swallowing his wounded pride, Maceo agreed to go along in a subordinate role. At the request of Flor Crombet, he readily agreed to meet with the new expedition commander. They reached an amicable agreement that twenty-three men would leave for Cuba. Aside from the machetes, only nine rifles were obtained in Costa Rica. The actions required to obtain these weapons alerted the Spanish officials, who put pressure upon the government to intern the rebels. Elizardo Maceo, José's son, was detained by the authorities, but the others were able to avoid this fate by exerting various influences. In addition, Maceo's activities were so closely watched that Crombet ordered the expedition divided into two groups until the time of embarkation, each of which would leave from a different port. But Maceo refused to leave the main group, and that was that.[12]

When the Costa Rican authorities, alerted by the Spanish representatives in the country, inquired of Maceo if he planned to invade Cuba, he assured the Secretary of State that he was going to New York rather than to Cuba. With this promise made, the rebels were allowed to proceed. Instead of being exhilarated, Maceo left in a despondent mood. On his last day in Costa Rica, he wrote to his wife:

> I have experienced untold bitterness, disgust, and displeasure brought on by those who shelter avarice in their hearts, disguised by the polish of goodness. How often men with a poor sense of loyalty deceive their friends! With you also I want to remain silent; I don't want you to suffer, too, with the horrible tempest which has begun to mount in my head. You must not be tormented with doubts and fears; I want you to be happy, ignorant of everything. There you have my correspondence; it explains much, and what I am including for you completes the work. Guard these papers with great care. They will have the task of saying what I prefer not to say.

Maceo's farewell to his wife closed with this exhortation: "The Nation above all! Your entire life is the best example. To continue forward is duty; to retreat is ignominious shame. Forward, then, for the sake of the native land, for the glory of sacrificing everything!"[13]

Crombet, Maceo, his brother, José, and twenty other rebels left Costa Rica on the *Adirondack,* an American craft, ostensibly bound for New York. The Spanish consul in Costa Rica was not fooled, however, and following his warning, the *Adirondack* was kept under a close watch by Spanish cruisers. On the night of March 29, the captain of the *Adirondack,* fearful of possible reprisals, broke his promise to land the insurgents in Cuba, and deposited them instead on Fortune Island, in the archipelago of the Bahamas. There they finally prevailed upon the American vice-consul, Farrington, to rent them his schooner, the *Honor,* and with three sailors as a crew, the twenty-three rebels sailed for Cuba on the afternoon of March 30. The following day, the schooner was hit by a bad storm, but the seasick rebels recovered sufficiently, on catching sight of the beacons of Duaba and Baracoa, to break out their weapons and ready the cargo for landing. The schooner was wrecked in the landing on the beach near the town of Baracoa. But the first expedition had succeeded in reaching Cuba. The rebels were greeted with joy by the farmers in the area, and the word spread immediately: *"Maceo is here! Viva Cuba Libre!"*[14]

Maceo knew that the presence of the rebels would soon be known to the Spaniards and that they would be pursued by strong enemy forces. To avoid encirclement and destruction while trying to join up with other rebel forces, Maceo led the expeditionaries through the mountains and forests toward the district of Guantánamo. Living on berries and drinking water from streams, the small group of rebels made their way up and down the hills, through tangled undergrowth, and dense woods. During a skirmish with Spanish soldiers, Crombet was killed. Maceo then split the rebels into groups, and, with five followers, moved ahead.

Soon only three of the six were left, and eight days later, after suffering extreme hardships, these *insurrectos* stumbled into the camp of Brigadier Jesús Rabí. Of the original twenty-three invaders who had left Duaba twenty days before, only thirteen were still alive, and most of these were prisoners of Spain.

On the very night that Maceo reached the rebel camp, on the verge of exhaustion, he issued a general order to the forces of Oriente announcing that he had arrived and had assumed command of the entire province. The following day, April 21, he ordered all rebel officers "to hang every emissary of the Spanish government, Peninsular or Cuban, whatever may be his rank, who presents himself in our camps with propositions of peace. This order must be carried out without hesitation of any kind or without attention to any contrary indications. Our motto is to triumph or to die."[15]

The same day Maceo issued a proclamation to the people of Cuba urging all of them to rise in arms. The response to this call was most gratifying. On April 30, Maceo wrote to his wife:

> I have 6,000 men, well-armed, and with much artillery . . . by the 15th of the month, I will have 12,000 armed men, and much territory conquered.
>
> Three days ago José [Maceo] told me of the arrival of Gómez, Martí, Borrero, Guerra and two others on the beaches between Guantánamo and Baracoa.[16]

On April 11, 1895, Gómez, accompanied by Martí, landed at Cajobabo. The chief veterans of 1868 and the ideological leader and moving spirit of the revolution were at last in Cuba!

At La Mejorana, near Santiago de Cuba, on May 4, Martí, Gómez, and Maceo met to decide on the strategy to be followed in the war. Among the topics discussed was the question of civil *versus* military control of the revolution. Martí expressed himself strongly in favor of civil superiority over the military authority, and proposed calling a convention of all the civil and military leaders to form a civil government and to elect its officials. As on previous occasions, he maintained that complete military control would be a very bad precedent for a postwar independent republic. He feared that the war might end with Spain expelled from the island, but with a Cuban military dictatorship in control.

This time, Gómez sided with Martí. But Maceo took a strong stand for a military *junta* until victory had been achieved. He felt that the weakness, dissension, petty rivalries, and incompetence of the civil government during the Ten Years' War had interfered with the prosecution of the revolution, and had ultimately contributed to the collapse of the rebellion. He argued that, in order to avoid this error in the new revolution, the war should be conducted under the control of a small group of the highest military leaders.

The question of civil versus military control of the war was not fully decided. Martí's viewpoint was more or less adopted, for agreement was reached among the three men that Gómez was to be commander-in-chief of the army, Maceo military chief of Oriente, and Martí supreme leader of the revolution abroad and in nonmilitary matters.[17]

On May 18, Martí wrote from Dos Rios to Manuel Mercado, his friend in Mexico. He began his letter: "I am now, every day, in danger of giving my life for my country."[18] The letter was never finished. On May 19, the Spaniards attacked. Although ordered by Gómez to remain with the rear-guard, Martí rode forth to his first encounter with the Spaniards. As he rode through a pass, Spanish soldiers shot him down. His companion, Angel de la Guardia, tried to rescue the body, but failed. Gómez's attempts to retake Martí's body were equally futile. The Spaniards carried it away to Santiago de Cuba, where, on May 27, 1895, José Martí was buried.

Martí's untimely death in battle led the Spaniards to believe that the revolution would now collapse, and, needless to say, Martí's death was a staggering blow. He had exercised an ideological influence over the Cuban insurgents that none of his successors could hope to duplicate. Nevertheless, the opposite of what Spain had expected actually happened. Instead of the revolution falling apart, the memory of Martí's personality, of his revolutionary ideas, and of his many sacrifices on behalf of Cuba, stimulated the struggle. The "Apostle of Cuban Independence" became, as Gómez noted, "the soul of the Revolution,"[19] and his memory invigorated and inspired the revolutionary drive of the people.

12

Cuban Revolutionary Strategy

In March 1895 the Spanish government in Madrid learned that Antonio Maceo and Máximo Gómez were preparing to land in Cuba. Martínez Campos, the Spanish hero of the Ten Year's War, was questioned about the latest Cuban revolt. He answered gravely: "I attribute great importance to the fact that Maceo is embarking for Cuba, because I know the prestige he enjoys and the military skill he exhibited in the previous campaign."[1] The government in Madrid shared this concern; it immediately instituted determined measures to meet the situation. Even before Maceo and his twenty-two companions had landed in Cuba, an announcement was issued by Spain on March 31 that "General Martínez Campos is ready to leave for Cuba to take charge of the command. . . . On April 2 a battalion of marine infantry will depart from the Great Antilles and by April 8 forces up to 6,000 soon will depart."[2] In New York, the *World* greeted the announcement with the observation: "When Spain sends its great general Martínez Campos to put down the uprising in Cuba, it means that the trouble is serious."[3]

By the middle of April, Spain had followed up the appointment of Martínez Campos with the declaration of martial law in the eastern provinces and with continued requests by Prime

Minister Cánovas del Castillo for additional troops and credits. In July 1895, De Truffin, the Russian consul in Havana, reported:

> In spite of the tireless efforts of the famed commander [Martínez Canpos] and reinforcements brought in from the metropolis (30,000 men), the uprising is still *spreading.* Another 10,000 men are due to arrive from Spain soon; it is asserted that the Marshal had asked for another 25,000 men in September.[4]

By December 1895, 98,412 regular troops had been sent from Spain, and the number of volunteers on the island increased to 63,000 men. These forces were steadily augmented by fresh troops from the Peninsula, so that by the end of 1897, there were 240,000 regulars and 60,000 irregulars on the island.[5]

The total given for those who served for the insurgents during the entire war was 53,774. But in the early months of the conflict, the number actually engaged in fighting was much smaller. It was not until the western provinces were invaded late in 1895, and new recruits added from that area, that the revolutionary army attained its maximum strength. For the greater part of the war, the effective combatant force amounted to about 30,000.

The Cuban Liberating Army was completely integrated. A *New York Times* correspondent later recalled that "all regiments were made up of men of any and all colors. There were white Cubans, black Cubans, black and white Americans and natives of other countries. There was no regiment reserved for whites or blacks." Just what proportion of the army was constituted by black Cubans is difficult to determine, but that it was substantial is abundantly clear. In 1912, black leaders in Cuba claimed that they had provided up to eighty-five percent of the soldiers. Charles E. Chapman, in his *History of the Cuban Republic,* felt that these estimates were too high, but he agreed that "certainly the Negroes had provided a majority of the Army of Liberation."[6]

Not only did the strength of the Spanish army far exceed that of the *insurrectos,* but it was vastly superior in supplies of weapons and implements of war. From the time of the Ten Years' War, the possession of firearms by individuals in Cuba had been prohibited; arms found in the possession of the common people were confiscated. This practically eliminated private arms, except for those that had been hidden, as a significant source for the rebels. Aside from such arms and supplies as could be captured from the enemy or were turned in by deserters, all materials had to come from outside the country, and primarily from the United States. With the Spanish navy in complete control of the Cuban waters, the arrival of supply boats was perilous and uncertain. In addition, the government of the United States, while permitting Spain to buy freely all the munitions she needed, repeatedly prevented rebel expeditions from leaving its shores.

A number of such expeditions did manage to reach Cuba. But despite thousands of dollars sent from Cuba and many thousands collected in the United States, Europe, and Latin America, only a small part of this amount actually reached Cuba.[7]

The rebels had no uniforms, meager rations, and little ammunition. The Spaniards, on the other hand, had the great advantage of standardized weapons and artillery, and an ample supply of ammunition. The great diversity in types and ages of the rebel weapons was a constant source of concern for the leaders, since they often found themselves with arms of one type and ammunition of another. Each Spanish rifleman carried from 100 to 150 rounds of ammunition, while his Cuban counterpart might have four or five rounds, or none at all. Guns were harder to replace than men, and the *insurrectos* put special emphasis on weapons maintenance.[8]

Cuban artillery weapons were not plentiful, and the ammunition for them was even less so. The only standard weapon that was available in abundance was the machete. One contemporary wrote:

> There is a peculiar wild shrill cry the Cubans give that announces a machete charge—a "rebel yell" sure enough, fierce and prolonged—and it means going in at the high speed of horses, for "war to the knife," and there is no doubt and no wonder that the Spaniards are alarmed always by that battle-cry. There has been more hand-to-hand fighting in Cuba than in any war of modern times.

This type of hand-to-hand combat resulting from the skillful use of the machete enabled the rebels, unaided by other arms, to often terrorize Spanish troops equipped with artillery and rifles.[9]

The native Cubans were more or less inured to the climate and diseases, while the new recruits from Spain were highly vulnerable to both. According to official Cuban figures, 3,437 *insurrectos* died of disease, which was fewer than the 5,180 who died of wounds or were killed in battle. In contrast, it was estimated that ten of the Spanish conscripts died of disease to every one killed in battle. Small wonder that when Gómez was asked who were his best generals, he replied, "June, July and August." These were the months when yellow fever was rife. This does not mean that the Cuban forces were not hard hit by illness and epidemics, for large numbers were incapacitated for various periods. Nevertheless, the Cuban cases were not as serious as the Spaniards', and their recuperation was much faster.[10]

This immunity only partially reduced the vast disparity between the Spanish and Cuban forces in numbers and supplies. It is amazing that on an island 730 miles long and an average of 50 miles wide, the Cuban revolutionaries were able to battle so effectively against the vastly superior Spanish army for over three years without any aid from a single foreign power. The story of how this was accomplished is one of the great epics of modern military history.

The military strategy of the Second War for Independence was formulated by the aging Máximo Gómez, commander-in-chief of the Liberating Army. It was his belief that the basic reasons for the failure of the Ten Years' War were: (1) the fact that the revolution was confined to the eastern part of the island; and (2) that not enough damage had been inflicted on the Cuban economy to force the wealthy classes to put pressure on the Spaniards to seek peace, and to deprive Spain of the revenues with which to continue the war. Gómez resolved not to repeat these mistakes. He was determined to extend the struggle throughout Cuba, even to the very extreme western coast. He was similarly determined that the island should be made unprofitable to the Spaniards by destroying every possible source of revenue. A "scorched-earth" policy would make the whole island a great economic liability for Spain. True, this would wreak hardships on the Cubans, but it was the price they would have to pay for independence. "The chains of Cuba have been forged by her own richness," Gómez argued, "and it is precisely this which I propose to do away with soon." His chief object was the sugar industry, which constituted approximately seventy-five percent of Cuba's wealth and was the main source of the Spanish government's revenue from the island. As Gómez noted: "Sugar cannot be allowed because to work means peace, and in Cuba we must not permit working." A by-product of this policy would be the recruiting of the unemployed into the rebel ranks.[11]

As Gómez pointed out later in the war, this scorched-earth policy was "considered when planning my campaign long before landing in Cuba."[12] He did not wait long before putting it into effect. On July 1, 1895, Gómez strictly prohibited the transport of industrial, agricultural, and animal products to towns and garrisons occupied by Spanish troops. His circular added:

> The sugar plantations will stop their labors, and whoever shall attempt to grind the crops, notwithstanding this order, will have their cane burned and their buildings demolished. The person who, disobeying this order, will try to profit from the present

state of affairs, will show by his conduct little respect for the rights of the Revolution of redemption, and therefore, shall be considered an enemy, and treated as a traitor, in case of his capture.[13]

On November 6, 1895, Gómez issued a new order calling for "all plantations" to be "totally destroyed, their cane and outbuildings burned and railroad connections destroyed." Anyone resisting this order would be considered "traitors to their country," and, if found guilty, could be shot.[14]

Both decrees, as Gómez informed Estrada Palma, "have the same objective: the total paralysis of all labor in Cuba."[15]

Gómez was not completely insensitive to the lasting damage his policies might inflict on the Cuban economy. He tried to introduce a new plan for the relief of owners of sugar plantations that was intended to result in the saving of several million dollars worth of property that would otherwise go to ruin. Permits were issued to planters who asked for them, allowing them to plow and, in fact, to perform almost any work necessary for the preservation of their properties. However, this plan was advanced only to lessen the effects of his policies and as a means of hastening the rapid utilization of lands and equipment once the war was over. The grinding of sugar cane remained prohibited, as was any sort of production which might accrue to the revenues of Spain.[16]

This policy caused considerable dissension among the civil and military revolutionary figures, and even the latter were not in agreement. Some were of the opinion that valuable properties should be subject to a type of "protection" fee which owners would pay in order to keep their properties from being damaged. Others expanded upon this with the idea that sugar mill operators should be allowed to grind cane and produce their product in exchange for regular substantial contributions to the revolutionary cause.

The radical prohibition of sugar production ordered by Gómez first met with opposition from Maceo, his second in command. Maceo believed that the revolution would be better served if the planters were allowed to grind sugar cane in exchange for payment of certain fixed and regular contributions to the rebels. In addition, he stipulated, they must neither aid the enemy nor hamper the progress of the rebellion. If the sugar producers did not agree to these conditions, their machinery and other resources should be ruthlessly destroyed. Maceo was also worried lest the effects of Gómez's intransigent policy should jeopardize the chances of recognition of its belligerency outside Cuba, and convert foreign property owners in Cuba from friends into enemies of the revolution. At the least, he felt, the prohibition against grinding should be applied only to those who refused or failed to pay a war tax or who disobeyed revolutionary orders.[17]

Maceo did not allow Estrada Palma to persuade him to "go easy" with the properties of men who might prove helpful to the revolutionary cause because of their "influence with members of the Congress and with prominent people [in the United States]." He informed Estrada Palma that it was necessary to treat each case equally and to avoid favoritism which would only injure the revolutionary cause. It was only necessary to know if a planter had paid his full tax, "so that if he has not, fire can be applied to his property with a minimum of delay."[18]

Soon after assuming command in Oriente, Maceo made a number of such agreements with the sugar cane growers and mill operators. These agreements facilitated the acquisition of funds by the revolutionary delegation in New York and provided some implements of war. Viewing this as a success, the mobile governing council in Cuba left the door open for individual leaders of the Liberating Army and the officials in the United States to make their own agreements with sugar producers on the same terms as those set forth by Maceo. This, of course, was precisely what Gómez wished to avoid. He insisted that, as long as there was no liberty on the island and Cuba had to suffer under the Spanish yoke, no one had the right to add to

Spain's capacity to maintain its tyranny. Despite his strong disapproval of them, Gómez did honor the contracts made by Maceo and others. "I am giving orders," he wrote to Estrada Palma, "to respect its [a sugar mill's] interest in grinding in view of the transaction completed by you to the effect of no less than $20,000." But then he showed his extreme disfavor for the whole policy by stating critically: "I value highly the Cuban blood that is being shed because of sugar, and if the amount is not adjusted soon, the torch will adjust it all."[19]

Gómez's objection forced the revolutionary government to examine the problem in detail. The examination produced the following analysis: First, that if the production of sugar crops was permitted, even though Spain benefitted, the revolutionists could obtain much-needed fees and taxes. And secondly, if cane grinding was not allowed, both sides in the war would suffer, but the *insurrectos* would be hit harder, since the Spaniards had greater sources of financing at their disposal. The civil government thus elected to permit sugar grinding for those mill operators who made fiscal arrangements with the revolution and who fulfilled their obligations on contributions. Those who did not contribute could not grind. Moreover, the cane fields and mills of all who showed any sympathy for Spain and who forfeited their properties thereby were to be burned and the owners declared enemies of the revolution.[20]

This policy, of course, was a serious blow to Gómez's general strategy. He envisaged a war in which Spain's economic losses would be so great that she would give up the island to stop the drain on her own resources. Wherever Gómez was in control, he relentlessly followed his policy. As he informed a New York delegation, he was "impeding the production of sugar and destroying plantations without entering into transactions of any kind, since on the contrary, even though they pay us interest, they prejudice us too much, and the triumph of the Revolution so far has been terrible and inexorable." The conflict of policies weakened the revolutionary struggle until other military leaders and government representatives aligned themselves with Gómez.[21]

Cuban military strategy, as developed by Gómez, was based on the premise that the huge disparity between the opposing forces made any decisive campaigns to defeat the enemy impossible. The war had to be won by making it impossible for Spain to continue the struggle. In carrying out this plan, Gómez continually placed his forces on the offensive, while forcing the enemy to remain on the defensive. This was done, first by forcing the Spaniards to disperse their forces throughout the island, and secondly, by concentrating all attacks upon the economy of the island, rather than against the enemy's military forces. Consequently, the great majority of Cuban actions occurred where and when Spanish forces were defending properties, towns, and communication and transportation facilities. Gómez instructed the Cubans to cut all railroad and telegraph lines, to destroy Spanish forces whenever the opportunity arose, and to attack any small Spanish outposts.[22] Of course, the shortages of ammunition also played a part in this policy, and while attacking Spanish positions, the Cubans were instructed to capture as many arms as possible.

Cuban strategy required that the *insurrectos* themselves never occupy a town or fixed position where they might be a target for superior enemy forces. Rather, the aim was to rout the Spanish garrisons when the rebels had superior numbers, to capture supplies and ammunition, and then to burn the towns in order to deprive the enemy of bases. Under this policy, women and children were given an opportunity to leave any towns that were attacked.

The strategy envisioned no fixed battle lines, no large campaigns, and no great concentrations of troops that could be overwhelmed by the Spanish army. (Only one large campaign was launched during the entire war. This was the invasion of the West, which lasted from October 1895 to January 1896.) Instead, rebels infiltrated areas strongly occupied by the

Spaniards; they assembled, struck, and then dispersed to later regroup and repeat the process.[23]

While the Cuban army operated in seemingly independent units, there was actually close cooperation and interdependence among the component parts. When attacks were planned on particularly strong positions, diversionary actions were planned to draw the attention of the Spaniards elsewhere. Rebel units that were threatened or trapped were able to escape through repeated multiple attacks by other units upon the rear and flanks of the Spanish attackers. Close coordination was made possible by the effective intelligency system maintained by the revolutionaries, which kept them fully advised of the enemy movements. The intelligence system owed its success to the fact that large numbers of the rural population sympathized with the *mambises.* Grover Flint, an American journalist and artist who spent four months with the Liberating Army in 1896, wrote: "No man is so poor that he cannot cheerfully give food for the army. This proves also the truth of saying here that the Spaniard owns only the ground he stands on. *The news of every movement of the Spaniard is quickly reported.*"[24]

Blending into the population, the *insurrectos* were impossible to isolate. Even when they were occasionally caught off-guard, the fleet-footed rebels were able to quickly vanish. Of course, it was easier to identify the cavalry, but they, too, were quartered by friendly peasants.

In addition to tested experience and good leadership, the *mambises* also had strong motivation. They understood why they were fighting and what they were fighting for. Night after night, the rebels would discuss the aims of the war as set forth in some article or editorial in one of the five papers they published: *El Cubano Libre* (in Oriente); *Boletín de Guerra* (in Camagüey); *La República* and *La Sanidad* (in Las Villas); and *La Independencia* (in Manzanillo). The printing shop for *El*

Cubano Libro, published under Maceo's direction, was visited by an American reporter, who wrote in the *National Magazine:*

> It must be extremely embarrassing [for the Spaniards] to receive with regularity a newspaper well edited, with twelve wide columns of news matter and editorial paragraphs full of unrestrained acrimony for Spain, and printed on territory which Spain still claims for her own subjugation!
>
> Time and time again the Spaniards have sent troops out in the vicinity of the fields where this paper was supposed to be printed, and equally as many times they have returned to their point of starting with ranks decimated, and without having silenced the most powerful voice on the Cuban fields—the voice that comes from the mountains of Cayo del Rey.
>
> The newspaper is circulated gratis in the ranks of the insurgent army. It has become an institution which does much to elevate the spirit of the *soldados de la manigua* (soldiers of the long grass), the Cuban insurgents. It is teaching the women, the children and the illiterate to read, who have not had the chance under the schoolless reign of Spain.[25]

Armed rebel teams wandered through the countryside, distributing copies of the insurgent papers to the peasants. They entered a village at dusk, when the peasants—both black and white—had finished their work and had time to listen, and they spent hours reading to them from the articles and editorials in the papers.

General Martínez Campos, the Spanish commander, was also a graduate of the Ten Years' War, and, having been successful in ending that struggle, he believed that by using the same strategy he could speedily triumph over the rebels. Martínez Campos' strategy was: (1) to distribute sufficient force at various points over the island to suppress the spread of the rebellion; (2) to concentrate troops west of Oriente to effectively wall in the *insurrectos* and confine them to a limited field of action, while preventing the destruction of property in that area; and (3) to push the rebels into a corner of Oriente, crush the penned-up Cubans by sheer weight of numbers, and end the war. In pursuance of this plan, Martínez Campos ordered the protection of sugar estates, railroads, and other valuable property. His forces were ordered to convoy provisions to those towns that needed them, and to attack Cuban forces when they were encountered.[26]

With the emphasis on defense, the backbone of his strategy was the use of the *trocha.* The eastern *trocha* was the most extensively fortified line ever constructed by Spain in the New World, stretching from coast to coast at the narrowest part of the island, from Júcaro on the southern coast to Morón on the north. An eyewitness description of this *trocha,* pictures it as a broad belt across the island, two hundred yards wide and fifty miles long. The space in the center had been cleared of timber, which was then placed in rows parallel to the two sides, "forming a barrier of tree trunks and roots and branches as wide as Broadway [in New York City] and higher than a man's head." Down the center of this cleared space was a single-track military railroad, equipped with armor-clad cars, to facilitate movement from one point to another along the fifty miles. Telegraph communication wires stretched along the railroad. On both sides of the *trocha* more than thirty large and small forts and blockhouses were constructed. The larger forts were placed at intervals of one-half mile, with the blockhouses and smaller forts placed at strategic points in between. A maze of barbed wire was placed so that "to every twelve yards of posts there were four hundred and fifty yards of wire fencing." Each fortification had adequate loopholes from which to observe and fire, and some were encircled on the outside by trenches. The forts were also equipped with iron or zinc roofs. As a final defense, bombs were placed at points most likely to be attacked, and were so wired that they could be set off in "booby trap" fashion.[27]

The eastern *trocha* was duplicated at other points on the island. It is not difficult to understand why Martínez Campos believed that this formidable system would make it possible for him to confine the Cubans to the east, and, just as in 1878, to overwhelm them by superior force. But he soon found that this plan was of no avail. Guerrilla warfare demands determined, disciplined, uncompromising, and selfless rank-and-file soldiers and leaders. Cuba was fortunate in its Second War for Independence that its revolutionary army possessed these qualities.[28]

13

The War in Oriente and Preparations for the Western Invasion

The war for the liberation of Cuba was characterized by few battles in which there were more than 2,000 or 3,000 men on either side. The Cuban forces, adhering to the principles of guerrilla warfare, avoided conflicts when they were outnumbered. But from the beginning, there were daily innumerable small engagements. By 1898, these clashes caused the total number of men killed in action to exceed the total number of Americans killed in the War of 1812, the Mexican War, the Spanish-Cuban-American War, and the war to crush the Philippine insurrection.[1]

Gómez pursued his strategy effectively in Camagüey, attacking and destroying the town of Altagracia on June 17, 1895, following this with attacks on the forts of El Mulato, and defeating Martínez Campos at San Jerónimo. There was, however, no greater master of this technique than Maceo. The Spanish soldiers sang derisively:

With the beard of Maceo
We will make brooms
To sweep the barracks
Of the Spanish troops.[2]

As the Spaniards soon discovered, it was easier to sing about defeating Maceo than to accomplish it. On May 23, 1895, in the course of an interview with a correspondent of the New York *Herald*, Maceo declared: "I march with 5,000 well-armed men. I have received various small but excellent expeditions. I have two mountain cannons with sufficient ammunition and soon I shall begin operations on a large scale."[3] Actually, this was an exaggeration for the sake of propaganda. Maceo had the men he claimed, but they were not well armed and they had very little ammunition. Nor did he have any artillery; indeed, during one of his maneuvers, his troops came across a printing press. When he saw it, Maceo exclaimed: "That is the artillery of the Revolution." (He had the press installed in a secure place, and published *El Cubano Libre*.)[4]

"Tranquility was not meant for me," Maceo wrote to his wife on June 30, 1895. "I live on a horse, running in every direction, organizing forces and prefectures."[5] During that month, he carried on repeated raids around Holguín and Gibara. He excelled at this type of warfare; striking here and there, he kept constantly on the move, never giving the enemy a chance to pin him down, always keeping him guessing. The cumulative effect of these actions was felt by the Spaniards. With the property owners thrown into a panic, the Spaniards were forced to place their main contingents in the Holguín region. This enabled Gómez to ride across the deserted lines and pass safely into Camagüey.

In mid-July, Maceo, while camped in Baraguá, received word from his scouts that the Spanish general Fidel Alonso de Santocildes was in Manzanillo, awaiting the arrival of Martínez Campos in order to conduct an important convoy to Bayamo. Maceo forthwith broke camp and led his 1,500 men to a place between Veguitas and Bayamo, known as El Tanteo or Peralejo. There he revealed part of his plan to his staff. If the Spaniards came by the main road, as could be expected, an ambush would be set and a surprise attack launched. Accordingly, Maceo placed Jesús Rabí's infantry in a favorable position at one point alongside the road, and that of Quintín Banderas, a black veteran of the Ten Years' War, at another. To the rear of these positions he placed the *impedimenta* (the cooks and camp servants), along with forty men. At another position, a little further removed and out of sight, was the cavalry led by Maceo. His strategy was clear. The infantry, applying the first pressure on the enemy, would close in on both sides. After the enemy responded, Maceo and the cavalry would move in and decide the conflict. He was confident that he would win a great victory over both Spanish generals—Martínez Campos and Santocildes—and capture them together with their valuable supplies.

But an unforeseen development marred Maceo's carefully laid ambush. While he was waiting for the enemy, two traveling salesmen were intercepted by his advance guards. After a brief interruption, Maceo, to the complete surprise of his staff, allowed them to leave. It was a costly mistake, for they promptly warned the approaching Spaniards of the rebel ambush. The Spanish forces struck swiftly from the rear of the *impedimenta*, the weakest and most vulnerable point of the rebel positions. The element of surprise, upon which Maceo had counted, was now with the enemy.

With the kind of quick decision for which he was famous, Maceo immediately rallied his forces and redirected the formation. At the head of his cavalry, which he had hoped to employ only after the battle was well under way, he furiously charged the Spanish troops who were attacking the *impedimenta*. The momentum of this wild, machete-wielding charge gradually rolled the Spanish infantry back and forced them to form a defensive square. With the pressure off his *impedimenta*, Maceo ordered Rabí and Banderas, with their infantry, to execute a flanking movement to the right and to place themselves between the enemy and the high grass at the rear. By this maneuver, Maceo hoped to keep the Spanish foot soldiers in the open and a target for his cavalry charges.

Before the Spaniards could grasp the consequences of Maceo's maneuvers, they were caught in the fire from the two groups of rebel infantry on the one side and the charges of the calvalry on the other. Seized with panic, the Spanish foot soldiers were about to capitulate when suddenly the sounds of furious fighting came from the outposts. Unknown to Maceo, the Spanish forces had been divided into two parts; the main body of troops had not been in the battle thus far and was now attacking from the rear of Maceo's cavalry. He turned his horsemen around to charge the new attackers. Now the battle swirled back and forth, with Maceo's forces barely managing to hold their own. All at once, the rebel commander was faced with the choice of disengagement or destruction.

At this critical moment, Maceo learned of a new and unidentified cavalry force approaching from the direction of Peniente. He sent Lieutenant Colonel Hector (Mariano) Lora to determine whether the new soldiers were Cubans or Spaniards. For what seemed an interminable length of time, Maceo waited anxiously for his report. Finally it came: the troops were the Cuban cavalry from Guá. With the cavalry reinforcements, Maceo charged a large detachment of Spanish infantry entrenched behind a tangled thicket. The thicket broke the momentum of the charge, and twenty-six of the horsemen were killed in front of the barricade. The cavalry squadron promptly reformed and, stampeding a herd of cattle in front of it, broke through the natural barrier. Maceo immediately ordered his infantry to advance in an irregular line against the entrenched Spaniards. The battle raged at close quarters, and the troops on both sides exhibited great spirit and courage. Shouts of *"Viva Cuba libre!"* and *"Viva España!"* could be heard above the sound of battle.

Without giving the enemy a chance to recover, Maceo ordered another machete charge against the enemy troops on the heights of Peralejo, which succeeded in dislodging the Spanish soldiers. Now in full command of the heights, Maceo could survey the positions of the Spaniards. He learned that Santocildes had died in the attack. With his expectations of capturing Martínez Campos and his whole column revived, he reorganized his forces for a final attack. Noting that the enemy had begun to withdraw toward Bayamo before the attack could begin, and wishing to prevent their escape, Maceo ordered an encircling movement, only to learn that Rabí's infantry troops had used up their ammunition.[6]

When the Cuban infantry ceased firing, the Spaniards retreated more rapidly. Maceo's cavalry followed the withdrawing enemy, but Martínez Campos' rear guard kept them engaged until the main body of the Spaniards could cross the Mabay River. With darkness falling, the Spanish column proceeded on a forced march toward Bayamo. One account has it that Martínez Campos escaped alive because, knowing that the Cubans never fired upon a seriously wounded enemy, he had himself slung in a hammock and carried on the shoulders of his men.

A few days later, Maceo sent a message to Martínez Campos, informing him that the wounded Spanish soldiers left behind on the battlefield had been lodged in the homes of Cuban families living near the scene of the conflict. He assured the Spanish general "that the forces you may send to escort them back will not meet any hostile demonstrations from my soldiers."[7]

After the battle of Peralejo, Martínez Campos took no further risks. He remained in Bayamo until a large force was assembled, and then moved to Havana.

Although Maceo did not gain the complete triumph he had hoped for, he did earn a great victory at Peralejo. In the last days of August 1895 he won a battle at Sao del Indio in Oriente, and, in following up their retreating troops, inflicted heavy casualties on the enemy besides capturing a large quantity of horses, ammunition, arms, and other materials. Gómez gave unstinting praise to these successes, especially the victory at Peralejo. He noted: "The personal defeat recently suffered by General M[artínez] Campos by Maceo's troops has resulted in his loss of credit and fame, and it is my opinion that the morale of his army is deeply hurt."[8] Maceo himself informed his wife that he considered the battles of Peralejo and Sao del Indio "superior to all of the past war, and . . . without equal in our fight for the independence of Cuba." He closed the letter: "The final contest will be in the port of Havana, where I will be within a few months."[9]

To the Spaniards, to the world at large, and even to most Cubans, any talk of fighting around Havana was just rebel propaganda. In all of thc ten years of the First War for Independence, the rebels had not come close to the province of Havana, much less to the capitol city itself. But the revolutionaries, led by Gómez and Maceo, were soon to surprise everyone.

As early as June 30, 1895, Gómez informed Maceo that he should prepare for a campaign into the western provinces where the revolution had faltered. Gómez was eager to begin as soon as the dry weather set in, and attack and destroy the plantations of the West in full harvest.[10] The "Old Chinaman"—his slanted eyes gave Gómez this nickname—declared that he could never think of beginning such an invasion without Maceo's "valuable cooperation." Maceo, however, replied that such a campaign should not be undertaken until some sort of government for the revolution had been settled upon. A few weeks later, when Gómez again asked Maceo to prepare for a western invasion, he once more hesitated, this time on the ground that he first wished to accumulate the substantial funds he was collecting from the sugar, coffee, and timber interests in Oriente and obtain "new elements of war."[11]

During the summer of 1895, Maceo sent more than $100,000 in money orders and promissory notes to New York to purchase arms and ammunition. Maceo sent a small amount of the money he received to his wife, including 300 pesos for his son's education. He felt he was justified in providing his family with these modest sums, since none of the officers of the Liberating Army received any pay.[12]

It will be recalled that at the conference with Gómez and Maceo at La Mejorana on May 4, 1895, José Martí had proposed calling a convention of all the civil and military leaders of the revolution to form a civil government and elect its officials. It will also be remembered that on that occasion, Maceo had taken a strong stand for a military *junta* until victory was achieved. Although Martí was selected as supreme leader of the revolution abroad and in nonmilitary matters, the issue of civil versus military control of the war was still unsettled. Moreover, Martí's untimely death prevented the selection of representatives to form a government. The delay in forming the government made foreign recognition of Cuban belligerency almost impossible, and caused a great deal of concern to the Cuban groups in the United States, who were engaged in campaigning for such recognition. These groups continued to urge the island rebels to organize a formal government. In the interim, Maceo had reconsidered his position and had decided that a government was essential, even though he still feared that its officials would hamper the war effort, by bickering among themselves and by their jealousy of the military commanders. He made it clear, however, that he neither desired nor would accept any post in the government, and that he would not even participate in the deliberations leading to its formation.[13] Salvador Cisneros Betancourt, who had been the second president of the Republic of Cuba during the Ten Years' War, wrote to Maceo, hinting that he might offer the general some high government post if Maceo supported him for president. Maceo wrote back:

> Do not forget the nature of my temperament if it should again occur to you to speak to me of posts and destinies which I have never solicited. As you well know, I have the satisfaction of never

> having held a post through favor; on the contrary, I have exhibited manifest opposition to the slightest suggestion of such a thing. The humbleness of my birth kept me from placing myself at the beginning on the heights with others who were leaders of the Revolution by birth.[14]

One does not have to read between the lines to understand that Maceo was reminding that he had been born a black—and a poor black, at that—and that aristocratic, wealthy Cuban revolutionaries had always looked down on him. They had also feared Maceo's rise to prominence in the revolution because it would enhance the role of black people in Cuban society. These fears now received added weight because the number of black *mambises* in the struggle was greater than during the previous war. In his description of the make-up of the Cuban army, Grover Flint, who spent four months with the Liberating Army, wrote that "half the enlisted men as you saw them together were Negroes, with here and there a Chinaman."[15]

On September 13, 1895, the Constituent Assembly, composed of delegates from Oriente, Camagüey, and Las Villas, met in Jimaguayú, Camagüey, to organize the Republic of Cuba and its government. The Assembly drew up and adopted a new constitution and elected the following officials: Salvador Cisneros Betancourt, President; Bartolomé Masó, Vice-President; Tomás Estrada Palma, Delegate Plenipotentiary and foreign representative; Máximo Gómez, General-in-Chief of the Army; and Antonio Maceo, Lieutenant-General. Upon being informed that there were rumors that he resented the fact that Gómez and not he had been elected general-in-chief, Maceo replied, "I was the first one in exile to give my vote and accept his authority because I recognized, as I now recognize, his indisputable authority and because that is my temperament of order and discipline."[16]

With the government formed, one of the two reasons Maceo had given for not preparing to go west no longer existed. He now intensified his efforts to remove the other obstacle—the lack of funds with which to obtain the badly needed war materials. While his brother José commanded the balance of his forces, Maceo busied himself with the collection of taxes from property owners. On September 22, he notified Estrada Palma that he was sending him a bank draft for more than $10,000 and urged him to quickly send along the arms and ammunition required for the coming western campaign.[17] A few weeks later, he again wrote to Estrada Palma: "Please do your best to send us, as quickly as possible, the weapons and ammunitions ordered, in order to enable us to fight effectively the winter battles which our enemies are preparing for us with so much display."[18]

Maceo was now ready to prepare for the western invasion. But a new difficulty arose. In organizing the invasion, Gómez had called for 1,100 men for each of the two corps of Oriente—the first headed by Maceo and the second headed by Masó. The latter had been designated by Gómez as commander of the second corps of Oriente, with responsibility only to the general-in-chief. As could be expected, Maceo was upset; since he was commander of the whole province of Oriente, he presumably had authority over all the troops of the area. Moreover, in making Masó's appointment, Gómez repudiated a prior agreement. Maceo's first order on landing in Cuba had been to designate himself as the supreme commander of Oriente. In the conference at La Mejorana, this action had been confirmed by Martí. By now designating Masó commander of the second corps, Gómez, who was notorious for overlooking his colleagues' feelings, had simply ignored the difficulties that were bound to arise. Perhaps, too, since Masó was a man of considerable importance and influence among the *insurrectos*, Gómez may have found it necessary to obtain a post for him, even though he must have been aware that it would anger Maceo.

Maceo bore no grudge against Masó; in fact, he had favored his election as president of the new government and had expressed this preference to the delegates from Oriente.[19] Maceo set about readying the forces from his own corps, and dispatched a message to Masó advising him to do the same. He was eager to go west, and his orders to the various units under his command instructed them to be ready to move by October 17.[20] As the days passed, Maceo received no answer from Masó, and this soon became common knowledge among the troops, causing a good deal of uneasiness in the ranks over the ability of the invading army to operate effectively. There was also concern that Masó's recalcitrance might encourage the troops to pull out of the invasion, since many of the soldiers had a strong sense of localism and provincialism and were not too happy about having to fight outside of their own area.[21] Since the majority of the soldiers were peasants who rarely traveled more than a few miles from their homes, their reluctance to fight in a strange area was understandable. This only complicated matters, as it had during the Ten Years' War.[22]

To meet these problems, Maceo asked for permission for himself and his brother, José, to send additional men from their own units. José did send some soldiers, but most of them were armed only with machetes.[23]

As Masó continued his delaying tactics, Maceo began to suspect that the revolution was being undermined, and that Masó might actually be delaying in order to negotiate peace with the Spaniards. Although he had nothing concrete on which to base this suspicion, Maceo could not forget that very early in the current war, leaders of the central *junta* of the propeace Autonomist Party, along with representatives of other political groups, had met with Masó at La Odiosa in order to halt the conflict. The delegates tried to convince Masó of the terrible consequences of another civil war, and he had asked for time to consult with other revolutionary leaders. The entire scheme collapsed when the Spanish commander at Santiago de Cuba refused to allow any further delay and ordered his troops to attack the rebels.[24] Perhaps, Maceo now reasoned, Masó was trying to delay the western invasion while negotiations got under way for a new Treaty of Zanjón.[25]

Meeting with President Cisneros and his cabinet near Baraguá, Maceo gave the government a complete account of the problem and demanded that it order Masó to send the troops requested. The government would only agree to send an emissary to Masó, ordering him to attend a conference to discuss the situation.[26] To placate Maceo, Cisneros advised him to begin his journey west with the understanding that the troops designated from the Second Corps would join the column en route. Maceo, impatient to move, agreed. On October 22, the soldiers for the invasion of the west staged a review, and the famous journey began.

Twelve days earlier, on October 10, 1895, the anniversary of the *Grito de Yara* was celebrated in New York's Chickering Hall. One Cuban patriot after another hailed Maceo's feats. Manuel Sanguilly gave him the name the "Bronze Titan," which was to be used thereafter to describe him. In a poem written during this period, R. Silva paid Maceo the following tribute:

I call him a glorious fighter
In the arduous business of life,
Who, in the fight for his beloved country,
Is like the iron fist of a colossus.
Of vigorous stature, on the radiant
State of Cuba, he shows
The uplifted face of a titan.[27]

On October 27, the column of soldiers commanded by the "Bronze Titan" arrived in Pestán. There he received several letters from officers of the Second Corps, revealing that they had not acted on Maceo's previous requests because Masó had intercepted the messages and had not delivered them. Maceo presented these letters to the government, and once again demanded that it act. (The members of the government had decided to accompany the column, much to Maceo's annoyance, since he did not want the responsibility for their safety.) Rafael Portundo, Secretary of the Interior, proposed dismissing Masó, but President Cisneros and the rest of the cabinet considered this too drastic. They decided to wait for Masó's answer to the order already sent by the government.[28]

These fruitless deliberations caused two days' delay on the progress of the march. The arrival of new units that swelled the ranks of the invading column partly compensated for the loss of time. On the third day, Masó's answer came. He could not comply with Maceo's order because he had no troops to spare for the mission. Masó probably felt that his orders should have come directly from Gómez and the whole controversy could probably have been avoided if he had issued orders directly to Masó. But Maceo, as commander of all the forces in Oriente, felt that he had sufficient authority. Enraged by Masó's refusal, he charged him with being in communication with José Ramírez, one of the Autonomist Party leaders who had been present at the La Odiosa meeting and who was still trying to arrange peace negotiations. When the government hesitated to take action, Maceo ordered Brigadier Rabí to take command of the Second Corps, to seize General Masó and send him to Maceo's headquarters, and then to fulfill the quota of men requested. At first, the members of the government were shocked by the order, but finally they went along and gave their approval.[29] In a letter to Estrada Palma on November 2, President Cisneros condemned Masó for sabotaging the war effort and praised Maceo for his decisive action in the matter. Nevertheless, the president and other members of his government still refused to order Masó's dismissal, and continued him in his office until Gómez could be consulted and render a decision. This, of course, put the problem where it had belonged from the beginning, but meanwhile Maceo's invading column lacked the reinforcements of the Second Corps.

The conduct of the government in the Masó affair naturally revived Maceo's original opinion that a weak civil government would only hamper the progress of the revolution. This feeling was strengthened by the action of the president and his cabinet in reversing their previous stand on the question of collecting contributions from the sugar producers. They now ordered that all sugar cane grinding should be prohibited, without exception, a policy that disturbed Maceo greatly. He feared that the expeditions financed by the contributions would be ended, and was concerned that his reputation would be jeopardized if the properties of the producers with whom he had made agreements were destroyed.[30] Although the government, in an effort to placate Maceo, agreed to review the entire matter, Maceo's opinion of the civil arm of the revolution did not change for the better. He still clung to the views he had expressed to Martí at the La Mejorana conference. He expressed this in a letter to Manuel Sanguily in the United States:

> We have not been very fortunate in the makeup of the new government. Again we have been victims of the vain effort of trying to give it the democratic forms of a republic already constituted when we have the enemy in front of us, and we are not the masters of the land we walk on. As you will understand, while the war lasts, there must only be soldiers and swords in Cuba, or at least men who know how to prosecute the war and how to achieve the final redemption of our people. When this is achieved, which is the objective to which our efforts are directed, the time will then be ripe for the forming of a civil government. Such a civil government should be eminently democratic and be capable of managing the public affairs with prudence and moderation, attentive to our own peculiar political and social requirements.[31]

Despite the bickering over the Masó affair, at least Maceo was now moving westward. On October 30, he wrote to Estrada Palma: "I am on the way to Las Villas province leading the invading army. The troops' spirit is excellent."[32] Maceo had moved toward Las Villas earlier than he had planned. Including his staff, his personal escort, a scouting unit, and a sanitary corps, the total number in the invading column was 1,700 men.

He considered this number inadequate, and was particularly desirous of having more cavalry, for the horsemen provided the mobility required for the hit-and-run operations he had in mind, and also gave the rebels an important advantage over the Spaniards, who relied primarily on foot soldiers.[33] But Maceo could not afford to wait for additional reinforcements. The Spaniards had learned of the invading column's plan to head for Las Villas, and since Maceo wanted to conceal his movements as much as possible, this development forced him to set the column into immediate motion. Ironically, they learned of the plan because the directors of Maceo's newspaper, *El Cubano Libre*, had indiscreetly published the news.[34]

Passing from the rough terrain of Oriente into the open plains of Camagüey province, Maceo was unable to completely hide his movements. He was also more vulnerable to a numerically superior opponent. Counting the volunteer native units, General Martínez Campos had nearly 200,000 soldiers at his disposal. Yet, in the first ten days of November 1895, during the passage from Oriente to Camagüey, the Cubans had only two small, though intense, engagements with the enemy. "I am on my way to the western province up to now without having faced any troubles," Maceo reported to Estrada Palma on November 21.[35]

As the column entered Camagüey, Maceo received two sensational reports from President Cisneros. One was that the United States government had just recognized the belligerency of the Cuban Republic. The other was that an American syndicate had offered a loan of $3 million "to meet the financial expenses of the war." This news was greeted with great joy by the government and the soldiers alike. Maceo, however, remained skeptical, saying "I have viewed it with a certain reservation due to the fact that the United States Congress is not in session and thus could not have acted on a recognition of belligerency, and because I belong to that group of men who say: If it comes, good; and if not, it's just as well."[36] He was far more pleased by the event on November 10. On that day, General Rodríguez brought two well-equipped regiments of cavalry to the invading column.[37]

As Maceo's column moved westward, he encountered none of the expected enemy resistance. ("In this Revolution," he wrote to his wife, "there is hardly any fighting.")[38] Because he moved so quickly, the Spaniards were not able to catch up with him when they tried to pursue him. In addition, the Spaniards were primarily concerned with Gómez's advance through the northern part of Camagüey. Alarmed western property owners, experiencing for the first time the actions of the "man of the torch," insisted that their plantations and mills be protected at all costs. In response, Martínez Campos ordered the Spanish forces to be concentrated in Las Villas. This left the path open for Maceo to advance without any resistance.[39]

The Spanish strategy did not halt Gómez's progress. From the beginning, Martínez Campos had given up any hope of preventing Gómez from moving west. On June 8, 1895, he wrote to the Minister of Overseas Affairs in Spain that while he hoped to confine Gómez to the eastern provinces, "if he wants to pass, he will pass." He based this conclusion on experiences "from the other war and a knowledge of Gómez's methods."[40]

Maceo moved forward rapidly until, on November 29, he found himself only five kilometers from Ciego de Avila, through which passed the *trocha* stretching from Júcaro to Morón. This *trocha* had been an obstacle to the invasion of the west during the Ten Years' War; and now, about 16,000 troops had been brought together by Martínez Campos to bar the rebels' way.

The effort to cross the line began during a dense early morning fog. Maceo ordered the local cavalry forces of Camagüey to execute a diversionary maneuver against one point of the line, while his invaders crossed at another. Within forty minutes, the 1,500 men of the invading column had completed the crossing without the loss of a man. The only shots fired were at the now retreating cavalry of Camagüey. The whole operation had been so swift that the Spaniards literally had no time to bring up reinforcements.[41]

In Lázaro López, still in Camagüey, but on the western side of the *trocha*, and only a short distance from the province of Las Villas, the two great revolutionary commanders, Gómez and Maceo—"the fox and the lion," as the Spaniards called them [42]—had their long-delayed reunion. Maceo had come from Oriente in the extreme east without any significant losses; Gómez, coming from Sancti Spíritus, had crossed the barrier further north also without any losses. The combined invading forces had a total of 2,600 men. Maceo had been appointed commander of the invading army by the government, and now Gómez confirmed the appointment. With the force of 2,600 men, headed by Maceo, Gómez predicted that Martínez Campos would be entombed in the West. Maceo added his view that at the end of the campaign, the Spanish general would be thoroughly discredited as a military leader.[43]

During the first night of the reunion, the insurrectos celebrated with song and music provided by the military band of the invasion. A military march, composed by Enrique Loynaz del Castillo, was dedicated to Maceo, who named it "The Invading Hymn." It opened:

> The beloved memory of Martí
> Offers honor to our lives,
> And the resplendent sword of Maceo
> Guides us to the Invader's advance.[44]

On the following day—November 30—Gómez, on horseback, spoke to all the assembled forces. In a harsh, fighting speech, he declared:

> Soldiers! The war begins now; the hard, pitiless war. The weak will fall by the wayside; only the strong and the intrepid will be able to stand the ordeal. In the full ranks which I see before me, death will open great gaps. The enemy is strong and tenacious. A

day which has no battle will be a day lost or ill-spent. Victory will only be attained by the shedding of much blood.

Soldiers! Do not be frightened by the destruction of the countryside. Do not be frightened by death on the field of battle. *Do* be frightened by the horrible picture of the future of Cuba if, by our weakness, Spain succeeds in winning the war. . . . I predict for Martínez Campos complete destruction, which already began for him in the savannahs of Peralejo, a prediction which will be fulfilled when the invaders reach the doors of Havana with the flag of victory. Soldiers! Let us reach the furthest limits of Occidente, wherever there is Spanish blood.[45]

Immediately after the general-in-chief's address, the invasion campaign began. The combined forces of Gómez and Maceo marched toward Las Villas and the west. It was the beginning of some of the most glorious pages in Cuban history.

14

The Western Invasion

The invasion campaign began on an auspicious note. On its first day, Gómez disposed of the Masó affair by ordering his dismissal from command of the Second Corps. In this way, notice was given that those who repudiated Maceo's command would not be tolerated.[1] This was to prove important when the invading column passed through Las Villas, where the tradition of localism was especially strong—strong enough to hinder the plan for a western invasion during the Ten Years' War. To avoid a repetition of that difficulty, Maceo directed a proclamation to all the people of Las Villas, calling upon them to think of the nation rather than their province: "Our mission is a high, generous, revolutionary one. We want the liberty of Cuba; we long for peace and the future well-being of all our children."[2]

The first problem facing Gómez and Maceo was that of crossing the province of Las Villas without dissipating the invading force. The Spanish high command was determined to destroy, or at least turn back, the invading column before it reached the three western provinces. To this end, Martínez Campos concentrated 25,000 troops in Las Villas in addition to the forces of the various garrisons and fortified estates already there. This Spanish force, under the command of Generals

Suáres Valdés y Molin, Fernando Oliver, Enrique Luque, Leopoldo Garrich, and García Aldave, had to operate over an area of almost 21,000 kilometers.[3]

Gómez and Maceo decided that the only way to prevent a Spanish blockade or encirclement was by the use of diversionary tactics, and that Las Villas was a large enough area in which to carry out such tactics successfully. The plan decided upon was to divide the column into two parts at Trillanderitas; 1,000 infantry soldiers, under Quintín Banderas, would penetrate the mountain range around Trinidad to the south of Las Villas, while the main body of the invasion force would continue through the center of the province. The troops under Banderas were to create as much destruction and confusion as possible in order to distract the Spaniards' attention, and were also to recruit new men for the invading army. After crossing the province, the two groups would reunite either in Matanzas or in the province of Havana. Both groups would be guided by Gómez's basic strategy: avoid large-scale actions with the enemy. This could be accomplished only by remaining constantly on the move and never getting pinned down.[4]

Although Maceo accepted Gómez's strategy of avoiding large and costly battles, he did so with a certain amount of reluctance. He was ever eager to defeat the Spanish troops in a major battle in the field. Throughout the entire invasion, however, he adhered to the fundamental strategy.

In the very first encounter with the enemy, this strategy was abandoned. On December 3, the main force crossed the Jatibonico River into Las Villas. Shortly thereafter, Gómez learned from some local peasants that a Spanish column was escorting a well-supplied convoy not far from Iguará. Gómez immediately saw the opportunity to surprise the enemy and capture much needed materials. He began to deploy his forces along the road over which the Spaniards had to pass. The ambush, however, was discovered before the trap could be sprung; still, Gómez decided to fight, even though he would be fighting entirely without infantry. An intense battle began. The battle of Iguará soon developed into precisely the type of action Gómez had planned to avoid. Although the Cubans finally forced the enemy to retreat to the fort of Iguará and thus scored a victory, it was a costly one. Both sides suffered casualties—the Spaniards left 18 dead on the field, along with 34 rifles, 800 cartridges and 20 fully-equipped pack mules; the Cubans lost 13 men, but the Spaniards could much better afford the loss of both men and supplies.[5]

The *insurrectos* buried their dead and moved forward. (At this point, the government party left the invading army and turned northward. Before leaving, President Cisneros presented the column with a war flag embroidered by the women of Camagüey, and directed Maceo to carry it to the westernmost part of the island.) When they came to the beautiful valley of Manicaragua, the rebels, after being greeted warmly by the inhabitants, decided to take a period of rest. But this was not to be. General Oliver and a large Spanish force were pursuing them. When Gómez discovered this, he ordered his soldiers to occupy better positions on the nearby Manacal Heights.

On the Manacal Heights, a battle began on December 10 that lasted for three days, with intervening nights of rest. The Spanish force consisted of some 1,500 men, and the Cubans had almost 1,600, but the Spaniards also had cavalry, artillery, and infantry, while the rebels had only cavalry. Cavalry was not effective in a fixed battle, but the Cubans had no intention of standing and fighting; their aim was to outmaneuver the Spaniards while continuing westward. As the Cubans moved on, the Spaniards remained in hot pursuit. Finally, the rebels erected an adequate defense position in the Quirre Mountains. At daybreak of the following morning, December 13, General Oliver began an artillery bombardment of the rebel positions. The Cubans withdrew, leaving Maceo to fight a continual delaying action, with ambush after ambush, against the closely pursuing enemy. By late afternoon, the Spaniards had had enough and decided to return to their base. The invading column, victorious but exhausted, spent the night in Siguanea.[6]

During the battle of Manacal Heights, Maceo had paused long enough to issue a moving proclamation to the people of the western provinces, which went in part:

> The war will be hard and desolating, but that is the way tyranny wants it. Yet there is more dignity and grandeur for the people in living free though poor, then rich and comfortable in a home besmirched by servitude and hatred.[7]

The battles of Iguará and Manacal Heights had practically exhausted the rebel's ammunition supply. Discussing this with Maceo, Gómez seriously questioned whether the western invasion could continue without more ammunition, especially in the face of the heavy concentration of Spanish troops that the invading column was certain to encounter. Maceo refused to consider the idea of abandoning the invasion. He told the general-in-chief that it must go on at all costs, and that he, for one, would march to the extreme western tip of the island even if he had to clear his way with a machete.[8] Gómez then turned to the ever-recurring problem of whether or not to allow the sugar mill operators to grind their cane. The old Dominican stood firm behind the policy of preventing any sugar production, while Maceo argued for permitting those mill operators who paid for the privilege to continue grinding. In addition to the usual argument that this would provide funds for the purchase of weapons and ammunition, Maceo also maintained that if the *insurrectos* could show that it was they, and not the Spaniards, who controlled what the operators could or could not do, the campaign to win recognition of Cuban belligerency by the United States would receive a tremendous impetus. Gómez brushed this new argument aside, just as he had done all previous ones. As far as he was concerned, all other arguments had to give way before the primary consideration of revolutionary strategy. Moreover, the Cubans must not count on foreign governments to achieve their victory; the only way they could defeat the Spaniards was by waging ruthless economic warfare.[9]

Maceo had to yield to his commander's policy, and he did so without equivocation. On the day after their conference, Maceo was the first to order the burning of the cane fields of the large plantation, "Teresa." The garrison guarding it offered no resistance.[10]

Maceo was pleased to learn at this time that the government had agreed to honor those contracts he had already negotiated in Oriente. But even these exceptions from the general rule could only be made if the owners involved promptly paid the stipulated contributions.[11]

Despite Maceo's determination to fight clear to the western tip of the island, he, too, was worried about the serious ammunition shortage. At the moment, the only way to obtain ammunition was by taking it from the enemy. With this in mind, the two rebel leaders decided to attack a well-supplied Spanish force in nearby Mal Tiempo. Informed that there was no ammunition for their rifles, and that they had to depend almost entirely on the machete, the Cuban cavalry charged with such fury and wild abandon that before the Spanish foot soldiers were aware of it, the rebels were upon them. The battle became a whirling scene of flashing machetes and bayonets. "It was all frenetic confusion," Gómez recalled later. "There was no one who could give orders or receive them, nor were there orders to give. The bugle would not have been heard. This type of wild attack is the explicit privilege of the Cubans."

The Mauser rifles of the Spanish infantry were of little use after the rebels, disregarding their losses in the charge, engaged the enemy at close quarters. The rearing, plunging horses of the Cuban cavalry, with their machete-wielding riders, spread first confusion and then terror in the Spanish ranks. The Spaniards were soon fighting in individual duels and isolated groups. Seeking hiding places in the short cane fields, they had only one thought in mind—to save their lives. The enemy was completely routed; those who were not killed or captured were dispersed in all directions.

The Spaniards left behind one hundred fifty Mauser and sixty Remington rifles. In addition, there were six boxes of munitions, with 10,000 rounds of ammunition, plus horses, mules, first-aid kits, and other articles. Even the regimental colors and records fell to the rebels. Included in the records was an order from Martínez Campos criticizing officers for concealing Spanish losses and for boasting of "victories over the Insurgents, tales I have never seen verified in the reports sent in later."

All in all, the battle of Mal Tiempo was a decisive one for the invasion. If the Cubans had not acquired the ammunition they received, they probably could not, as Gómez realized, have continued the western penetration. Indeed, they could not even have maintained themselves in Las Villas with only the machete. To be sure, even this booty was not enough to support a complete march to the westernmost extremes of the island, and more would have to be acquired along the way. But at least now the invading army could move forward with confidence.[12]

During the second half of December, the rebels crossed the Hanabanilla River and advanced into Matanzas province, fighting only minor skirmishes on the way. The revolution had now reached the western provinces. The *insurrectos* were warned by the peasants, upon whom they always depended for valuable information, that Martínez Campos was preparing unusually heavy concentrations of military units to block their advance, and that he personally was in the field to lead them. Gómez and Maceo worked out a strategy to avoid being caught in an enemy pincers movement. One device the rebels employed to make their escape was to send out wide-ranging units from the main column and set fire to all the surrounding cane fields. The fires served a tactical as well as strategic purpose, since the billowing clouds of smoke created great uncertainty as to the positions of the insurgents. Invariably, the tactic was successful.[13]

The invading column was accidentally divided into two parts for two days after crossing into Matanzas. Maceo led one column and Gómez the other. Both were fearful that the Spanish forces would isolate and destroy one or the other of the divisions. Fortunately, by an amazing stroke of luck, the two rebel divisions were reunited on December 23 at Coliseo, just before the arrival of Martínez Campos' forces.[14] The encounter with the 2,500 Spanish troops that ensued threatened the destruction of the reunited Cuban divisions. Before the Cubans could properly position themselves, the enemy attacked with unusual fury. Concentrating intense rifle fire on the rebels, the attackers created considerable confusion in the Cuban ranks. Several of the officers who formed Maceo's escort were felled in the first hail of bullets, and the *caudillo* had his horse shot from under him. Commandeering another, he organized a cavalry charge in an effort to drive back the enemy, but the Spanish fire was too intense and the charge was halted. Realizing that they were at a disadvantage, and still seeking to avoid a major battle, Gómez and Maceo sounded the retreat. Martínez Campos apparently mistook the withdrawal for an attempted flanking movement, and fearing a repetition of Peralejo, he failed to follow up his advantage. Consequently, the Cubans were able to disengage themselves and withdraw.[15]

Then began the famous Cuban countermarch. After the Cuban withdrawal, the Spaniards could not immediately relocate the *insurrectos.* They expected them to continue through the province in a northwesterly direction toward Havana province, passing through the large and important towns of Cárdenas and Matanzas. Hoping to intercept and trap the *insurrectos,* they concentrated their forces in the northern part of the province.[16] To avoid the trap, Gómez and Maceo executed a brilliant countermarch that lasted five days. Instead of turning to the right, or north, they turned to the left, southward, and then back eastward until they had once more entered the territory of Las Villas.[17] When Martínez Campos learned of this development, he jubilantly informed his government that the rebels had been blocked and forced back to the east. The danger to the west, he announced, had passed. *Diario de la Marina* of Havana carried this welcome news on January 1, 1896, and the Spanish element and their sympathizers, especially the wealthy property owners of the West, greeted the New Year with sighs of relief.

With their deception completed, the Cubans suddenly turned and reentered Matanzas, moving rapidly through the southern portion of the province. On January 1, the very day of the *Diario de la Marina* announcement, the invading army entered Havana province.

Martínez Campos had been completely outmaneuvered. Thinking that the rebels had gone eastward, he had broken up the powerful concentration of his troops in the eastern part of Matanzas province, and had dispatched a large portion of his army eastward by sea to the port of Cienfuegos, hoping to confront the rebels in that area. Meanwhile, the Cubans passed rapidly through the province or Matanzas with only moderate opposition, destroying cane fields, communications, wires, railroad stations, sugar mills, and other valuable property along the way. When they entered Havana province, they had left a wide smoking path of destruction clear across Matanzas.[18]

The invading army's feat was literally unprecedented. Still, the skillful maneuver had been costly. The ranks of the *insurrectos* were greatly thinned by casualties. Many of the wounded had to be left behind in hastily improvised, out-of-the-way places, like the swamp peninsula of Zapata in Matanzas, and a number of the best officers had been killed or wounded. Six had been wounded and four killed in action around Calimete, in Matanzas, on December 29, and after that skirmish the column carried sixty-nine wounded soldiers with it.[19]

The *insurrectos* more than made up their losses in the province of Havana. In the first week of the New Year, they covered 172 kilometers. In those seven days, they not only destroyed some of the most valuable property in Cuba, but reinforced their ranks with both men and supplies. The garrison of Güira de Melena, consisting of 300 volunteers, surrendered to the rebels after a hard fight, with all of its equipment intact. In a brief speech to the prisoners, Gómez contrasted Spanish and Cuban policy:

> Spaniards! If things were the opposite way and you were the victors, not a single one of us would remain alive to tell the tale. But it is the Cubans who triumphed, and neither Antonio Maceo nor I can find it in our hearts to kill prisoners of war. Both of us respect the vanquished, especially when the enemy, as you were, is courageous. So then, Spaniards, remain at complete liberty in spite of having shed our blood through a misunderstanding of your own interests. Tell your companions, the Spanish merchants, that the great Cuban Liberating Army will respect the persons and interests of those who obey and respect our Revolution. But those who oppose it will be crushed.[20]

It is clear that Gómez realized that the policy to be followed in the West, where revolutionary enthusiasm had always been weakest, had to be more lenient than that followed in other provinces. On January 10, he issued a public circular announcing that the Liberating Army would respect the peaceful population and agriculture.[21] By following this less harsh policy, Gómez hoped to attract more support for the insurrection. The invading columns could not maintain themselves long in the West without local help, and unless western recruits were forthcoming, the fighting in the west would die out when and if the invading columns were withdrawn.

In Alquizar, all the arms and other war supplies were turned over to the rebels without a fight, and in Ceiba del Agua, the *insurrectos* camped in the streets and were welcomed with band music.[22] On January 3, Martínez Campos sent a frantic cable to the Minister of War in Madrid:

> The enemy keeps advancing through the lines north and south of Havana. A numerous separatist force is in San Jose de las Lajas, a town situated twenty-nine kilometers from Havana. It comes destroying all. They burn the railroad stations. There are also parties in Guara. Similarly insurrectionary forces are in Melena del Sur, not far from Batabanó. Numerous families reach Havana fleeing from nearby villages. The panic is extraordinary.[23]

On January 6—Three Kings' Day—the Cuban forces entered Vereda Nueva and were received with cheers "for the Liberating Army and for the chiefs who came from far-off Oriente." Some of the Veredanos joined the insurrectionaries; others turned over the arms they had been hiding, waiting for the arrival of the rebels. The few pro-Spanish volunteers who lived in the village escaped, some abandoning their arms and ammunition, which were turned over to the Cuban army. A delegation even arrived from Havana to see the *mambises* and their famed leaders, Gómez and Maceo, in person.[24]

Following Vereda Nueva, in quick succession, the villages of Caimito, Punta Brava and Hoyo Colorado surrendered; again there was rejoicing in the streets, and again provisions, war supplies, and recruits were received.[25] "What is happening is really inconceivable," cried the *Heraldo de Madrid*. "The government should know that this situation cannot be prolonged."[26] In Havana, there was unusual excitement. For the first time since the outbreak of the revolution, the inhabitants of the capital city felt that a serious war was in progress. Up to that time, the wealthy had lived their usual gay lives as though nothing unusual were happening. Like other large coastal cities, such as Santiago de Cuba and Matanzas, Havana was able to receive sufficient supplies by sea to offset the partially restricted trade with the interior. Upon their arrival in Havana, American correspondents had been amazed to find cafés, shops, and places of entertainment all doing a thriving business, and the residents acting as if times were normal.[27] But now the rebels were within sound and sight, and there was panic in the capital, coupled with demands that its defenses be strengthened.[28]

Under increasing criticism in Spain for his failure to stop the rebel advance, Martínez Campos declared a state of war in the provinces of Havana and Pinar del Río "in order to repel ultimately, rapidly, and energetically any aggression whatsoever and to choke off every seditious internal movement." He also dispatched eight columns of troops to combat the rebels, and strengthened the fortifications and the warning system around Havana.[29] But try as he might, Martínez Campos simply could not cope with the situation. For one thing, he had to comply with the insistent demands for protection raised by alarmed property owners and to set aside troops to defend their holdings. For another, Spanish units sent to pursue the rebels were too slow to keep up with the fast-moving, fast-striking *insurrectos.* Added to all this was the fact that valuable information and aid was given to the rebels by the country people. Consequently, the *insurrectos* were better informed than their enemy. Finally, Martínez Campos could not shift his forces about quickly because the rebels had destroyed the swiftest means of transportation. Early in the war, he had authorized the Spanish army to assume command of the railways, and they remained theoretically in the hands of the Spanish government. But in actuality, they were controlled by the insurgents. Only armored cars got through, and soon even these could not pass because of the destruction of rails and blown-out bridges. For the same reason, telegraph lines were more often down than up.[30]

The final result, as De Truffin, the Russian consul in Havana, noted in a dispatch early in January 1896, was that Martínez Campos' strategy ended "in a sad fiasco," and the general's prestige had been "considerably shaken."[31] At about this time, the following song ran through Cuba:

> Martínez Campos,
> Sweeping over the mountain
> With pieces of artillery,
> Believed that Cuba would belong to Spain.
> And Maceo said to him,
> "You go away to Havana,
> And I with my Cuban troops,
> With Máximo Gómez up front,
> Will make Cuba independent
> With American gunpowder."[32]

On January 7, 1896, Gómez and Maceo arrived near the northwestern border of Havana, where they held a strategy conference. They agreed that Maceo should take part of the invading army and carry the invasion into the province of Pinar del Río, while Gómez, remaining in Havana with the largest portion, would keep the capital province in a turmoil and prevent the Spaniards from sealing Maceo off in the western extreme of the island. At a previous conference after entering Havana province, Gómez and Maceo had agreed that the latter should take steps to reorganize and strengthen his depleted forces. Maceo had sent General Serafín Sánchez back to Las Villas to take charge of the war of devastation in that area, and he dispatched an order to General "Mayía" Rodríguez in Camagüey to bring a picked force of 200 men to Havana without delay. Finally, Maceo sent Colonel Roberto Bermúdez ahead with a small but well-armed force to act as a scouting and organizing unit. Bermúdez was ordered to enlist recruits, to destroy property, to choose locations for making camp, to discover where supplies and arms could be obtained most easily, and to collect any other information that might prove to be valuable.[33]

With the decision made to separate, all the soldiers were drawn up in review and the two leaders proceeded to choose their forces. The contingent agreed upon for Maceo consisted of slightly less than 1,500 men. With this force, he was expected to march to the western end of the island and to maintain an active campaign. It was an indication of Gómez's confidence in the brilliant general that he was given the difficult assignment of completing the invasion of the western provinces. Another indication was the fact that Gómez appointed Maceo Chief of the Invading Army, Chief of the Western Department, and Chief of the Sixth Corps.[34]

The Spaniards spread the word that Gómez had deliberately sent Maceo into Pinar del Río with a limited force "so that he might fall into a trap," that Maceo resented this, and that a serious split had developed between the two generals. When the correspondent of the *Washington Star,* then in Cuba, asked Maceo if there was any foundation to the Spanish story, Maceo wrote to the editor of the paper:

> In the first place, there could not exist such a disagreement, a split as you wish to call it, between General Gómez and myself. He is the General-in-Chief and his laws are, as laws, accepted and respected by me. I am only the Lieutenant General of the Army, and at all times, and in whatever place and for whatever reason, I am subject to his orders. Our army is not composed of riff-raff in which the man who shouts the loudest is the chief. It is organized under a plan of a modern military force in which order and discipline are maintained and superiors are respected. But apart from the rules of military discipline, there is not a soldier in the Cuban army who for one instant would disobey the orders of Máximo Gómez. The whole army trusts implicitly his patriotism and his military ability. We who have known him and followed him in other wars are convinced of our comparative smallness compared to his knowledge and rectitude.
>
> With respect to the assertion that he assumed the command and left for the province of Havana, abandoning us . . . in the

"quagmire," I have nothing to say about this. We have our campaign plans in the Cuban war and it is not necessary for the whole world to know about them. The Spanish government would love to know why . . . we make certain moves and do not make others. When the Spanish authorities cannot see a plausible reason in some important movements of the rebel forces, they immediately invent some agreeable theory and throw it out to the four winds. However, we have no complaint if they receive some satisfaction from this, nor does it disturb us. We let them enjoy their theories. . . . Still they do not realize that they are making themselves ridiculous in the eyes of the world because what could people of good sense believe who, having read the official Spanish dispatches saying that the Revolution was insignificant, on the following day read in the newspapers that in Spain more troops were reembarking to reinforce the army of more than 100,000 men that they have here.[35]

With his force, Maceo set out for Pinar del Río. He did not move in the due west direction that was the shortest route to his destination. Instead, he went on a reconnoitering mission in the northwest corner of Havana province and to the very outskirts of the capital city itself. This mission had two purposes: one was to search for the weakest points of the *trocha* across the narrow coast of the island near the border of the two western provinces, and the other was to determine if he could successfully invade the suburbs of the city.[36] Maceo, a keen student of public opinion, was aware that the whole world would sit up and take notice if the Liberating Army could pose a serious threat to the capital city of the island. It was the sort of daring, spectacular venture that most appealed to Maceo.[37]

Maceo approached the city from along the western coast, passing by the beach of Baracoa and going as far as the edge of Marianao, the principal suburb of Havana. There he learned that the city was too heavily fortified for an attack by a force as small as the one he commanded. In fact, it was only by skillful maneuvering that Maceo was able to prevent the entrapment of his troops. The Spanish General Prats had discovered

Maceo's presence, and tried to pin him against the ocean between the beach of Baracoa and Havana. Maceo managed to escape only after fighting a running battle with the Spanish troops, and at the cost of several wounded, including Colonel Francisco Pérez Carbó, his chief of dispatch. When the Spaniards had been outdistanced, Maceo stopped at the sugar mill, "Luisa," whose owner, Señor Perfecto Lacoste, was sympathetic to the revolution. There, Colonel Pérez Carbo and the other wounded rebels were left to receive medical attention.[38]

Señor Lacoste told Maceo that the story making the rounds in Havana was that "if you pass the *trocha* of Mariel you will be greater than Hannibal." To this the confident general replied: "I do not know where the fortified line is, but give me tomorrow and I will be situated in Pinar del Río."[39] Of course, Maceo not only knew the exact location of the *trocha,* but had already figured out exactly how to pass through it. He knew that it, like the others in the system, was surrounded by thick wooded areas, undergrowth, and swamps, so that his troops could creep near the line before making their charge. (On open terrain, the Spaniards would have been able to detect his approach in advance.) Maceo also knew that he would have well-informed guides lead him to where the Spaniards would least expect him. As good as his word, on the next day, January 8, Maceo passed through the *trocha* and was camped in Pinar del Río, Cuba's most western province.[40]

When one considers the thoroughness with which the *trochas* were constructed, one wonders how the rebels could have passed through them with such apparent ease. An American who actually crossed most of the western *trocha* explained how his small Cuban party accomplished the feat. From his experience, the most important requirement for success in this endeavor was a well-chosen guide. This man had to be so familiar with the area that an isolated spot could be selected at a time when no Spanish patrol was passing.[41]

The Spanish authorities were at first not too alarmed by the news that Maceo was in Pinar del Río. They were confident that they had only to concentrate enough troops to crush the 1,500 rebels.[42] They were also convinced that their propaganda would turn the people of Pinar del Río against the *insurrectos.* Spanish propaganda pictured Maceo as a crude, barbaric *caudillo,* who delighted in all sorts of inhuman practices forbidden by the recognized rules of warfare. Moreover, the Spaniards made ample use of the fact that Maceo was a black, and hammered away at the theme that he was leading an invasion of predominantly black troops from the East, who were bent on subjecting the white Cubans of the West to a reign of terror, rape, pillage, and murder, with the ultimate objective of establishing a black republic, headed by Maceo himself.[43]

On neither point were the expectations of the Spaniards fulfilled. Maceo, by following a zigzag course, avoided contact with the numerically superior forces pursuing him. Nor were the peasants of Pinar del Río frightened by the picture drawn by Spanish propagandists of the invading army and its leader. On the contrary, wherever news spread that Maceo was in the vicinity, group after group of peasants traveled miles by horseback just to see, speak to, and shake hands with the most celebrated and fabled of all the *insurrectos.*[44] For the black peasants, the opportunity to meet Maceo was the fulfillment of a life's dream. To the colored people of Cuba, Maceo was their idol and their acknowledged leader.

If the Spaniards believed that Maceo's march would be halted by resistance from the towns of the province, they were quickly disillusioned. Time after time, as Maceo's column approached a town, the municipal officials, either because of the sympathy of the populace with the revolution or because the wealthier citizens were anxious to avoid the expected pillage and destruction, actually gave him the keys to the town. In the few cases where the towns did not welcome him, Maceo sent a note to the authorities informing them what they could expect if his troops were not supplied with arms, ammunition, and supplies. Usually he got what the locality had to offer, for only the most strongly fortified and best garrisoned municipalities could afford to resist the rebels.

Although Maceo burned some towns that resisted, he disproved the propaganda depicting him as a ruthless conqueror. Realizing that the people of Pinar del Río feared that his troops would "destroy their tobacco harvest," Maceo saw to it that the column avoided passing through tobacco fields, since their "passage through would have ruined them."[45] He also countered the Spanish propaganda that pictured him as a black leader bent on dominating the white population by exercising extreme care in dealing with civilians and by requiring iron discipline of his troops. A measure of Maceo's discipline was displayed on December 27, 1895, in Las Villas, during the famous false retreat from the West. Four of Maceo's soldiers invaded the home of the colonel of the Spanish volunteers, and when they threatened the family, the colonel killed one of the rebels. He was brought before Maceo expecting to be executed. But when Maceo learned the facts of the incident, he congratulated the man who had killed one of his soldiers and ordered the three surviving *insurrectos* to be shot. The Liberating Army, he made it clear, must respect family homes.[46] During his stay in Pinar del Río, Maceo insisted on the same type of conduct by his troops. He permitted no plundering, and his orders were followed to the letter.[47] In his famous account of the invasion, General José Miró wrote:

> In Guane no farms were destroyed nor were any commercial establishments occupied. No one was denied a safe conduct or the necessary documents for goods, and all work tools were respected. . . . Men of the highest importance talked with Maceo, measuring and admiring him, surprised to find themselves in his presence, and even more astonished that he was an affable and kindly man.[48]

During his two-day stay in Guane, Maceo ordered that the municipal funds be used to pay the back salaries of teachers in the primary schools.[49]

On January 22, 1896, the ultimate goal of the campaign of invasion was achieved. Maceo's column left Guane in the morning, and at three in the afternoon arrived at Mantua, the westernmost town on the island. The invading army was met on the outskirts of the town by an official body, headed by the major. Miró continues the story:

> One hour later, at four in the afternoon, the Liberating Army made its triumphal entry into Mantua, the last Spanish bulwark of the far west. . . . The glorious campaign of invasion was ended, and the wishes of our famous *caudillo* [Maceo] were fulfilled. . . . In the column entering Mantua, with the bells of the town tolling, there came men from the Sierra Maestra; from Bayamo; from Santiago de Cuba; from Manzanillo; from Holguín; from Mayarí; from Guantánamo, and from Baracoa. What an achievement. These men had changed horses in Camagüey, in Las Villas, in Matanzas, in Havana, and on the highway of Pinar del Río. . . . Only Maceo, first soldier of America, only he, audacious warrior, intrepid captain, tireless soldier, always in the lead, could have opened the road to victory and imposed his indisputable authority on these men from the Sierra of Guantánamo and the pine groves of Mayarí, wild and brave men like the peaks of these mountains.[50]

People congregated on the streets of Mantua to see the fabled *caudillo* and his soldiers, and Maceo, aware of the historic occasion, had his troops form a parade to make a grand entrance into the town. Aware also of local feelings, he wisely accorded his newly formed cavalry of natives of the province the honor of leading the procession. Immediately behind the cavalry of Pinar del Río, at the head of his veterans, came the proud general, mounted on a splendid horse, stiffly erect, and as always perfectly groomed.[51]

Many Mantuans greeted the Liberating Army joyously, but the volunteers and other Spanish sympathizers had fled the town, convinced that their lives would be taken and their property confiscated by the "black Devil." Maceo immediately dictated an order to his troops designed to maintain public order and respect for the lives and property of all classes. He also commissioned one of his officers to go to the neighborhood to which the frightened Mantuans had fled, and authorize them "to return to their homes with their arms or without them, with the security that they would not in the least be molested by any Cuban force." He urged them, moreover, "to dedicate themselves to the care of their families, separating themselves from their political work in which they had served to sustain an iniquitous and shameful enemy government." All returned to their homes, and thirty rifles and more than 4,000 cartridges were turned over to Maceo.[52]

Those who had been taken in by the Spanish propaganda were literally astounded by Maceo's behavior. Describing one scene, Miró wrote:

> The most important of the Spanish sympathizers, fearing Maceo and observing him carefully, were very much surprised to find him conversing freely with them, and they appeared even more amazed at his fine manners and agreeableness. He spoke to them (about the Revolution) without reference to origins or opinions, all the while trying to draw them over to the cause of the Revolution, but without the slightest inferences of offense.[53]

On January 23, 1896, official ceremonies were held during which a document was signed by representatives of all classes, the parish priest, and the heads of the invading army. It read in part:

> First, that the town of Mantua is situated at the extreme west of the island in the province of Pinar del Río.
>
> Second, that General Maceo, with the forces at his command, has occupied the town and municipal terminal: lives and goods of all kinds having been respected by his troops, public order having been maintained, and the authorities and employes which the Spanish government had placed there having been left in the exercise of their functions, and that the actions of the Liberating Army and its chief will redound not only to the benefit of this

region, previously impoverished by multiple exactions of which it has been the victim, but also to the benefit of the whole country, which has been suffering from the same bad treatment.

Following the signing of this document, the mayor offered a champagne toast to Maceo. The general graciously declined the glass offered him, saying, "I do not drink any kind of liquor." Offered a cigar from Vuelta Abajo, the area that produced the best tobacco in the world, he again graciously refused, stating, "I am sorry not to be able to please you, but I do not smoke."[54] On this note, the official ceremonies marking the great invasion of the West ended.

The invasion of the West received much attention in the world press. Editorially, the papers had expressed considerable doubt about the ability of the invading army to achieve its goal. Writing to his wife, Maceo noted with deep satisfaction: "The Invasion which here and abroad was thought impossible has been realized and without great difficulties and with few losses, despite hard fighting every three days."[55] In ninety days and in seventy-eight marches from Baraguá to Mantua, the invading army had covered 1,696 kilometers; twenty-seven battles had been fought, twenty-two important towns taken, and fifty-nine known towns burned and destroyed; more than 2,000 rifles, 80,000 rounds of ammunition, and 3,000 horses had been captured; and in Mantua, two mountain cannons had been acquired. All this was accomplished by a few thousand devoted Cuban patriots, without help of any kind from outside the country, against an enemy who, according to the official report of the Ministry of War in Madrid, had available in Cuba during these three months 124 infantry battalions, 40 squadrons of cavalry, 16 batteries of field artillery, 6,701 general and other officers, a navy that controlled the coast, and an elaborate "system of defenses and *trochas* thought up by expert military engineers."[56] What is more, the last part of the invasion took place in areas favorable to the Spaniards. As De Truffin correctly noted in a dispatch on January 8, 1896:

> The part of the island which the insurgents have just captured is a vast cultivated plain without any forest at all. In these conditions, the enemy who moves in columns of 2,000 or 3,000 men each, apparently ceases to be elusive. Nevertheless, he is not routed, and apart from a few skirmishes in which he lost less than a few hundred men, nothing prevented him from advancing and leaving a trail of ruins.[57]

The campaign of invasion was a remarkable achievement. One military historian has compared it with "Hannibal in Italy, and the marches of San Martín, Sherman and Napoleon."[58] Clarence King, a leading American student of military history, describing the invasion in an article published in the *Military Review* of Brussels, called it "the most audacious military feat of the century."[59]

While the invasion campaign, as a whole, gained worldwide admiration, the operation conducted by Maceo in Pinar del Río won special praise. Even the Spaniards were amazed. Juan Ortega y Rubio, the Spanish historian, wrote: "Our historical impartiality obliges us to say that the campaign carried out by Antonio Maceo in the province of Pinar del Río is a glorious page in the history of that valiant *caudillo*. . . . With extraordinary activity and pursued always by our columns, Maceo went from one end of the province to the other."[60] Pablo Picasso recalled that Maceo was so famous at the time that even children in Málaga, Spain, would assume his name when playing soldiers.[61]

Five days after the official ending of the invasion in Mantua, Maceo replied to a question posed by the *Washington Star* as to what had been accomplished by the campaign. "Much," he wrote. The rebels had been able to march from one end of the island to the other "without a single hitch," proving to the Cuban people and the world that Spain's boast that the revolution had been crushed was a myth. They also had shattered the Spaniards' boast that the system of *trochas* would keep the revolution confined to the eastern provinces and would doom it to an early death: "We crossed them and rendered them useless forever." Furthermore, the revolutionary cause had gained many new supporters: "Since we reached this province, the Cuban army strength has grown twenty-five percent in other areas. Ten thousand patriots have been recruited to our flag." Unfortunately, the liberating army simply did not have enough arms for all who offered their services; indeed, as many as 35,000 men could have been recruited in the provinces of Havana and Matanzas alone:

> But we lack sufficient arms to give them, and it is useless to say that we have them, since we do not gain anything by throwing out boasts like the Spaniards. Our soldiers are not well armed by measure. If they were, there would not exist today a single Spanish column outside of the cities of Havana, Matanzas, and Santiago de Cuba.

The invasion had improved the *insurrectos'* capacity for fighting, and had demonstrated for all to see that the war could never be won by Spain. As Maceo put it:

> It might last a few months or several years, I cannot say. But what is certain is that the red and yellow flag of Spain will never wave again over a Cuba enslaved. Cuba must be free. This oppressed people has consecrated its life to the work of emancipation, and God in heaven will strengthen its arm.[62]

15

Weyler versus Maceo

On January 7, 1896, Martínez Campos resigned his post as captain general. The Spanish government, furious over his failure to crush the *insurrectos,* agreed to accept his resignation and announced the appointment of General Valeriano Weyler y Nicolau as his successor. Sabas Marín became the acting captain general until Weyler's arrival from Spain.

When Maceo heard the news of Martínez Campos' resignation, he could not hide his emotion. The man who had defeated the revolutionaries in 1878 had now been completely routed by his old adversaries. Nothing could have demonstrated as well to the world the strength of the revolution as the failure of Spain's ablest general.[1] Maceo also saw another advantage for the revolution in the turn of events. Since Martínez Campos had resigned amidst a great clamor in Madrid for sterner measures against the *insurrectos,* they could now expect a more ruthless policy from the Spaniards, especially since the man designated to apply this policy was General Weyler, who had gained a reputation for harsh military policies during his two years' service as a subordinate general in the Ten Years' War. Maceo felt that the new Spanish policy of repression might be beneficial to the revolutionaries, since it would finally force the autonomists and other Cuban neutrals to choose sides. In the type of war Weyler could be expected to launch—a war of extermination—there could only be Cubans and Spaniards. There was now little prospect of a peace offensive such as might have been expected under Martínez Campos; this, Maceo feared, would have met with a favorable response from the fainthearted, just as it had in the last stages of the Ten Years' War. Now there could only be total war.[2]

Ever the daring warrior, Maceo was eager to stage an attack at the very gates of Havana at the moment of General Weyler's arrival. Making his way to Havana, Maceo looked forward to an opportunity to clash with the enemy in a major battle even though this meant forsaking Gómez's basic strategy. Not only did he long to defeat the Spanish army in the field, but he believed that if he could win an important victory before reaching Havana, he would deliver a crushing blow to Spanish morale, already sagging as a result of the triumphant invasion of the West.[3]

Unknown to Maceo, however, his decision to engage the enemy coincided with a change in Spanish tactics. With the departure of Martínez Campos, more Spanish columns were operating on the offensive, and under persistent prodding from the home government, they were demonstrating more aggressiveness. This was to complicate Maceo's plans to achieve a decisive victory.

During an unexpected and unplanned encounter with the Spaniards at Paso Real, the Cubans drove the attackers off after hard fighting, but sustained looses they could ill afford. The Spaniards suffered one hundred killed and wounded, including General Luque, who was seriously wounded. The Cubans lost fifty-five killed and wounded, which was a considerable loss. Maceo moved to attack and capture Candelaria, one of the two important fortified towns on the railroad lines from the West. (The other was Artemisa.) Maceo hoped to obtain here his important victory, and launched a savage attack on the town.

His determination to capture the town increased when he learned that many of the defenders were blacks, fighting with the Spaniards. Nothing infuriated Maceo more than to have his own people fighting with Cuba's oppressors, even though such cases were not frequent. Abandoning his usual chivalrous regard for enemy prisoners, Maceo gave the order that all the black defenders should be killed by the machete when Candelaria fell. The blacks fighting inside the town put up a ferocious defense. Just at the point when this stubborn defense was about to be overcome, strong enemy reinforcements arrived from Artemisa. The rebels were forced to retreat after twenty-six hours of intense fighting.[4]

Compelled to flee, Maceo laid a trap for the Spanish column that had frustrated his plan. He moved to catch the troops by surprise when they returned to Artemisa. It worked very well, and Maceo was again at the verge of a decisive victory, when Spanish reinforcements once more arrived at the scene. Furious at the prospect of having victory snatched from his grasp twice, he refused to leave the scene of battle, even in the face of mounting odds. Not even when his horse was shot from under him and he himself suffered a bullet wound in the right leg, would he stop fighting. Mounting a new horse, whose fine performance caused him to name the animal "Liberator," Maceo continued to personally lead machete charges. At nightfall, both sides ceased fighting, and the battle was over. The Spaniards left seventeen dead on the field of battle, in addition to the many wounded they carried away with them, but this time, the Cubans had suffered greater losses than the enemy. Maceo's determined stand, in the face of superior numbers and firepower, was an indication of his great courage, but it had been costly as well. During the battle, his officers had become alarmed and had agreed that prudence dictated a rapid retreat. But, as General José Miró later reported, no one dared to question Maceo's decisions in the midst of battle.

Before Maceo could move toward Havana, he learned that

Weyler had already landed on February 10. The attack that had been planned before the arrival of the new captain general had to be shelved. (Actually, the recent losses in battle, the shortage of ammunition, and the increased concentration of Spanish troops around the capital had rendered the planned attack impractical.) Nonetheless, Maceo led his column toward Havana, determined to show the world that he was active in the vicinity of the capital, despite the vaunted Weyler, with his long and imposing military record.[5]

As Maceo had predicted, the arrival of the notorious General Weyler initiated a new phase of Spanish military strategy. Weyler had only contempt for what he called "the benevolence" of Martínez Campos, and believed that he should have been initially selected to deal with the insurrection.[6] He decided to make up for lost time. While he continued the *trocha* policy and the holding of garrisoned towns and forts, he determined to remove one of the chief obstacles facing the Spanish forces in their effort to corner and annihilate the rebels—the aid the *insurrectos* received from the Cuban peasants. Reasoning that when there would be no large groups of country people to provide information, food, and other aid to the rebels or inhibit the Spanish forces' freedom of movement, Weyler decided that the peasants had to be removed from the countryside. He also initiated a campaign to destroy all crops, cattle, horses, empty houses, or any other materials that might furnish aid to the *insurrectos.*

Immediately after his arrival, Weyler proceeded to issue a seemingly endless series of proclamations relating to practically every phase of Cuban life. The most important of these were embodied in the infamous order of *reconcentración.* Under this decree, all inhabitants outside of the fortified areas were given eight days to move into the towns occupied by the Spanish troops; the transport of food from one place to another was forbidden; and all cattle were to be brought into the towns. The proclamation closed with an offer of clemency for any insurgents who surrendered during the eight days, provided they brought in their arms and furnished information about the enemy.[7]

Weyler's brutal scheme, which was to earn for him the name "Butcher," coincided with Maceo's prediction. It brought total war, a war of extermination, to Cuba. Many Spanish and American historians have attempted to justify Weyler's policies by arguing that he was applying a military strategy that had already been put into practice by Máximo Gómez. In other words, he was simply fighting fire with fire and outmaneuvering the rebels at their own game. This rationalization ignores the fact that while Gómez did move some women and children into the hills from towns, his policy was basically directed against the economy, and not against individuals—against property, not people—and that when the rebels entered the western provinces, they took care to protect the lives of the inhabitants of all towns they conquered, including the volunteers and other Spanish sympathizers. Weyler's policy, on the other hand, made no distinction either between people and property, or between those who aided the rebels and those who were neutral. Certainly, the *insurrectos* did not prohibit anyone, least of all old people, women, and children, from working the soil and keeping cattle in order to feed themselves.

Immediately after his arrival, Weyler also reorganized the Spanish army in Cuba, dividing it into three corps and improving its intelligence service. But he did not abandon the Spanish strategy that was primarily defensive in nature. The Spanish forces were still concentrated in the cities, towns, and fortified areas, and especially along the *trochas.* Instead of placing his huge numbers of troops in the field, he sent out relatively small units to search out the rebels.[8] His fundamental aim was to compress the insurgent forces in the western provinces into a small area and then smash them against the anvil of the *trocha.* This process was then to be repeated between the western and eastern *trocha,* and finally, with the enemy troops confined to the extreme east, the whole Spanish army could overpower them. Meanwhile, the policy of *reconcentración* would work to deprive the rebels of peasant support, and, by the sheer misery it created, diminish the will of the Cuban people to resist.[9]

On February 19, two days after Weyler issued his orders, Gómez and Maceo met in Soto to discuss the decrees. Both agreed that the common people would now fully appreciate both what Spanish rule really meant and the importance of the rebels' struggle to overthrow it. (A few days earlier, Maceo had written to his wife: "The importance of the Campaign of Invasion had been understood by the foreigners and the Spanish militarists, but not by the plain people.")[10] Both agreed, too, that for the time being, they must avoid encounters with the concentration of troops Weyler was forming against them in that part of Havana. They decided that both columns should reenter Matanzas and operate in that region.[11]

In fulfillment of this plan, Maceo marched northwardly and Gómez southeasterly toward Matanzas. In accordance with their plan, Gómez would operate in the central provinces of the island and Maceo would continue to carry on the war in the western provinces. The revolutionaries could not afford to allow a period of inactivity in either area, and particularly not in the West. Maceo's immediate assignment was to distract attention from Gómez's column. By February 23, Maceo was already operating in Matanzas. On the following day, his forces camped at the "La Perla" sugar mill, in the valley of Guamacro. There they observed the first anniversary of the revolution with a simple ceremony.[12]

Maceo's disappearance from Havana province immediately produced a rumor that he was dead. The Spanish had spread reports that Maceo had been killed in battle as early as May 1895. These reports continued, with the new touch now being added that the famed general had committed suicide. From reports from "La Perla", on February 25, the Spaniards learned to their sorrow that the newest rumor of Maceo's death had no more truth than its predecessors. Two days later, Maceo joined the cavalry regiment of General José Francisco Aguirre at Cayajabo. After reviewing Aguirre's well-armed cavalrymen, the two generals sat down to exchange information and discuss the progress of the war. Aguirre informed Maceo that since Weyler had assumed command, the number of atrocities and war crimes had increased sharply, and that "mass acts of barbarism were committed daily by Weyler's troops." Even though he had felt at first that a savage policy would help the revolution, Maceo was so enraged by this news that he wrote an open letter to the Spanish commander-in-chief.[13] He began by asserting that he had at first believed that the reports of atrocities and crimes were being spread by the Spanish general's enemies. He had therefore expected Weyler "to give the solemn lie to your detractors," and to adopt "the generous system followed from the beginning by the forces of the Revolution with the Spanish wounded and prisoners of war." But this had not happened. Not only had Maceo learned of massacres of the wounded and prisoners of war alike, but he had received reports that even civilians were being treated savagely. He then went on to warn Weyler that while, in the interest of humanity and in keeping "with the spirit of the Revolution," he would never "take reprisals which would be unworthy of the prestige and strength of the Liberating Army," nevertheless, "at the same time, I warn that such abominable conduct on the part of you and yours will provoke in the not too distant future, private vengeance which will be practiced without my being able to prevent it, even though hundreds of innocents may suffer from it."

Maceo urged Weyler to reverse his policy and "reprimand with a severe hand those deeds, if they were committed without your sanction. In any case, avoid the shedding of a single drop of blood outside of the field of battle. Be kind to all those unfortunate noncombatants, and we shall proceed in the same way."[14]

Maceo's moving appeal fell on deaf ears. An era of terrible human misery descended upon Cuba, and the revolution rapidly developed into total war.

Confident that his policies would produce the desired results, Weyler publicly prophesied late in February that Pinar del Río province would soon be completely pacified, and he assured the sugar producers that they could begin grinding cane.[15] As Maceo phrased it, he could not allow "Weyler's dreams to come true"; therefore, he issued orders for the destruction of all sugar crops in the two westernmost provinces. In a report to Estrada Palma in New York, he pointed out that he had been compelled to take this extreme step and "spread the necessary terror so that plantation owners are sufficiently frightened and do not develop their sugar crop." Maceo carried out his own orders. Everywhere he passed while returning to Havana province, he cut a wide swath of destruction of sugar plantations and mills. After making a devastating circle throughout the province of Havana, Maceo returned to Matanzas on March 5, 1896, outmaneuvering a powerful column that Weyler had sent against him.[16]

On March 10, Maceo joined Gómez at El Galeón. It was to be the last meeting between the principal leaders of the Cuban revolution. The two generals agreed that Maceo would continue his campaign in the West, while Gómez would direct operations in the central part of the island. Both agreed, too, that the tempo of destruction must be accelerated, since it was becoming clear that Spain could not much longer bear the tremendous financial burdens of the war. In parting, Gómez promised to send Maceo desperately needed war supplies.[17]

Upon leaving El Galeón, Maceo set out for Pinar del Río to give the lie to Weyler's prediction that the province would soon be pacified. ("Due to the fact that many landowners were inclined to trust Weyler, I had to invade the province again," he wrote to Estrada Palma.)[18] His rapid passage across Havana province could be traced by the fires along the way. By March 15, he was once more in Pinar del Río, and on the following day, he announced his presence in a special proclamation designed to make Weyler's claims look ridiculous.[19] The Spaniards felt Maceo's presence even more concretely in his battle with them on March 20 at El Rubí, where, despite his lack of ammunition, he forced a numerically superior opponent to retreat. At this battle, the "Bronze Titan" had only 500 men. In his desire to stimulate fighting throughout the province, he had split his forces into several units.[20]

In spite of the continuing scarcity of ammunition, the indomitable Maceo fought a series of clashes and continued his work of destruction through the last week of March and the first week of April. He suffered only one defeat: at La Palma, where a treacherous guide led his unit into a trap and he lost thirty-nine dead and eighty-eight wounded, a heavy loss considering the small size of the unit.[21] Despite this setback, Maceo proudly reported to Estrada Palma that he had "successfully destroyed every piece of property that might be a source of revenue and assistance to our enemies," and deflated Weyler's reputation by making a mockery of his promise to pacify the province.[22]

Weyler was not one to take such an affront lightly. He prepared a new device to seal off Maceo in the extreme western province. Weyler was building a modernized *trocha,* equipped with electric lights, across the narrow waist of the island from Mariel to Majana, on the border of Havana and Pinar del Río provinces. Along this line, he stationed 14,000 soldiers in fortified positions.[23] When he learned about this, Maceo wrote Gómez, with typical audacity: "If I crossed *trochas* coming here, I can cross them again whenever I choose to do so. I am more worried about new Zanjónes than about *trochas.*"[24] To prevent another Treaty of Zanjón, Maceo issued orders threatening the death penalty to any rebel officer or soldier who initiated discussions with the enemy.[25]

Weyler was not content to build a wall at one end of the province to contain the rebel leader. Ignoring the war everywhere else in Cuba, he concentrated all his energies on crushing Maceo. He sent 3,000 veteran troops, under the command of General Suárez Inclán, to attack Maceo's forces, which numbered only 250 men! (As we have seen, Maceo had dispersed many of his troops throughout the province.) Yet the bold Cuban, with only this small number of men, without adequate ammunition, with a vastly numerically superior army exerting every effort to trap and annihilate him, and with the Spaniards publicly predicting that they would finish him off during May,[26] exuded his usual confidence. He wrote to Estrada Palma on April 14, 1896, that he could hold out "until Spain is exhausted." Three days later, he assured his wife that he would outwit the enemy, and that Spain would see the hopelessness of its situation in August, and abandon the island.[27]

Until he could obtain more ammunition, Maceo decided to avoid the Spanish forces sent against him and take refuge in the Tapia Mountains. From April 18 to 26, the Spaniards repeatedly attacked this natural defense position, but each time Maceo repulsed them. Learning of the landing of the *Competitor* carrying an expedition with war materials from the United States, Maceo left his retreat, outmaneuvering the enemy that was waiting for him, and hurried in search of the new arrivals.[28] At Cacarajícara, he was delayed by the battle that his company, now down to 170, had to fight against a Spanish column of nearly 1,000 soldiers, led by General Suárez Inclán. At a critical point in the conflict, Colonel Juan E. Ducasse, from the newly-arrived expedition, reached the scene with reinforcements, rifles, and 10,000 rounds of ammunition. With shouts of *"Viva Cuba!"* the rebels quickly forced the enemy column to retreat.[29]

The auspicious arrival of the reinforcements, and the defeat of the Spaniards at Cacarajícara, led Maceo to issue a communiqué declaring that victory was in sight and that economic necessity would soon compel Spain to stop the war. At precisely the same time, De Truffin was writing to the Russian ambassador to Madrid that the news of Maceo's victory "gives ground to assume that Spain's cause in Cuba is a lost one."[30]

Returning to his bastion in the Tapia Mountains, Maceo fought a series of small but fierce engagements. On May 23, he attacked the fortified town of Consolación del Sur, and left it in flames. Two days later, he won a victory over the forces of General Valdés, the supreme commander of the province. In the fighting, the Spanish general was seriously wounded.[31]

The entire world now rang with paeans of praise for the Cuban general. Poems ridiculing Weyler and hailing Maceo were published in all the Latin American countries. From Havana, Colonel Charles E. Akers, correspondent of the London *Times,* sent the following dispatch, appearing in early June:

> In the province of Pinar del Río, at some eighteen miles from the center of the Spanish lines, is encamped since last March the rebel General Antonio Maceo with his army. Here are the rebels almost in view of 60,000 Spanish soldiers. There is no pretense of not knowing the position of Maceo since a Spanish general indicated to me the precise point where the insurrectionaries' encampment was. The frequently repeated Spanish boast that Maceo will not be able to cross the *trocha* is already worn out and useless. Undoubtedly, whenever it suits the insurrectionary leader, he will succeed in breaking the line, and meanwhile, it is enough for him to stay where he is and compel more than a third of the entire Spanish army to remain on the defensive.[32]

Weyler now decided that the only way to retrieve his reputation was by entering the field himself. He organized a force made up of 12,000 troops and twelve cannon to launch against the 500 men fighting under Maceo's immediate command. At

San Gabriel de Lombelle, the battle between these forces raged back and forth as Maceo tried to prevent the Spanish battalions from pinning him down. On June 24, he sustained his twenty-fourth battle wound when a rifle bullet broke a bone in the lower portion of one of his legs. With their general out of action, his troops again took refuge in the Tapia Mountains.[33]

Maceo was taken to the house of a rebel civilian in the Rosario Mountains, where he was treated by his medical aide for nine days. During his convalescence, he wrote to Estrada Palma, pointing out that to a large degree his actions against the Spanish forces of the west had been fought with the arms he took from the enemy. He complained that favoritism was being shown toward the east in the matter of military supplies, and demanded adequate shipments of arms. This was not Maceo's first complaint on this score. On March 21, 1896, he had written to Estrada Palma:

> Since I organized the contingent for the invasion with the resources allowed me by the state of the army in Oriente, sufficient for the campaign until now, I resent that you people have not taken advantage of the facilities offered you by this whole western coast to make small and frequent expeditions which would have been of the greatest use to me.

In late June, Maceo wrote to Gómez:

> Until now I have received no resources, absolutely none. I am making war with what I have taken away from the enemy. To this is owed the fact then that I see myself personally resisting more than once intentions to make me abandon this province, which I have defended in hand-to-hand fighting against an enemy—numerous, strong and skillfully directed by its principal leaders.[34]

It is clear from Maceo's letters that he was convinced that "the privileged ones" in the army were being favored, and that he was being neglected. It is not difficult to discern in this correspondence that Maceo believed that he was being discriminated against because he was black. He was soon to discover that there were ample grounds for this suspicion. Gómez shared Maceo's views and made several efforts to prod the government into sending the much-needed supplies, but for a long time he was simply ignored. Maceo wrote scornfully to General José Rodríguez that while the men under his command were keeping the revolution alive,

> the gentlemen of the government were watching from behind the barriers with impassable indifference, the sacrifice this army was making without any other help than its own strength, to save itself from the ruin which constantly threatened it. Hardly any one is alive and uninjured from the invading column which I took out from Oriente and Las Villas. Is this the way a government fulfills itself? Or patriots? Or soldiers?[35]

One other theme runs through Maceo's correspondence at this time: the determination that Cuba must be kept free from *all* foreign domination—by the United States as well as by Spain. José Martí had feared American intervention, knowing from personal experience, derived from his long residence in the United States, that among the North Americans were influential economic and political forces who sought increased profits through either direct annexation or indirect control of Cuba.[36] Martí was determined to keep Cuba free of all foreign domination, and he had timed the outbreak of the Second War for Independence so as to prevent "the annexation of Cuba to the United States." As for American assistance in the form of armed intervention, Martí had expressed his opinion tersely: "Once the United States is in Cuba, who will get it out?"[37]

Most of the leaders of the revolution shared Martí's determination to keep Cuba free of all foreign domination, and after "the Apostle's" death, they continued to uphold his principles. Henry A. Hinley, a New York merchant who was interested in the "Occitania" estate and had frequent discussions with the leaders of the revolution, made this point clear in a letter to U.S. Secretary of State Richard B. Olney in April 1896:

> the insurgents not being annexationists (neither the ones who are in Cuba, nor those who are in the United States) they do not see that in case a war did arise between the United States and Spain, and that the first came out victorious, it would have been foolish of them to have spent their money and spilled their blood in order to make a present to the United States of the Island without reaping any benefit from the conflict.[38]

None of the revolutionary leaders were more determined to follow Martí's principles regarding United States intervention than the military commanders in the field, and none more so than Maceo. He favored a declaration by the United States recognizing the belligerency of the Republic of Cuba, realizing how important this was for the acquisition of military equipment, as well as for its moral effect. But there he stopped. "All I want to obtain from the United States is the recognition of the belligerency of the Cuban Republic." He informed the New York *World*: "I should not want our neighbors to have to shed their blood for our cause. We can do that for ourselves if, under the common law, we can get the necessary elements to overthrow the corrupted power of Spain in Cuba."[39]

Coupled with this hope for American aid *only* in the form of ability to purchase arms in the United States, Maceo looked forward to assistance from the Latin American republics. In October 1895, he wrote identical letters to the presidents of Venezuela, Mexico, and several other Latin American countries in an effort to obtain a joint loan of $1 million, as well as the recognition of Cuban belligerency. On November 24, 1895, Maceo wrote enthusiastically to General José Manuel Capote and Jesús Rabí:

> All the news which Señor Estrada Palma has communicated to me and which I have read in the foreign newspapers is most promising. The recognition of belligerency appears an assured thing when the American Congress inaugurates its session which will be the 4th of the coming month. In Latin America there have been large demonstrations of sympathy for our cause; in Caracas,

> a meeting of 5,000 persons took place under the statue of Bolívar. Chile and Peru have openly shown their desire to intervene in the question. The president of Costa Rica has been urged to convene the government heads of the rest of the Republics to agree on a collective intervention for the purpose of recognition of the independence of Cuba by Spain.
>
> As you see by the news, we are travelling with the wind behind us and everything makes us believe that it won't be long before the Revolution triumphs.[40]

Maceo's joy over what he believed was the imminent recognition of Cuban belligerency by the United States soon vanished. The administration of President Grover Cleveland consistently maintained a policy of doing everything possible to sustain Spanish sovereignty over the island and to prevent a victory for the Cuban revolution. According to General Miró, this stand neither surprised nor disappointed Maceo, for he felt that Cuba would receive more help from the Latin American republics collectively "than from the big power of the North [the United States]."[41] Unfortunately, the kind of support Maceo envisaged receiving from Latin America never materialized.

Two opposing feelings operated side by side in Latin America during Cuba's Second War for Independence. One was sympathy for the Cuban struggle; the other was solidarity with Spain. For several years prior to the outbreak of the Cuban revolution, the Pan-Hispanic movement had been fostered by a group in Spain whose object was to promote solidarity between that country and the Hispanic nations of America, largely for the purpose of combatting the growing aggressiveness of the United States. Its imperialist policies, before and during the Cuban revolution, made the propaganda of the Pan-Hispanists more effective. During these years, as Walter La Feber points out,

> the American business community began systematically opening Latin American markets. . . . American investment, composed

> mainly of surplus capital accumulated from the home market's collapse (during the depression which began in 1893), flowed into Latin American in increased amounts during the 1893–1898 period. New steamship lines, heavy investments in Latin American railroads, the movement of American bankers into Santo Domingo and the expansion of the Guggenheim interests in Mexico exemplified this southward advance of the dollar.[42]

United States arrogance toward Latin America intensified the fears created by the "advance of the dollar," and to many Latin Americans, Spain appeared an ally against the threatening Yankee colossus.

Although several Latin American republics had recognized the Cuban government during the Ten Years' War and had even cooperated in an effort to force Spain to relinquish Cuba, the situation during the Second War for Independence was quite different. This time, no Latin American republic recognized Cuban belligerency; many of them even displayed indifference, and one—Argentine—openly side with Spain. The Cuban revolutionaries, therefore, had to depend solely upon supporters in the United States for assistance in the forms of arms and ammunition.[43]

Maceo feared that the future Republic would be born a cripple if its freedom was achieved through the military intercession of any other country. He insisted that only by wresting freedom through its own power could Cuba develop as a truly independent nation. Other nations could help the Cubans by providing financial assistance and by allowing them to transport it to the island. But the fighting had to be done by the Cubans themselves.[44] So important did Maceo consider this issue that in the midst of continual fighting, he repeatedly took time out to press his point of view on Cuban officials both on the island and in the United States. In April 1896, he wrote to Estrada Palma, criticizing the latter's policy of seeking American support for the Cuban rebellion:

> Already I read in the papers a discussion on whether the United States should intervene in the war to bring it to a swift end, and I suspect that you, inspired by patriotism, are working without tiring to do all for Cuba that you can, but as I see it, we do not need intervention in order to win this war. If we want to reduce Cuba in a few days, send us twenty-five or thirty thousand rifles, a million rounds of ammunition and one, or at the most two expeditionary forces.

Maceo concluded by pointing out that if the United States were genuinely interested in Cuba's welfare, she would give full support, even tacitly, to this program.[45]

Maceo always had doubts about the United States government's genuine interest in Cuba's welfare. He told J. Syme Hastings, correspondent for the *Journal of the Knights of Labor,* that while he did not doubt the sympathy of the American people, he feared that "your Government may doubt the discretion of recognizing our belligerency." When Hastings remarked that Americans had had to fight for their own liberty, Maceo smiled and answered: "Ah, yes, but I doubt if we will have a Lafayette to aid us in this unequal struggle."[46]

On July 14, 1896, Maceo wrote to Francisco Pérez Carbó:

> From Spain I never expected anything. She always despised us, and it would be undignified to think otherwise. Liberty is won with the edge of the machete; it is not asked for. To beg for rights is the domain of cowards incapable of exercising these rights. Neither do I expect anything from the [North] Americans. We must depend on our own efforts. It is better to rise or fall without help than to contract debts of gratitude to a neighbor so powerful.[47]

And two days later, he wrote to José Dolores Payo, Delegate of the Revolutionary Government in Key West:

> What do you say about the extraordinary merit of this invading force? When historians write in the future, a brilliant page will

have to be devoted to it. . . . We have no factories, no hospitals, no replenishments, nor do we obtain any consideration from the barbarous enemy. Notwithstanding this situation which began at the outbreak of the war and still exists today we made our rations go further, and we have healed our wounds perfectly. And if today we have gone from triumph to triumph, it is because we have been able to receive some war supplies thanks to the activities of the *junta* of New York. *Why do we need and of what advantage to us is foreign intervention and foreign meddling? Cuba is winning its independence by the arms and hearts of its sons. It will be free in a short time without needing any other help.*[48]

That same day, Maceo developed this theme more fully in a letter to Dr. Alberto J. Díaz, then residing in Louisville, Kentucky:

The official recognition of our belligerency does not seem to me to be such an important thing, if in order to achieve it we have to concentrate so much of our effort in that direction. Nor is American intervention so advantageous to the future of Cuba as most of our compatriots think. I believe rather that the secret of our final triumph is intertwined with the efforts of Cubans who are working for the independence of our country, and that only if the final triumph is achieved without this foreign intervention will it bring us complete happiness.[49]

This was Maceo's last word on the subject before his death several months later. As Cuba's history after United States intervention was to prove, it was a truly prophetic analysis.

16

The Death of Maceo

In mid-September 1896, Maceo learned of the arrival of Colonel Francisco Leyte Vidal's expedition, and he went off to obtain the much-needed supplies. On September 18, he met Leyte Vidal and received from the expedition 500,000 rounds of ammunition, 1,000 rifles, 2,000 pounds of dynamite, one cannon, and 100 cannon shells. With the pneumatic cannon came three American artillerymen. Francisco (Panchito) Gómez Toro, the young son of Máximo Gómez, also came to join Maceo, who had been his hero from childhood. Clearly Maceo's and Gómez's complaints that the warriors in Pinar del Río were being abandoned had produced some results, although hardly enough to fill the need.[1]

The happy shouts over the arrival of the war material were abruptly stilled when everyone noticed Maceo's face. He had been handed a copy of the *Boletín de Guerra* of July 15, which announced that on July 5, José Maceo had been killed in battle at Loma del Gato in Oriente. It may seem incredible that it should have taken so long for the news to reach Maceo. It was, rather, an indication of the indifference of the government toward its greatest warrior. The officials had simply neglected to inform Maceo of his brother's death. The only communication Maceo received from government officials during the entire western campaign was a criticism for making a number of appointments and conferring ranks "without first submitting them to the Governing Council for their approval."[2]

Maceo received hundreds of letters of condolence from his friends abroad, but except for one or two replies, it was fully two months before he could bring himself to acknowledge receipt of these expressions of sympathy.[3] Despite his sorrow, Maceo, having been fortified by the supplies from the Leyte Vidal expedition, made preparations to engage in extensive battle activity. On October 14, De Truffin wrote:

> At present being better organised and well supplied with arms and ammunition, they [the rebels led by Maceo] have altered their tactics, and are offering resistance to the royal troops. Five rather serious clashes have taken place in the last few days. . . . The bitterness with which both sides fought is an indication that the war has entered an entirely new and more active phase.[4]

Maceo's first combat after receiving the new supplies took place in Montezuelo on September 23–24. There he drove the Spaniards from the battlefield at the cost of sixty-eight casualties. The next day, he had another clash at Tumbas de Estorino, and on October 1, he was momentarily trapped by three Spanish columns at Ceja del Negro. Making effective use of the new cannon, however, he not only broke out of the Spanish encirclement, but forced the enemy to retreat. In the three day battle, Maceo won a notable victory—but it cost him 227 casualties. After the battle was over, he had only 200 fighting men left. Nevertheless, the "Bronze Titan" had once again demonstrated his extraordinary skill and ferocious tenacity.[5]

Throughout the rest of October, Maceo continued his rapier-like thrusts at the enemy in Pinar del Río. On October 27, in San Cristóbal, he delivered what was to be his last address to the troops under his command. He urged them to take heart and prepare for whatever sacrifices might arise. He assured the few score men that they could wear down the Spaniards in the West and open the way for final victory.[6]

But as he spoke, Maceo did not know that his days of campaigning were numbered. On October 29, in El Roble, he received a letter from Gómez urgently requesting that he break through the *trocha* and return to Camagüey.

This was not the first time that Maceo had received a request from the general-in-chief that he join him. During his convalescence in the Rosario Mountains, he had been asked by Gómez to leave for Camagüey, due to the difficulties the latter was having with the government.

There was really nothing new about that either. For many months, certain members of the civil government had become extremely irritated by Gómez's strong individuality; the general obstinately insisted on enforcing the policies he regarded as essential for victory. The government officials objected to Gómez's summary dismissals of their plans for obtaining finances through making exceptions to his policy of destruction. Gómez resisted all efforts to moderate what he considered the basic strategy for winning the war: the destruction of all wealth. The dispute even threatened to split the revolutionary leaders into two opposing camps. However, Gómez triumphed and his opponents gave in.[7]

Members of the civil government remained dissatisfied over the basic issue of authority. The conflict was brought to a head over a matter involving the Maceo brothers, Antonio and José—and behind it lurked the question of racism. As we have seen, Cuban blacks comprised a majority of the Liberating Army, although the exact percentage is a matter of some doubt. Moreover, it has been estimated that about forty percent of the generals and colonels were blacks. But less than two percent of the civilian administrators were black. The same percentage applied to the representatives of the revolutionary government in New York, Washington, Philadelphia, and Paris.[8] Against this background the charge was raised that the Maceos were trying to monopolize the revolution. Only a determination to prevent blacks from asserting a serious influence in the policies of the revolution could have led to so ridiculous a charge.

The accusation surfaced when Gómez placed José Maceo in command of Oriente province. This action infuriated President Cisneros, who raised the cry that the Maceos—one in the East and the other in the West—were seeking to take control of the war. He also charged that their occupation of key positions would strengthen Spanish propaganda accusing the rebels of seeking a black-dominated Cuba. He further charged that the campaign for United States recognition of Cuban belligerency would be seriously impaired if the impression spread in that country that the rebel cause was dominated by blacks and was being carried through mainly in their interest. This charge against Maceo was by no means a new one; it had been spread by the Spaniards during the Ten Years' War, and then as now, had been accepted by too many elements in the revolutionary ranks.

Cisneros decided to reduce the Maceos' influence. He did this, first, by demanding that Gómez replace José Maceo with Calixto García, and secondly, by stopping all Gómez's efforts to send replacements and material aid to Antonio Maceo. Although Gómez refused to remove José Maceo, the latter resigned his post in favor of Calixto García early in July 1896 in order to prevent the dissension over his position from further hindering the war effort. His untimely death in battle a few days later disposed of this issue as far as the government was concerned.

Encouraged by its "victory" in the case of José Maceo, the civil government began interfering with Gómez's conduct of the war by issuing orders directly to the commanders in the field. Gómez expressed his opinion of these actions in a note which he wrote on the back of a communication he had received from one of the leading government officials informing him that military commands would thereafter be issued by the governing body: "I believe we should be sensible and recognize that while Cuba is not free, we should recognize the military power as the only supreme power."[9]

This, then, was the background of Gómez's first message to Maceo asking him to return east. But Maceo was not interested in becoming involved in political disputes, even though he was furious over Cisneros' clear demonstration of racial prejudice in the treatment of his brother. In addition, as he informed Gómez, his departure "would prevent the realization of our plan to crown the work of the Invasion with a Cuban Ayacucho."[10]

Maceo was referring to the Battle of Ayacucho in Peru on December 9, 1824, where the Spanish forces were decisively defeated. This battle was the final blow to Spanish rule on the continent; after it, only Cuba and Puerto Rico were left to Spain. Maceo frequently referred to his desire to liberate Cuba from Spain by climaxing the invasion with a "Cuban Ayacucho."

In El Roble, Maceo learned that the rebel government had dismissed Gómez from his post as general-in-chief of the revolutionary armies, and had taken over the direction of the war. Gómez now insisted that Maceo leave for Camagüey—that the very existence of the revolution depended on his return. Reluctant though he was to leave, Maceo decided that he must return to the East as quickly as possible.[11] He did so—to a senseless death.

It had not been easy for Gómez to order Maceo to abandon his campaign in the West. He was fully aware of the significance of what he was accomplishing there. As Gómez noted in a letter to Estrada Palma, the fact that the Spaniards had to concentrate so many of their troops against Maceo had weakened them in many other strategic places, "thus giving us the opportunity and more time to prepare operations in areas like Santiago de Cuba, Guantánamo, and Camagüey." Maceo had built an efficient organization in Pinar del Río made up of "well-trained men," and had effectively destroyed the myth of the invulnerability of the *trocha* system. These were important contributions "to the final triumph."[12]

In view of this, Maceo must have realized that Gómez's request had come only after the most careful analysis of all the factors involved, and that he would have to yield to his judgment. As Gómez told his officers, referring to the crisis in the revolutionary government: "Whatever our sacrifices for independence and whatever the fate reserved for us in the future, however bad it may be, it is preferable to be resigned to it than to continue suffering the dishonor of being governed by unworthy people from a foreign soil."[13]

Just what Maceo intended to do after he rejoined Gómez is not known. It is known that he did not intend to lead a revolt against the government, even though he had little respect for it. His old friend and adviser, Eusebio Hernández, who held a post in Cisneros' cabinet, urged Maceo to take over the direction of the revolution, assuring him that he would have sufficient support to carry this through. However, Hernández overlooked two important facts: that Maceo prided himself on his disciplined obedience, and that he had never revolted against the revolutionary government during the Ten Years' War, despite his opposition to many of its policies. It was typical of Maceo that he not only rejected Hernández's suggestion, but commented that his friend must be out of his mind to think that he would have responded favorably. He added: "We [rebels] are our own worst enemies."[14]

Immediately upon making his decision to join Gómez, Maceo began marching toward the *trocha* of Mariel, not far from the city of Havana. General Weyler's favorite *trocha* was now a truly formidable military line, equipped with electric lights, artillery, and innumerable forts, and garrisoned by some 14,000 soldiers. In addition, Weyler had collected more than 10,000 troops to surround Maceo as he moved westward and to pin him against the *trocha.* Maceo did not seem to realize how much strength Weyler was sending against him, nor did he expect to encounter much difficulty in passing through the *trocha.* As he moved toward the fortified line, he sent a message to Commander Baldomero Acosta in Havana province, ordering him to prepare fresh horses for the long journey eastward. He advised Acosta to expect him on November 11.[15]

On November 9, Maceo encountered the advanced columns of Weyler's encircling force in the Tapia valley. With great effort and skill, he broke away from these columns, but lost seventy-seven of his two-hundred-thirty men in the process. On the following day, he was almost completely encircled by the main body of the Spanish force, made up of eighteen infantry battalions and six battalions of artillery—a total of 6,000 men, under the command of General Weyler himself. To oppose this formidable enemy, Maceo had exactly one hundred fifty-three men—but again the brilliant general managed to snatch his forces from the enemy's pincers.[16]

On November 11, the day on which he had expected to meet Acosta across the *trocha,* Maceo reconnoitered the fortified line seeking the best place at which to cross. He became increasingly uneasy as he discovered the true strength of the *trocha* and realized that it would not be an easy matter to effect a crossing. Nevertheless, he was still determined to break through the massive fortified line, and he sent new orders to the rebel units of Havana for a concentration of forces at a predetermined place on November 27.[17]

While preparing for the task ahead, Maceo wrote a series of letters to friends in the United States, reaffirming his faith in the ultimate victory of the Cuban cause, but at the same time recognizing the problems still facing the revolution. He wrote to Clarence King in New York on November 22, thanking him for praising his military achievements, but stating modestly that these were due more "to the abnegation and heroism of the Cuban army than to my skill, which is very little." Maceo noted that the Cuban rebels still faced "very superior forces who are provided with all the elements of war". And added: "No other people of the Americans, upon fighting for their independence, have had to confront the formidable obstacles facing the people of Cuba . . . not even the English colonies of North America." Even if Spain should triple the number of its soldiers, he declared, it could not succeed in forcing the Cubans "to submit to foreign domination."[18]

On November 25, Maceo talked to three soldiers who claimed knowledge of a weak spot in the *trocha,* but after questioning them for half an hour, he was dissatisfied with their information. On the following morning, Maceo made another reconnaissance of the military line, searching for an escape route. He continued this until December 3, when he decided that the best plan was to go around the *trocha* by water at the port of Mariel. Carlos Soto, a local civil official in the revolutionary organization, agreed to furnish the boat and to act as guide. Maceo then chose seventeen men to accompany him around the line and to the East. José Luciano Franco, the Cuban authority on Antonio Maceo, records that the men who were not selected to accompany their beloved leader "wept and begged for the honor of accompanying him."[19]

At 11:30 on the night of December 4, Maceo and his men successfully circled the *trocha* within sight of a Spanish garrison. The feat required four trips of the small boat. Once on the other side, Maceo could not locate the delegation appointed to meet him, and the small group took refuge in an abandoned sugar mill, "La Merced." By the morning of December 6, the horses for Maceo's group had still not arrived. By midday, Maceo would wait no longer, and even though he had developed a high fever by aggravating both his old and recent leg wounds from the long walking, he gave orders to begin marching toward the "Garro" sugar mill. On the road, they met Acosta's contingent with the long-awaited horses. Maceo quickly placed his fine saddle, which he had brought with him, on one of the animals. The group continued to Garro and remained there until nine o'clock that night. Then Maceo decided to join the forces of Colonel Silverio Sánchez Figueras, chief of the brigade of southern Havana, at San Pedro de Hernández.[20]

In San Pedro, the "Bronze Titan" revealed that he had a new plan. He had heard from Acosta and others that his actions in the West had caused so much concern among the officials in Madrid that an attack on any community around Havana would bring about the removal of Captain General Weyler and possibly the end of his brutal policies. Before leaving the West and continuing toward Las Villas, Maceo wanted to strike a blow that would hasten the departure from Cuba of the hated captain general. Maceo's plan was to assault the town of Marianao on the outskirts of the capital itself, and he issued orders for all the rebel forces in the area to gather for the operation.[21]

After formulating his plans for the night's action in Marianao, Maceo, still suffering from his recent wound, stretched out in a hammock to rest. He asked José Miró to read from the Crónicas de Guerra, which his chief of staff was then compiling. He particularly wanted to hear Miró's account of the Battle of Coliseo. Maceo's revolver and machete were close at hand, and his horse was standing unsaddled. As Miró read, the group was startled by sudden sounds of gunfire. Before Maceo and his companions could move from their positions, enemy bullets were whistling around them. Somehow the Spanish troops had evaded the rebel outposts. One of his aides helped the still ailing Maceo out of his hammock. In a few minutes, the general was astride his horse, armed with his machete and revolver. A group of Cuban cavalrymen from the Santiago de las Vegas regiment had heard the shots and were now forcing the vanguard of the attackers back.

But the ever-daring Maceo was not content. He determined to pursue and annihilate the invaders. Sighting another group of enemy infantrymen behind a wire fence to his left, Maceo ordered the forty-eight men around him to charge. The horsemen were detained by the fence, and the Spanish foot soldiers concentrated heavy rifle fire on them. Maceo ordered Commander Juan Manuel Sánchez to cut the fence and sent Brigadier General Pedro Díaz with a small group on a flanking movement to the right. After giving these orders, Maceo leaned toward Miró and shouted, *"Esto va bien!"* (This is going well!) Those were his last words. A bullet struck him in the face. Dropping his machete, the *caudillo* fell heavily from his saddle while at the same time, some twelve men from Commander Sánchez's escort likewise fell.

With the strength of the enemy fire increasing, some of the rebels tried to help Maceo, and others tried to drive the Spaniards back. Colonel Nodarse tried to put Maceo, still alive, on a horse in order to remove him from the scene. But as two men lifted Maceo to put him on the horse, the *caudillo* received another bullet wound—this time in the chest. The rider trying to hold Maceo was also shot from his saddle. Lieutenant Francisco Gómez Toro, the young son of Máximo Gómez, rushed to help. Nodarse and Gómez carried Maceo away. When Gómez was shot in the leg, Colonel Nodarse ordered him to leave, but Gómez refused. The young lieutenant was then shot again and fell over Maceo's body. Nodarse was also wounded, but managed to escape the advancing Spaniards.

The "Bronze Titan's" body had to be abandoned to the enemy. The Spaniards removed the clothes and other valuables from Maceo's body and from those of the other rebel dead. Evidently the Spaniards did not recognize his body, for they would have relished the opportunity to display the corpse in Havana. Before they learned that one of the dead was Maceo, it was too late. The Cubans in the area reorganized and, after driving the enemy troops away, recovered the bodies. Maceo's body was taken to an abandoned house nearby. At three o'clock in the morning of December 8, 1896, the black hero of Cuban independence was buried, together with Panchito Gómez Toro in a place called Cacahual in Santiago de las Vegas.[22]

Several days later, Weyler learned of Maceo's death and celebrated. He gathered his officers and supporters around him, and they feasted, drank, and prematurely toasted a Spanish victory. They could not imagine that the rebels would continue to fight once they had lost the superhuman figure of Maceo. This view was widespread.[23]

In his general order of December 28, 1896, announcing the death of Maceo, Máximo Gómez, doubly grief-stricken over the death of both his son and his comrade-in-arms, wrote: "The army is in grief and with the army its General-in-Chief. Now the country mourns the loss of one of its most mighty defenders, the most glorious of its sons, and the army, the first of its generals." Gómez pledged that the liberating army would not rest until it had achieved the goal for which Maceo had laid down his life—a free and independent Cuba.[24]

Antonio Maceo did not live to see his country liberated from Spain by a combined United States-Cuban force four months after the United States Congress declared war on April 11, 1898. (Of course, as we have seen, the Cubans had been fighting and dying for their independence since 1868, and it was they who had brought the war to a point where it took only four months to end it.) Nor did Maceo live to see his and Martí's worst fears confirmed, as the United States deprived Cuba of the type of independence they had been seeking, and instead converted the island, if not into what Leland H. Jenks described in the title of his 1928 book—*Our Cuban Colony*—at least without any question into a semicolony.[25]

17

Conclusion

Antonio Maceo was one of the truly great figures in the history of the Hispanic-American wars of independence. For twenty-seven years—his entire adult life—all of his thoughts and actions were conditioned by the cause of Cuban independence. He sacrificed everything—his family and countless opportunities to lead a life of ease and luxury—to the cause. Continuing resolutely toward his fixed goal, suffering insult and criticism because he was a man of color, sustaining twenty-five wounds, he fought bravely and brilliantly for his country, *and never once lost a battle.* Neither bullets nor sickness stopped him; at the time of his death, his body was racked with constant pain, and he was able to walk only with a great deal of effort. But his thoughts were fixed on how best to defeat the enemy.

Uneducated and of humble circumstances, Maceo rose from obscurity to heights of great fame and prestige, and he accomplished this under the continual burden of race prejudice. Maceo's career began in a movement dominated by the white aristocracy—the elite of Oriente province. Yet against imposing obstacles, he became a hero of his country and an idol of his people.

From the first battle until his death, Maceo's life quite literally belonged to his country. His military instincts, his personal bravery, and his qualities of leadership were legendary. Having volunteered to fight in the army of liberation as a simple soldier, he rose rapidly and eventually became the major military official, next to General-in-Chief Máximo Gómez. The two military leaders worked together closely during both the Ten Years' War and the Second War for Independence, and they frequently found themselves at odds with the more conservative political leaders of the rebel government. The politicians opposed Gómez because of his unwavering insistence on the need to extend the war from the east to the economic heartland of the island in the west. They opposed Maceo not only because of his close cooperation with Gómez, but also because they felt threatened by his popularity among both blacks and the poor.

Maceo's race was a constant source of political controversy. During both wars, the Spaniards capitalized on existing racist attitudes among white Cubans and spread malicious rumors about the alleged secret ambitions of the black leader. While these rumors were consistently denied by all who fought with and knew Maceo, they were widely believed and were a factor in undermining the unity of the Cuban insurgents. For his part, Maceo usually maintained silence when he was informed of the slanders against him. He considered racism incompatible with the goals for which he was fighting—a republic based on equality and fraternity—and he deeply regretted the division among Cuban fighters. Maceo did once break his silence and expressed his views on the problem of race and racism, in a letter to then President Cisneros on May 16, 1876. In this letter, he reviewed his record of service to the rebel republic and noted that the racist insinuations that were being cast about him were both unjust and divisive. Speaking of himself, he said:

> And since I belong to the colored race, without considering myself worth more or less than other men, I cannot and must not consent to the continued growth of this ugly rumor. Since I form a

> not inappreciable part of this democratic republic, which has for its base the fundamental principles of liberty, equality, and fraternity, I must protest energetically with all my strength that neither now nor at any time am I to be regarded as an advocate of a Negro Republic or anything of the sort. This concept is a deadly thing to this democratic republic which is founded on the basis of liberty and fraternity. I do not recognize any hierarchy.

Maceo believed that the acquisition of equal rights for blacks would have to await political independence. Therefore, he fought on while others tried to undermine his position.

Of all Maceo's achievements, one in particular made him an enduring hero to all generations of Cuban patriots: the Protest of Baraguá in February 1878. When virtually all the political leaders of the republic-in-arms, and most of the military commanders as well, were ready to agree to peace in the Treaty of Zanjón, Maceo alone refused to surrender. Rejecting the minor political concessions the Spaniards were willing to make, he openly defied the Spanish general, Martínez Campos. Although he was soon obliged to cease fighting and to join the other leaders in exile, Maceo's defiance had two important consequences: first, zanjón, instead of being considered a peace treaty, came to be viewed as no more than a truce; secondly, Maceo's act strengthened the determination of his countrymen to renew the war as soon as possible.

It took seventeen years for this opportunity to present itself. Maceo spent these years going from one Caribbean country to another, and to the United States. With others in exile, he devoted his energies to the task of reorganizing the rebel forces for the eventual resumption of the war. To judge from his own writings, Maceo grew both intellectually and politically during his period in exile, which he spent traveling, working, and reading. He was able to develop his own distinctive social vision, which went well beyond his patriotic passion at the time of Baraguá. By the time he was fighting again in Cuba, Maceo saw his goals in terms of well-defined concepts of anti-imperialism, social justice, and human responsibility.

Before returning to do battle, Maceo made one important visit to Cuba in 1890. On that occasion, he was greeted throughout the island with enormous enthusiasm. Although the Spanish authorities forced him to cut his stay short, the response to his visit demonstrated the readiness of the Cuban people to renew the struggle and indicated that Maceo himself had been endowed with the status of a hero. It is unlikely that any other nonwhite would have been welcomed so warmly by white high society, nor is it likely that anyone but he could have so inspired Cuban youth who barely remembered the Ten Years' War.

When hostilities broke out again in 1895, Maceo was among the first to return to Cuba. He forthwith met in La Mejorana with his former commander-in-chief, Máximo Gómez, and the writer, poet, political theorist, and organizer, José Martí, to undertake the task of setting out the political objectives of the future republic. However, Martí was killed shortly thereafter, and Maceo and Gómez soon found themselves in precisely the same position they had been in during the previous war. Again, despite their efforts, power remained in the hands of ambitious, competing politicians: again their military plans were subject to constant political interference, and again Maceo was accused of having racist ambitions. Just as in the previous war, however, Maceo devoted all his thoughts and activities to only one objective—the achievement of Cuban independence.

Maceo lived long enough to accomplish another feat that assured his fame forever. At the end of October 1895 his army began the long march westward—a march that realized Gómez's longtime insistence that the revolution must be brought to the inhabitants of the rich agricultural lands in the provinces beyond Camagüey. The Cuban insurgents fought their way from the eastern end of the island to its western end in Pinar del Río, a distance of over 800 miles. The unexpected success of the Cuban western invasion forced the Spanish to reorganize their activity. On February 11, 1896, the new commander-in-chief of the Spanish forces, General Valeriano

Weyler, entered Cuba. His first military efforts were devoted to the destruction of Maceo. Maceo, on the other hand, fought, evaded, and frustrated Weyler for almost a year. Ironically, he met his death near Havana in a skirmish that was more an ambush than a battle. Characteristically, the last words he was heard to utter were *"Esto va bien!"*

Maceo was beloved by his soldiers and feared and respected by his enemies. On December 14, 1896, De Truffin, the Russian minister in Havana, wrote:

> Maceo's accidental death in a clash at the gates of Havana . . . is undoubtedly a great success for our Governor General [Weyler] . . . . It is not to be denied that the death of the most popular insurgent leader is a grievous blow to the revolutionary cause, because the deceased, quite apart from his military qualities, enjoyed great influence among his men.[1]

General Fidel Alonso de Santocildes, the Spanish general who later died fighting Maceo, made a point of personally telling Maceo that he was the most capable officer he had ever faced.[2] During the Ten Years' War, General Martínez Campos said, "Maceo is the key to real peace."[3] And at the beginning of the revolution of 1895, the Spaniards admitted "the great importance of the landing of the leader Maceo in Cuba."[4]

After the death of Martí, Maceo and Gómez embodied the spirit of the Cuban revolutionary movement. Maceo's name became a household word among all Cubans wherever they lived, and his exploits were discussed again and again in the *bohios* of peasants. Too often, even in Cuba, he was pictured in one-dimensional terms, "solely as a great warrior, a man of action but not of ideas."[5] But his correspondence demonstrates how diligently he pursued his self-education, even in the midst of military campaigns, and how well he succeeded. He was reported to have acquired a fair knowledge of several languages, including English. Those who heard him speak reported that he could converse with some assurance on history, political science, and military theories. Maceo recognized and respected the need for education, and wherever he went, he surrounded himself with those from whom he could learn and thereby improve himself. The extent to which he succeeded is testified to by Martí's statement in *Patria* of October 6, 1893, that "Maceo has as much strength in his mind as in his arm."

Maceo also made important contributions to the ideology of the revolution. It was his Protest of Baraguá that kept alive hopes for independence. When the rebel leaders wished to rekindle the Cuban spirit, they invariably pointed to Maceo and his Protest. During the Second War for Independence, whenever Cubans wanted to demonstrate the invincibility of their cause, they used the example of the undefeated Maceo to humiliate the Spaniards. On an island averaging no more than fifty miles in width, they found it impossible to contain him, and general after general was recalled and replaced because of this failure. Even the famed and feared General Weyler was on the verge of being summoned home when Maceo was killed. In the Ten Years' War, Maceo aroused international attention with his Protest of Baraguá. In the Revolution of 1895, the world rang with praise for the fabulous exploits of Maceo and the western invasion, Maceo and the threat to the capital, Maceo and the campaign in Pinar del Rio.

Maceo symbolized and embodied the hopes of the black people of Cuba, and he fully justified their faith in him. In every statement he uttered, he stressed the dual cardinal principles: independence for the nation, and freedom and equality for blacks. The emancipation of the slaves in 1887 did not by any means eliminate racial inequality in Cuba. When Maceo fought for independence after 1895, he also fought for racial equality, convinced that the latter could not be achieved without the success of the former. He was thus able to rally to the revolutionary cause the thousands of blacks and mulattoes who joined the *mambí* forces in such large numbers and whose support was so important for the struggle against Spain.[6]

By steadfastly refusing to place himself above the revolution, Maceo reassured some of those who feared that he might lead a struggle for black domination in Cuba. Maceo always insisted that there were no black or white soldiers—all were Cuban warriors and all should work together to establish and build the republic. In 1895, a pamphlet was published (in Spanish) in the United States entitled "The Program of Maceo," and subtitled, "Ideas of Maceo, Head of the Black Race in Cuba." It emphasized that Maceo saw himself as the spokesman for black Cubans and that his special mission was to establish, with his sword, the dominance of the black race in an independent Cuba.[7] Nothing, however, could have been further from the "ideas of Maceo," and it is clear that the pamphlet was just a clever device on the part of Cubans, in league with Spain, to create confusion and disarray in the ranks of the independence fighters. An accurate reflection of Maceo's true ideas is the following observation by the African historian Joseph Ki-Zerba, who wrote in 1972:

> It was a general of African descent, Antonio Maceo, who was to conduct the liberàtion struggle against Spanish domination. When a Cuban of Spanish descent advised him to organize his regiments with whites and nonwhites (separately), Maceo replied: "If you weren't white, I would have you immediately shot; but I don't like the idea of being accused of being a racist like you. Get out. But I warn you—next time I won't be so patient. The Revolution has no color."[8]

Like Martí, Maceo was also the symbol of a free Cuba—equally free from the domination of Spain and of the United States. He was ready to lay down his life for only one cause—the genuine independence of Cuba. Nor could he accept any other solution for the Cuban people, black or white. Indeed, when his lawyer and consultant, Antonio Zambrana Vázquez, broached the idea that evolution, rather than revolution, and autonomy under Spain, rather than independence, might be the best solution for Cuba, the "Bronze Titan" broke off both their friendship and their business relationship. When Maceo learned in June 1896 that the United States and Spain were discussing the possibility of granting Cuban autonomy and not independence, he wrote to Perfecto Lacoste: "The [North] Americans and Spaniards can make whatever agreements they wish, but Cuba will be free in a short while and can laugh at the negotiations which do not favor its independence."[9]

It could hardly be expected that Maceo was without any weaknesses. He was considered somewhat irresponsible in the handling of money and valuables, and as a result, rebel leaders hesitated to trust him with them. When he did have money, he spent it quickly and often unwisely. But he never profited from his revolutionary activities; in fact, just when he had achieved his goal of economic stability and prosperity in Costa Rica, he abandoned it all without hesitation when he was called upon to join the revolutionary movement organized by Martí. Because of his impeccable dress and the fact that he cherished fine objects, Maceo was often considered vain. His enemies repeatedly attacked him on this score, but those who knew Maceo testified that it was pride, not vanity, that prompted his behavior. His manners were courteous, and he was always respectful of the opinion of others. He reacted with great sensitivity to ridicule heaped upon him because of his color and lack of formal education, and there is no doubt that he sought, through his impressive appearance, to achieve the respect and social position denied him by racism, whether Spanish or Cuban in origin.

To a remarkable extent, he succeeded, and achieved a degree of social mobility almost unique in Cuban society for a man of his origins. There were many black officers in the wars for independence, like José Maceo, Flor Crombet, Guillermo Moncada, Quintín Banderas, Cecilio González, and Pedro Díaz. While they were able to move up in the ranks of the revolutionary army despite barriers of prejudice, none of them rose to

Maceo's heights as a military commander or attained his fame and popularity. Nor did any of them acquire the international reputation that Maceo won during his travels through the Caribbean countries and in the United States. Both in Cuba and abroad, Maceo appears to have been better known in his time than even Martí. Writing in the *New York Times* of September 16, 1900, Dorothy Stanhope, the *Times'* special correspondent in Havana, observed: "Maceo, one of the Cuban idols in the war of independence, was a black man. All Cubans, of whatever color, look upon him as one of the noblest of their countrymen."

Yet one must be careful not to view Maceo's well-deserved reputation as typical of the status achieved by the mass of black Cubans. The Cuban historian Jorge Ibarra exaggerated when he wrote: "The fact that Antonio Maceo was recognized at the end of the revolutionary war of '95 as the national hero of Cuba . . . is the most obvious manifestation of the fact that the revolution had ethnically integrated the broad masses of peasants and workers of the country."[10] While the symbol of the "Bronze Titan" helped perpetuate the myth that the independence struggle had produced an integrated Cuba, with equality for blacks, nevertheless black Cubans in general, and ex-slaves in particular, found the Republic imposed by the United States under the notorious Platt Amendment a very hostile environment. The spurious independence fostered by the Platt Amendment served to intensify the patterns of racism in Cuba, for on top of the island's long-established discrimination, there was now imposed the more obvious racism of the United States. As early as 1899, the New York *Tribune* reported that signs inscribed, "We cater to white people only," were going up in Havana at the insistence of American officers and soldiers, and that Cuban blacks were alarmed by talk of "what they understood to be the favorite American pastime of 'nigger lynching.'"[11]

It was not until the Revolution of 1959 that Cuba achieved

the kind of independence envisaged by Martí and Maceo—independence from the United States as well as from Spain. For the first time in the island's history, one could say, as Maceo did in upbraiding a racist: "Young man, here there are no whites and no blacks, only Cubans."[12]

Maceo was probably the best known Cuban of his time, and the news of his death brought reactions from afar. In distant Kiev, Russia, *The Illustrated World* carried the following article:

> Antonio Maceo
>
> In one of the last skirmishes of the Cuban insurgents with the leading Spanish forces of General Weyler, in the battle of Punta Brava, the principal leader of the insurgents on the island of Cuba fell, General Maceo. The news of the death of the valiant warrior was received with great joy in Madrid, since Maceo was the most dangerous enemy of Spain in Cuba. Associated with the name of this Cuban hero were numerous legendary reports referring also to his own family, outstanding for their extraordinary revolutionary spirit.
>
> Maceo, fallen in battle against the enemy under the command of Cirujeda, defended himself long and tenaciously, surrounded by Spanish troops in the province of Pinar del Río. In the wars of Cuban liberation he received no less than twenty-seven wounds. Several times the balls whistled past him, from side to side, and the doctors who examined his body could not conceive how he had succeeded in surviving with so many and such serious lesions.
>
> Truly admirable was the destiny of this man who personified the destiny of his country, his fatherland, and who fell in heroic battle for its independence. . . . The appeal of Antonio Maceo among his people was irresistible. They venerated him as an unearthly hero, and his loss is for the Cubans completely irreplaceable.[13]

In Chile, the article, "Quien era Maceo?" (Who was Maceo?) awakened public recognition of a man who "above all and more than all was a citizen . . . a precursor of independence, father of his country and founder of a nation." Upon learning of Maceo's death, Antonio Rosado, a Cuban black working in the nitrate plants of Iquique, Chile, contributed his life savings of 1,000 chileons, and his 20-year-old first-born son joined the Cuban Liberating Army.[14] The tiny Cuban settlement in Managua, Nicaragua, collected $135 (U.S.) as a special tribute to Maceo. And in Paris, a Cuban named his newly-born son Antonio Maceo "to conserve the name and soul of Maceo."[15]

When Eugenio María de Hostos, Puerto Rico's greatest social philosopher, wrote that Maceo was "the most genuine representative of embattled Cuba," he voiced an opinion that was shared throughout Latin America. A cable to New York from workers and students in Buenos Aires, dated December 17, 1896, carried the information that at a tremendous mass meeting held in that city the night before, profound sorrow was expressed at the news of the death of Maceo, and in his honor "there was the greatest demonstration in favor of the cause of the independence of Cuba." Guillermo Valencia, the Colombian poet, and Guillermo Matta, the Chilean poet, both dedicated poems to Maceo. In Santo Domingo, Alejandro Woss y Gil, an officer in the government of President Ulisses Heureaux, wrote mournfully:

> The Cuban cause has lost its greatest bulwark. . . . Unfortunately, nature does not produce such men every minute. It is certain that at the present time there is simply no one capable of filling the void which the death of this titanic figure has caused in the Cuban revolutionary movement.

Robert Love, the gifted black Jamaican lawyer, praised Maceo as "the pedestal on which the independence of the Cubans was raised," and hailed the cause he had died for as "the highest and noblest of causes, for the greatest of the rights of man."[16]

In 1925, Lugo Viña delivered a lecture at the Central University of Madrid, in the course of which he mentioned Antonio Maceo without any further explanation. Primero de Rivera, who was chairing the lecture, interrupted the speaker, and observed: "I, General of the Spanish Army, son of a general and nephew of generals, feel very honored to have been wounded in battle against Antonio Maceo, the greatest of the Spanish generals born in Cuba."[17]

Almost half a century later, in the midst of the United States intervention against the Vietnamese people, *ABC*, the conservative paper published in Madrid, issued the following warning to the Americans:

> Beware that you do not have happen to you what happened to us in Cuba. We sent 250,000 of Spain's best soldiers, with the best military equipment of the time; and 3,000 ragged men, commanded by Gómez and Maceo, finished us off. That is why the people of Madrid sing:
>
> Por culpa de estos dos mulatos
> -Pasamos muy malos ratos.
> (Because of those two mulattoes
> -We had a very bad time.)[18]

So legendary had Maceo's fame become in Madrid that it was taken for granted that Gómez, too, was a man of color!

So great was Maceo's reputation for invincibility in the United States that for a considerable period, many people insisted that he must have met his death at the hands of the Spaniards through foul play. The headline in the New York *Journal* of December 13, 1896 read: "Massacre, Ambush, or Poison?" Senator Wilkinson Call, of Florida, introduced a resolution into Congress denouncing "the Maceo assassination," and a Senate committee was appointed to investigate the affair.[19]

An eloquent tribute to the fallen Cuban hero was published in the *Journal of the Knights of Labor.* In its issue of December 17, 1896, J. Syme-Hastings, who had met and interviewed Maceo in Cuba, wrote:

I consider him the greatest hero of the nineteenth century—aye—even in history. Caesar crossed the Rubicon; Napoleon crushed the world; Alexander crossed Hellespont; William III caused the Boyne to run blood; Skobeloff forced leagues of rockbound ravines and crossed the Balkans; but all had armies; all had arms; all levied strict discipline; all had room in which to operate. With a handful of untrained men, armed with machetes, without any discipline save loyalty to the cause, cut off from food, water and shelter, and operating in a few square miles of territory, Maceo routed the flower of the Spanish army again and again. He has gained control of the whole island. With 20,000 men he has not only kept over 200,000 well trained, well disciplined and well armed men at bay, but he has routed and crushed them repeatedly and forced a passage from one end of the island to the other.

To Maceo fear was a myth. He was absolutely devoid of the sense which we call fear. Every nerve, every sense, so tingled and vibrated with keen foresight, certainty of victory, and love for his country, that he never gave the slightest heed to personal danger. I have wondered if other generals were like Maceo but history fails to show any light. I have crouched down behind a tree when the air was red with bullets, when showers of clipped leaves and pieces of bark fell on me like flakes of snow, and I have watched Maceo's face as he sat firmly on his horse waiting for his ambushed, crawling followers to get close enough to the enemy to allow him to give the charge signal. Had I stood up I should certainly have been filled with Mauser bullets, because I feared them. But there was no fear on that face—his bright eyes roamed calmly from the ambushed enemy to where his men were, and back again, his horse restlessly snorted when the bullets singed him, but Maceo merely patted and calmed it. God! that was a memory; each moment I waited to see him fall with a hole in his high forehead, but it never came to pass. That is why the Cubans win their engagements with such a noble figure for a leader, even a band of cowards could sweep all before them

I loved him best when the lion was dormant and he grew reminiscent. He was one of those immortal characters who cause one to forget for the time that he is but a man. His was a soul of strong magnetism and great character—poetical like all of his race—and ever surrounded by that strength of refinement which denotes genius.

I have seen him carry five wounded men from the field after a battle and care for them with all the tenderness of a sister of charity—yet this was the same man whose cool, bloody fighting made each field after an engagement look like a dissecting room in a hospital.

He was the life of every camp—was, in fact, one of the men—he would share his water and food with anyone who was short, often he wrote letters home from many of the "Cubes" who were unable to do so. His heart was as big as his massive frame. Therefore, one cannot wonder that he was idolized and that his men would gladly die fighting under him.

Writing in Yiddish, Morris Rosenfeld, Jewish working class Socialist poet, paid tribute to the fallen black in his poem, "Antonio Maceo (The Cuban Hero)" which went in part:

Madrid, the old capital, pride of the Dons,
Revives with a jubilant clanging
Of bells, a hosanna of bugles and guns,
Silk banners from balconies hanging.

A mighty procession has come into view.
Each face is enthralled and inspired.
Hearts hammer: What is it they're going to do?
Another Jew put to the fire?

The pious Castilian, what gladdens him so?
Why else would his march be so merry?
But no! this all happened a long time ago!
Long since, Torquemada was buried.

Then why such rejoicing? such hymns to their Lord
Darkhooded Dominicans bawling?
"At last we have splintered the enemy's sword:
At last the great Cuban has fallen!"

The sharp-edged machete is orphaned at last—
The blade which Maceo the Valiant

Swung fiercely to pay old Castile for her past,
Unpeopling her proudest battalion.

The eyes are extinguished, which turned against Spain
The stare of contagious defiance,
The brave one is broken, the hero lies slain
Who tore at his foe like a lion.

For this, old Madrid's making merry: the threat
Is smashed by her bloody despoiler,
Maceo at last has been caught in a net,
The net of that arch-demon Weyler.

That fiend, on whose features are graven again
The inquisitors' venomous rancor—
Astonishing, so the historian's pen
Spits out their story in anger!

On them, and on him, and on all who rejoice
Tonight, falls a deep execration;
For over the tumult a terrible voice
Gives notice of Spain's desolation.

And up from the earth spring Marranos and Moors
And Cubans . . . In harrowing legions,
On foot and on horseback, to settle old scores
They come from mysterious regions.

A throng of dead marchers! invincible comes
Their phantasmagorical thunder!
Each foot moves in time to the festival drums;
Maceo's their man, their commander.

And laughing they pour through the streets of Madrid
—The city hellbent and polluted
Which did as her God and his ministers bid,
Whose credo in bloodshed was rooted.

And heaven and earth laugh aloud, and from thrones
Long lost comes a roar of derision. . . .
O festive old beggar-maid, glamorized bones
Of "Bygones"! Accurst inquisition![20]

The Detroit *Journal,* upon learning of his death, called Maceo "the greatest colonial fighter since Toussaint L'Ouverture."[21] As for black Americans, they honored Maceo during his lifetime, immediately after his death, and long afterward. In a poetic tribute published in *The Freeman,* a black weekly published in Indianapolis, Dr. W. A. Majors wrote:

No, Maceo, man of Negro blood!
Great general, leader, stem the flood.
Thou art not dead, thou canst not die.

Thy race bemoans thy ill-timed fate
And bubbling o'er with murderous hate
For Spain, traducer, with bloodful lust
Erases her name from 'mong the just.
The world looks on with eagle eye
And saw thy sword 'tween earth and sky,
When urging men to bravely fight
For freedom, Maceo, man of right,
The world to-day, yes, all do know,
How thou hast fought, brave Maceo.[22]

A leading guest house in New York's black community in the late 1890's was named "Hotel Maceo," and many black Americans gave their male children the first name "Maceo."[23] In the *Colored American Magazine* of November 1900, S.E.F.C.C. Hamedoe described Maceo as "the greatest hero of the nineteenth century."[24] In his speech accepting nomination as presidential candidate of the National Liberty Party in 1904, George Edwin Taylor, the first black American to be nominated for the presidency of the United States, referred to "General Maceo, the greatest Negro soldier and general of modern times."[25] One of the ships in Marcus Garvey's Black Star Line in the early 1920's, originally the *Kanawha,* was renamed the *Antonio Maceo.*[26]

Of all the tributes in the black American conmunity, probably the most meaningful was one that appeared in the *Church*

Review of the African Methodist Episcopal Church soon after Maceo's death. It read:

> Keen, thoughtful, reserved, brave, he deserves to rank with Toussaint L'Ouverture. In his calling, he will rank as high as the solon Dumas in his, or President Juarez of Mexico, or that famous black Russian whose poems are sung so often amid the steppes and mountains of Russia as our own Whittier's are in the vales and hills of America. We believe as the years go by his name and record will acquire a deeper, holier meaning to everyone who loves liberty. How can patriots ever consign to oblivion a man with such heroic elements in his nature, such statesmanlike views, such marvelous gallantry, such majestic faith in his countrymen? We colored Americans need the inspiration of Maceo's memory. In these degenerate days when the gods of our land are silver and gold, instead of liberty and freedom, we need the remembrance of some former deeds of such a hero.[27]

In 1935, Dr. Carter Goodwin Woodson, the father of the organized effort to collect and disseminate Afro-American history, and founder twenty years earlier of the Association for the Study of Negro Life and History, as well as editor of its *Journal of Negro History* until his death in 1950, wrote a preface to *Negro History in Thirteen Plays,* one of which was entitled, "Antonio Maceo." In it, Dr. Woodson referred to Maceo as one of the "great men of African blood who had done much for the benefit of mankind," and praised the play about him as showing that black people were "a factor in the development of Greater America."[28]

In 1959, Raúl Castro was the speaker at the Cuban ceremonies commemorating the anniversary of Antonio Maceo's death in the first of what was to become an annual event on the island. Castro described how the example of Maceo had inspired the revolutionaries in the Sierra Maestre, and how truly he had represented the still-strong spirit of the Cuban people. He then went on: "What will we do about the men and women of dark skin for whom Maceo fought? . . . We know what to do because we take as our own the promises of José Martí and Antonio Maceo."

Raúl Castro also suggested that too much emphasis had been placed in the past on Maceo's role as a warrior, and not enough on his contributions as a statesman who fought not only with his machete, but also with his pen, which "altogether simple—as Maceo was simple—faithfully interpreted his revolutionary thought."[29]

In a tribute to General Antonio, Che Guevarra pointed to Maceo's two greatest achievements: the Protest of Baraguá in which he continued the battle for Cuban independence alone against impossible odds, and his amazing conduct during the invasion of the West in 1895 when he proved himself the greatest of revolutionary guerrilla fighters. "The spirit of Antonio Maceo is the spirit of Cuba," Che Guevarra exclaimed.[30]

Today, Martí is still considered the principal "intellectual author of the Revolution,"[31] but far more attention than before is being paid to Maceo's ideas.[32] A reflection of his intellectual clarity is found in his profound antiracism and anti-imperialism, both of which grew with his experience. Unlike many other Cubans who fought for independence but welcomed the intervention of the United States, Maceo understood clearly that North American influence would have a negative, retarding effect on the struggle for genuine independence. He is therefore justifiably considered a pioneer, both in deed and in thought, in Cuba's century-long anti-imperialist struggle.

In a speech commemorating the hundredth anniversary of the *Grito de Yara,* which marked the beginning of the Ten Years' War, Fidel Castro declared: "Nothing could better teach us . . . to understand what the term 'Revolution' means than an analysis of the history of our country, a study of the history of our people, of our people's revolutionary roots."[33] The homage in present-day Cuba to Antonio Maceo is evidence of this understanding. Today, nearly half of the Cuban population is either black or mulatto, and the vast majority of Cubans come from the poorer sections of the population. It is understandable, therefore, that Maceo's accomplishments should be such a source of general pride. But Maceo's heroism transcends his rise as a man of color from humble origins to unexampled heights of rank and achievement. It lies, too, in the fact that he was an unwavering fighter for independence and against imperialism.

At the funeral ceremonies in honor of Antonio Maceo organized by the *Club Radical* of Santiago de Chile, the great Chilean poet, Guillermo Matta, read the following tribute he had composed for the occasion:

> . . . Al fin obtendrá victoria
> de Cuba el largo suplicio;
> y entonces tu sacrificio
> será un altar de gloria
> Maceo! . . . Altar de la historia
> Que en fulgente irradiación
> dará forma a toda acción,
> dará lustre a toda hazaña;
> y será, pese a la España
> Altar de Cuba—Nación!
>
> . . . In the end after your
> long torment
> the victory of Cuba will be attained
> And then your sacrifice will
> be an altar of glory
> Maceo! . . . an altar of history
> which in shining radiance
> will give form to every action,
> will give lustre to every heroic feat;
> and it will be in spite of Spain
> an altar of Cuba—a nation![34]

Reference Notes

Preface

1. Arthur A. Schomburg, "General Antonio Maceo," *The Crisis* 38 (May 1931): 155–56, 174.
2. Fermín Sarcusa Peraga, *Bibliografia de Antonio Maceo y Grajales* (Havana, 1946).
3. Maceo is barely mentioned in a footnote on p. 767 in *Blacks in Colonial Cuba 1774–1899* by Kenneth F. Kipple (Gainesville, Fl., 1976), a curious book since, despite its title, it is not a study of Afro-Cubans but an analysis of Cuba's census data. Maceo is casually mentioned as "Gomez's able mulatto subordinate" in *A Yankee Guerrillero: Frederick Funston and the Cuban Insurrection 1896–1897* by Thomas W. Crouch (Memphis, Tenn., 1976), p. 43. This is also a curiously titled book since, unlike the Cuban *mambises*, the guerrilleros of the 1890's were pro-Spanish Cuban irregulars.

   There are exactly two references to Antonio Maceo in *Marriage, Class and Colour in Nineteenth-Century Cuba* by Verena Martinez-Alier (London, 1974).

   A much more extensive and useful treatment of Antonio Maceo is to be found in Donna Marie Wolf, "The Caribbean People of Color and the Cuban Independence Movement," (Ph.D. diss., University of Pittsburgh, 1973).

4. The full article is reprinted in Philip S. Foner, "A Tribute to Antonio Maceo," *Journal of Negro History*, 60 (January 1970): 65–71.
5. Luis Rolando Cabrera, *El centenario de Maceo, 1845–14 de Junio, 1945* (Havana, 1945). Cabrera himself was a mulatto.
6. José Antonio Portuondo, ed., *El pensamiento vivo de Antonio Maceo* (Havana, 1962), p. 7.

   The publication of this and similar works since the Revolution of 1959 makes ridiculous the statement by Eldridge Cleaver in a 1976 interview that all he heard while he was in Cuba was that "José Martí was the brain and Antonio Maceo was the brawn" of the Cuban independence struggle. ("Eldridge Cleaver on Cuba, Interview by Skip Gates," *Yardbird Reader* 5 (1976): 208.)

1. Prologue

1. Some authorities accept 1845 and others 1848 as the year of Antonio Maceo's birth. After his death on December 7, 1896, the Cuban revolutionary journal, *Patria*, published in New York, accepted the date of Maceo's birth as June 13, 1848 on the ground that it was the date given by Maceo in the biographical files of the Cuban Army. (*La Patria*, December 15, 1896.) But the baptismal entry made by the priest of the Church of Santo Tomás Apóstol where Maceo was baptized on August 26, 1855 states that he was born on June 14, 1845. (A copy of the baptismal record, as certified by church officials, is in the Maceo Collection of Francisco de Paula Coronado, Central University, of Las Villas. Hereafter cited as Coronado Collection.) Gerardo Castellanos in his *Panorama histórico* (Havana, 1934), p. 10, selects the date of Maceo's birth as June 14, 1845, asserting that it "appears to be most exact."
2. William Robertson, *The Beginnings of Spanish-American Diplomacy* (New York, 1910), pp. 236–37.
3. Laurence R. Nichols, "The 'Bronze Titan,' The Mulatto Hero of Cuban Independence, Antonio Maceo," (Ph.D. diss., Duke University, 1954), p. 38. For a discussion of the reasons why Cuba remained faithful to Spain during the Wars for Independence, *see*

Philip S. Foner, *A History of Cuba and Its Relations with the United States*, vol.1 (New York, 1962), pp. 81–89.

4. José María Zamora y Coronado, *Biblioteca de legislación ultramarina*, vol. 3 (Madrid, 1845), pp. 126–27; Hubert H.S. Aimes, *History of Slavery in Cuba, 1511–1868* (New York, 1907), pp. 77–78. The treaty abolishing the slave trade to Cuba remained a dead letter; indeed, more slaves were imported into the island following the signing of the treaty than ever before. (Foner, *History of Cuba*, vol.1, pp. 172–78, 181–87.)
5. José Luciano Franco, *Antonio Maceo, apuntes para una historia de su vida*, vol. 1 (Havana, 1951), p. 11; Manuel Sanguilly y Garrite, "Antonio Maceo," in *Discursos y Conferencias* (Havana, 1919) 2: 197.

   The slave revolts of 1844 were actually a large-scale conspiracy in Matanzas on the part of free Negroes, slaves, and a handful of white Cubans. They organized a revolutionary uprising aimed at social betterment for free Negroes and liberation for the slaves. The goal was the establishment of a republic in which slavery would be abolished and Negroes would enjoy full equality with whites. Although the insurrection, known as *La Escalera*, was exposed in January 1894, and never got beyond the planning stage, 4,039 individuals were arrested—2,166 free blacks, 972 slaves, and 74 whites among them. About 300 were put to death, including the talented black poet Gabriel de la Concepción Valdés, known as "Plácido." (Foner, *History of Cuba*, vol. I, pp. 214–28.)
6. Franco, *Antonio Maceo*, vol. 1, pp. 23–27; Gonzalo Cabrales, *Epistolario de héroes* (Havana, 1922), p. 179; Rafael Marquina, *Antonio Maceo, heroe epónimo; estudio biográfico* (Havana, 1943), pp. 14–22.
7. Franco, *Antonio Maceo*, vol., p. 29. There is, as in the case of the date of his birth, considerable confusion as to the exact date of Maceo's marriage. The date cited in this study is based on information obtained by José Luciano Franco who has made a careful study of the available evidence.
8. The summary of Cuban history prior to the outbreak of the Ten Years' War is essentially a summary of material in my *History of Cuba and Its Relations with the United States*, vol. 1 (New York, 1962) and vol. 2 (New York, 1963). Other sources worth consult-

ing are Hugh Thomas, *Cuba: The Pursuit of Freedom* (New York, 1971), and especially Franklin Willis Knight, *Slave Society in Cuba During the Nineteenth Century* (Madison, Wis., 1970).

See also Franklin W. Knight, "Origins of Wealth and the Sugar Revolution in Cuba, 1750–1850," *Hispanic American Historical Review* 38 (May 1977): 231–53.

9. José Pérez Moris, *Historia de la insurrección de Lares* (Barcelona, 1972), pp. 212–13, 333.
10. Gerardo Castellanos, *Panorama histórico* (Havana, 1934), p. 22.
11. Emilio Bacardi y Moreau, ed., *Cronícas de Santiago de Cuba*, 7 vols. (Santiago de Cuba, 1908–1924) 3: 33–4; Manuel Sanguilly y Arizti, *Páginas de historia,* vol. 1 (Havana, 1929), pp. 10–12; Franco, *Antonio Maceo,* vol. 1, pp. 27–28, 33, 35–36; Ramiro Guerra y Sánchez, *La Guerra de Diez Años*, vol. 1 (Havana, 1950), pp. 50–54. *El Boletín de la Revolución, Cuba y Puerto Rico* (New York, no. 5, December 31, 1868).
12. *El Boletín de la Revolucion, Cuba y Puerto Rico* (New York), no. 5, December 31, 1868.

2. The Ten Years' War: Part 1

1. Philip S. Foner, *A History of Cuba and Its Relations with the United States*, vol. 2 (New York, 1963), p. 166.
2. Manuel Sanguilly y Arizti, *Páginas de historia*, vol. 1 (Havana, 1929), pp. 31–32; Gonzalo Cabrales, *Epistolario de héroes* (Havana, 1922), p. 179.
3. *Ibid.*
4. María Cabrales to Francisco de Paula Coronado, San José, May 6, 1897, Francisco de Paula Coronado Collection, Central University of Las Villas, Cuba. Hereafter cited as Coronado Collection.
5. Sanguilly, *Páginas*, vol. 1, p. 44.
6. *Ibid.*, p. 47; María Cabrales to Francisco de Paula Coronado, San José, May 6, 1897, Coronado Collection.
7. Quoted in Félix Lizaso, *José Martí: Martyr of Cuban Independence,* trans. by Esther E. Shuler (Albuquerque, New Mexico, 1953), p. 20.
8. During the first and second wars of independence, the Cuban

guerrilla fighters were commonly called *mambises*. The word originated in Santo Domingo. Juan Ethninius Mamby, a black Spanish officer, joined the Dominicans who were fighting for independence against Spain in 1846. The Spanish troops called the Dominican guerrilla fighters, "the men of Mamby." Then the word "mambies" was applied to all Dominicans fighting against Spain. When the Ten Years' War broke out in Cuba, Spanish soldiers were sent from Santo Domingo to help put down the revolution, and they called the Cuban revolutionary fighters *mambises*. The word was taken over by the Cuban revolutionists. ("Los Mambises," *Bohemia* (Havana), June 4, 1965, p. 102.)

9. *Facts About Cuba. Published under the Authority of the New York Cuban Junta* (New York, 1870), pp. 3–4.

   It is difficult to arrive at any exact estimate of the size of the Cuban army at any given time during the Ten Years' War. This is due to the widely different reports that appeared in various sources, and, while the Spanish authorities tended to minimize the size, the Cubans generally exaggerated it.
10. Máximo Gómez, *Diario de Campaña* (Havana, 1940), pp. 4–7, 11–12; Máximo Gómez to Andrés Moreno, February 6, 1897, in Emilio Roig de Leuchsenring, ed., *Ideario Cubano; Máximo Gómez* (Havana, 1936), pp. 68–72.
11. Gerardo Castellanos, *Panorama histórico* (Havana, 1934), p. 61.
12. Gómez, *Diario*, pp. 10–11, 85–87; James J. O'Kelly, *The Mambi-Land, or, Adventures of a Herald Correspondent in Cuba* (Philadelphia, 1874), pp. 87–102; Foner, *History of Cuba*, vol. 2, pp. 184–87.
13. Cabrales, *Epistolario*, p. 179; Emilio Bacardi y Moreau, ed., *Cronícas de Santiago de Cuba*, 7 vols. (Barcelona, Spain, 1908–1924), 3:53.
14. Juan Bautista Rondón, Maceo's first commander, deserted to the Spaniards and was succeeded by Juan Monzón, a native of the Canary Islands. He was executed by the rebel forces because of his cruelty and barbarity in the successful assault on Mayarí. Maceo then came under the command of General Donato Mármol.
15. Fernando Figueredo Socarrás, *La revolución de Yara* (Havana, 1902), pp. 31–33.
16. *Ibid.*, pp. 33–35.
17. *Ibid.*, p. 40.

18. José Luciano Franco, *Antonio Maceo, apuntes para una historia de su vida*, vol. 1 (Havana, 1951), p. 47.
19. *Ibid.*, p. 50.
20. Máximo Gómez to the Secretary of War, General Headquarters, Nov. 7, 1870, original in Archivo Nacional, Havana. Hereafter cited as AN.
21. Sanguilly, *Páginas*, vol. 1, pp. 73–74
22. Franco, *Antonio Maceo*, vol. 1, pp. 50–51; Laurence R. Nichols, "The 'Bronze Titan,' The Mulatto Hero of Cuban Independence, Antonio Maceo," (Ph.D. diss., Duke University, 1954), pp. 80–81.
23. Quoted in Franco, *Ibid.*, p. 52.
24. Cabrales, *Epistolario*, p. 180.
25. María Cabrales to Francisco de Paula Coronado, San Jose, May 6, 1897, Coronado Collection.
26. Leonardo Griñán Peralta, *Antonio Maceo; Análisis characteriológico* (Havana, 1936), p. 34; Sanguilly, *Páginas*, vol. 7, pp. 51–53.
27. Franco, *Antonio Maceo.*, vol. 1, pp. 51–52; Nichols, "The 'Bronze Titan'," pp. 80–81.
28. Enrique de la Osa, "Una interpretación materialista de la guerra de los diez años,. "*Bohemia*, October 8, 1961, pp. 54–57; Raúl Cepero y Bonilla, *Azúcar y abolición; apuntes para una historia critica de abolicionismo* (Havana, 1948), p. 107; *El Boletín de la Revolucion. Cuba y Puerto Rico*, December 10, 16, 31, 1868.
29. Cepero, *Azúcar y abolición*, p. 124.
30. Eugenio Alaiso y Saturjo, *Apuntes sobre los projectos de la abolición de la esclavitud en las islas de Cuba y Puerto Rico* (Madrid, 1874), pp. 44–46; Cepero, *Azúcar y Abolición*, p. 109.
31. Alaiso y Saturjo, *Apuntes sobre los projects*, pp. 48–50; Willis Fletcher Johnson, *The History of Cuba*, vol. 3 (New York, 1920), pp. 158–60; Cepero, *Azúcar y abolición*, p. 111.
32. Translation of decree attached to Hall to Washburne, Consular Despatches, National Archives, Washington, D.C. Hereafter cited as NA.
33. *Constitution of the Republic of Cuba, April 10, 1869, at Guaimaro, Provisional Capital of Republic,* New York City, Nov. 17, 1869.
34. Johnson, vol. 3, *History*, pp. 163–64.
35. *La Revolución* (New York), May 29, 1869; José Morales Lemus to

Hamilton Fish, Aug. 18, 1869, Hamilton Fish Papers, Library of Congress, Washington, D.C.

36. Antonio Pirala, *Anales de la guerra de Cuba,* vol. 2 (Madrid, 1896), p. 52; Cepero, *Azúcar y abolición* pp. 117-18.
37. Antonio Zambrana, *La República de Cuba* (Havana, 1922), pp. 50–52; Plumb to Davis, Aug. 31, 1869, Consular Reports, NA.
38. Pirala, *Anales*, vol. 1, p. 642; Cepero, *Azúcar y abolición*, pp. 129–30.
39. Gómez, *Diario*, pp. 12–15; Franco, *Antonio Maceo*, vol. 1, p. 53.

3. *The Ten Years' War: Part 2*

1. Máximo Gómez, *Diario de campaña* (Havana, 1940), p. 11–22.
2. Máximo Gómez to the Secretary of War, General Headquarters, November 7, 1870, Archivo Nacional, Havana, caja 116, no. 12, 347. Hereafter cited AN.
3. Gómez, *Diario*, pp. 18–19.
4. Máximo Gómez to the Secretary of War, General Headquarters, November 7, 1870, AN, caja 116, no. 12, 347.
5. Fernando Figueredo Socarrás, *La revolución de Yara* (Havana, 1902), p. 83.
6. Enrique Ubieta, *Eféme rides de la revolución cubana*, vol. 1 (Havana, 1910), p. 123.
7. Emilio Bacardi y Moreau, ed., *Cronicas de Santiago de Cuba*, 7 vols. (1908–1924), 3:103.
8. Gómez, *Diario*, pp. 25–26.
9. Bacardi, *Santiago de Cuba*, 3:135.
10. Gómez, *Diario*, p. 26.
11. *Ibid.,* p. 487. *See also* José Antonio Franco, *Antonio Maceo, apuntes para una historia de su vida*, vol. 1 (Havana, 1951), pp. 60–61.
12. *U.S. Statistical Abstract*, 1878, p. 55.
13. Gómez, *Diario*, p. 26; Raúl Cepero y Bonilla, *Azúcar y abolición: Apuntes para una historia de abolicionismo* (Havana, 1948), p. 179.
14. Philip S. Foner, *Abraham Lincoln: Selections from His Writings* (New York, 1944), pp. 20–21.

15. Benjamin F. Butler (1818–1893), antislavery politician and Union general. After the Civil War, he was an antimonopoly and prolabor political leader.
16. Juan Arnao, *Páginas para la historia de la isla de Cuba* (Havana, 1900), p. 226; Cepero, *Azúcar y abolición*, p. 127.
17. Gómez, *Diario*, p. 26.
18. Antonio Pirala, *Anales de la guerra de Cuba*, vol. 3 (Madrid, 1896), p. 932, Cepero, *Azúcar y abolición*, p. 179.
19. Gómez, *Diario*, p. 504.
20. Gonzalo Cabrales, *Epistolario de héroes* (Havana, 1922), p. 181.
21. The original letter, Céspedes to Colonel Antonio Maceo, April 16, 1872, is in the Archivo Nacional, and reprinted in part in Franco, *Antonio Maceo*, vol. 1, p. 64.
22. Figueredo, *La revolución*, pp. 113–15.
23. Gómez, *Diario*, pp. 30–31.
24. *Ibid.*, p. 31; Franco, *Antonio Maceo*, vol. 1, pp. 65–66.
25. Figueredo, *La revolución*, pp. 20–22; Franco, *Antonio Maceo*, vol. 1, p. 167.

    Years later in a dispute with his old commander, Maceo reminded Gómez of his loyalty on this occasion. (Antonio Maceo to Máximo Gómez, Kingston, August 31, 1886, in Cabrales, *Epistolario*, pp.100–5.)
26. Figueredo, *La revolución*, pp. 120–22.
27. Quoted in Franco, *Antonio Maceo* vol., pp. 66–67.
28. Antonio Maceo to the Secretary of War, General Headquarters, August 27, 1872 (including reports of August 18 and 21), Coronado Collection; Antonio Maceo to Calixto García, Baraguá, November 11, 1872, and December 6, 1872, in *La Independencia* (New York), March 1, 1873, p. 1; "Documentos históricos," *Revista Cubana* 7 (Havana, 1902): 539–40; Figueredo, *La revolución*, pp. 118–19.
29. Pirala, *Anales*, vol. 1, p. 203.
30. Laurence R. Nichols, "The 'Bronze Titan,' The Mulatto Hero of Cuban Independence, Antonio Maceo," (Ph.D. diss., Duke University, 1954), p. 99.
31. Philip S. Foner, *A History of Cuba and Its Relations with the United States*, vol. 2 (New York, 1963), pp. 232–33.
32. Gómez, *Diario*, pp. 47–48.

33. For a discussion of the Virginius incident, *see* Foner, *History of Cuba*, vol. 2, pp. 244–47.
34. Figueredo, *La revolución*, pp. 130–31.
35. Cabrales, *Epistolario*, p. 181.
36. Figueredo, *La revolución*, p. 134; Franco, *Antonio Maceo*, vol. 1, pp. 77–78.
37. Gómez, *Diario*, pp. 54–55; Franco, *Antonio Maceo*, vol. 1, pp. 79–80.
38. Foner, *History of Cuba*, vol. 2, p. 234.
39. *Ibid.*, pp. 234–35.
40. Manuel Sanguilly y Arizti, *Páginas de la historia*, vol. 1 (Havana, 1929), p. 128; Franco, *Antonio Maceo*, vol. 1, pp. 81–82.
41. Sanguilly, *Páginas*, vol. 1, pp. 140–42; Gómez, *Diario*, pp. 56–57.
42. Ramón Roa, *Con la pluma y el machete*, vol. 1 (Havana, 1950), p. 266.
43. Publicaciones del Archivo National de Cuba, *Antonio Maceo, documentos para su vida* (Havana, 1945), pp. 1–17.
44. Gómez, *Diario*, p. 58; Franco, *Antonio Maceo*, vol. 1, p. 86.
45. Franco, *Antonio Maceo*, vol. 1, p. 87; Cepero, *Azúcar y abolición*, pp. 159–60; Ignacio Mora, *Diario durante la guerra de los diez años* (Havana, 1910), pp. 198–99.
46. It was also not unusual for troops of one region to refuse to fight outside their area, a tendency which weakened the Liberating Army.
47. Franco, *Antonio Maceo*, vol. 1, pp. 87–88.
48. Emilio Roig de Leuchsenring, *Máximo Gómez, el libertador de Cuba y el primer Ciudadano de la República* (Havana, 1959), pp. 20–21.
49. Cepero, *Azúcar y abolición*, pp. 127–28; Don José Ferrer de Couto, *Cuba May Become Independent* (New York, 1872), pp. 47–50.

4. The Ten Years' War: Part 3

1. Enrique Collazo, *Desde Yara hasta el Zanjoń* (Havana, 1893), p. 213.

2. A *trocha* is a ditch with an embankment on one side and entanglements of wire projecting over the edge to prevent the passage of an army. A large area in front of the ditch is cleared away, and fortresses and watch towers constructed at intervals of about a mile.
3. Máximo Gómez, *Diario de compaña* (Havana, 1940), p. 70.

   In carrying out this campaign, Gómez was fulfilling his main purpose in joining the Cuban revolutionary struggle. In August 1896, in the midst of the Second War for Independence, Gómez told Fermín Valdés Domínguez that the exploitation of the black slaves had moved him to join the Cuban Liberating Army, hoping thereby to end these "shameful and intolerable injustices." (Antonio Pirala, *Anales de la guerra de Cuba*, vol. 3 (Madrid, 1896), p. 218; Emilio Roig de Leuchsenring, *Máximo Gómez* (Havana, 1936), p. 20.)
4. Collazo, *Desde Yara*, p. 213; José Luciano Franco, *Antonio Maceo, apuntes para una historia de su vida*, vol. 1 (Havana, 1951), pp. 90–91.
5. Collazo, *Desde Yara*, p. 213.
6. Philip S. Foner, *History of Cuba and Its Relations with the United States*, vol. 2 (New York, 1963), pp. 254–55.
7. Antonio Maceo to Gaspar Betancourt Cisneros, June 29, 1875, Pirala, *Anales*, vol. 3, p. 245.
8. Fernando Figuereda Socarrás, *La revolución de Yara* (Havana, 1902), pp. 152–54.
9. Gómez, *Diario*, p. 96.
10. Jorge Gaspar, "Influencia del Tabaquero en la trajectoria revolucionaria de Cuba," *Revista Bimestre Cubana* 39, (January-February 1937): 105–6.
11. Raúl Cepero y Bonilla, *Azúcar y abolición: Apuntes para una historia critica de abolicionismo* (Havana, 1948), pp. 133–35.
12. Allan Nevins, *Hamilton Fish: The Inner History of the Grant Administration* (New York, 1957), pp. 180–81.

    For the details of the Grant Administration's role in the Cuban war against Spain and the special influence on the part of Spain exerted by Hamilton Fish, *see* Foner, *History of Cuba*, vol. 2, pp. 198–223, 240–52.
13. José A. Lemus to Fish, Aug. 1869, Hamilton Fish Papers, Library

of Congress, Washington, D.C.; Gabriel Rodríguez, *La España del siglo XIX*, vol. 3 (Madrid, 1883), pp. 283–85.

14. Hamilton Fish Diary, Oct. 29, Nov. 5, 1875, Library of Congress, Washington, D.C.; Fish to Cushing, Nov. 5, 1875, Jan. 15, 1876, Hamilton Fish Papers, Library of Congress, Washington, D.C.; "Report of Senate Committee on Foreign Relations Relative to Affairs in Cuba," *Report 885*, 55 Cong., 2nd Sess., pp. 44–52, 160–62.
15. Franco, *Antonio Maceo*, vol. 1, pp. 107, 117.
16. Emilio Roig de Leuchsenring, *Revolución y república en Maceo* (Havana, 1932), pp. 31–32.
17. Maceo to the President of the Republic, Baraguá, May 16, 1876, Biblioteca de la Sociedad Económica de Amigos del País, *Documentos manuscritos de interes*, vol. 1 (Havana, 1885), p. 44.
18. Antonio Maceo to Félix Figueredo, Baraguá, May 18, 1876, "Documentos históricos," *Revista Cubana* 3 (1888): 533–34.
19. Aguas Verdes, *Antonio Maceo, ideología política* (Havana, 1922), pp. 85–86.
20. Pirala, *Anales*, vol. 1, p. 271.
21. Ramón Roa, *Con la pluma y la machete*, vol. 1 (Havana, 1950), p. 281.
22. Figueredo, *La revolución*, p. 271.
23. Antonio Maceo to Vicente García, San Agustin, July 5, 1877, Coronado Collection, yr. 1877, José Antonio Portuondo, ed., *El pensamiento vivo de Maceo* (Havana, 1962), pp. 20–21.
24. Quoted in Franco, *Antonio Maceo*, vol. 1, p. 117.
25. Gómez, *Diario*, pp. 102–03.
26. T. Ochando, *Martínez Campos en Cuba* (Madrid, 1878), pp. 37–52.
27. Figueredo, *La revolución*, pp. 184–85.
28. Hamilton Fish to Daniel E. Sickles, April 26, 1872; Hamilton Fish Diary, Oct. 24, 1872, both in Library of Congress, Washington, D.C.

    United States government policy toward Cuba was not changed by Fish's resignation as Secretary of State. This policy was summed up in a brief but accurate statement by the Cuban League of the United States issued in August 1877: "Until now, it appears that the Administration at Washington has had for its object a continuation of Spanish dominion in Cuba." (*The Present Condition of Affairs in Cuba. A Report of a Special Committee of the Cuban League of the United States. . . . , August 23, 1877* (New York, 1877), p. 11.)

29. Ramón Domingo de Ibarra, *Memorias revolucionarias* (Madrid, 1880), p. 232.
30. Figueredo, *La revolución*, p. 182; Gómez, *Diario*, p. 123.
31. Gómez, *Diario*, p. 125.
32. Tomás Estrada Palma to Calixto García, Iniguz, Cádiz, December 21, 1877, Guerra de 1868, AN, caja 115, no. 10, 523.

    Estrada Palma was now a prisoner so that even the revolutionaries in prison camps had heard of Maceo's fabulous exploits after he was so severely wounded.
33. Franco, *Antonio Maceo*, vol. 1, pp. 123–25.
34. General Rafael Rodríguez to Félix Figueredo, New York, February 21, 1878, Guerra de 1868, AN, caja 114, no. 5, 232.
35. Gómez, *Diario*, p. 125; Willis Fletcher Johnson, *The History of Cuba*, vol. 3 (New York, 1920), p. 299.

5. The Protest of Baraguá

1. Jorge Ibarra, *Ideología mambisa* (Havana, 1967), p. 57; Raúl Cepero y Bonilla, *Azúcar y abolición: Apuntas para una historia critica de abolicionismo* (Havana, 1948), pp. 221–22.
2. Máximo Gómez, *Diario de campaña* (Havana, 1940), p. 125.
3. Willis Fletcher Johnson, *The History of Cuba*, vol. 3 (New York, 1920), pp. 299–300; José Luciano Franco, *Antonio Maceo, apuntes para una historia de su vida*, vol. 1 (Havana, 1951), pp. 140–41; Gómez, *Diario*, pp. 136–37.
4. *Annual Register*, 1878, p. 372.
5. Enrigue Collazo, *Cuba heroica* (Havana, 1912), p. 137; Cepero, *Azúcar y abolición*, p. 181.
6. Franco, *Antonio Maceo*, vol. 1, p. 140.
7. Antonio Maceo to Bargés, La Llanada, February 6, 1878, Antonio Pirala, *Anales de la guerra de Cuba*, vol. 3 (Madrid, 1896), p. 574.
8. Fernando Figueredo Socarrás, *La revolución de Yara* (Havana, 1902), pp. 172–74.

9. *Ibid.*, pp. 175–76.
10. Franco, *Antonio Maceo*, vol. 1, p. 138; Figueredo, *La revolución*, p. 180.
11. Gómez, *Diario*, pp. 136–37; Franco, *Antonio Maceo*, vol. 1, p. 141.
12. Maceo indicated to Gómez that he was interested in holding an interview with Martínez Campos, and Gómez commented that he understood that Maceo wanted to secure a truce in order to reorganize for a continued fight. He added that Maceo should try to secure a long truce since "with time and place many things could be done." (Gómez, *Diario*, pp. 136–37.)
13. Maceo to Barges, February 21, 1878, Pirala, *Anales*, vol. 3, p. 615.
14. Martínez Campos to Maceo, Puerto Principe, February 24, 1878, Coronado Collection; Figueredo, *La revolución*, pp. 191–93; Franco, *Antonio Maceo*, vol. 1, pp. 144–45. My emphasis, P.S.F.
15. Figueredo, *La revolución*, p. 185.
16. Maceo to Colonel Fernando Guevera, Baguanos, February 27, 1878, "Antonio Maceo," *Revista de historia cubana y americana* 7 (1916): 91–92.
17. Maceo to Flor Crombet, Baraguá, March 4, 1878, Biblioteca Cuba, *Antonio Maceo, de la campaña* (Havana, 1916), p. 12; José Lacret to Maceo, Cristo, April 28, 1878, Coronado Collection.
18. Pirala, *Anales*, vol. 2, pp. 39–40.
19. Figueredo, *La revolución*, pp. 192–93; Franco, *Antonio Maceo*, vol. 1, pp. 150–51.
20. Franco, *Antonio Maceo*, vol. 1, pp. 146, 150, 154–58; Figueredo, *La revolución*, pp. 196–200.
21. José Antonio Portuondo, ed., *El Pensamiento vivo de Antonio Maceo* (Havana, 1962), p. 24; Emilio Bacardi y Moreau, ed., *Crónicas de Santiago de Cuba*, 7 vols. (Barcelona, 1908–1924), 6:109–10.

    Donna Marie Wolf points out that the "reference to a union with thc Republics of Santo Domingo and Haiti must certainly have alarmed the white Cubans." She adds: "However, there is no evidence of any such plot. There was a brief theoretical plan to unite the islands formulated by several intellectuals and revolutionaries in Santo Domingo known as the Confederation of the Antilles." ("The Caribbean People of Color and the Cuban Independence Movement," (Ph.D. diss., University of Pittsburgh, 1973), p. 96*n*.)

22. Juan Arnao, *Páginas para la Historia de la isla de Cuba* (Havana, 1900), p. 247; Franco, *Antonio Maceo*, vol. 1, p. 163.
23. *La Verdad*, April 6, May 4, 1878; Franco, *Antonia Maceo*, vol. 1, p. 161–62; House of Commons, April 15, 1878, *Hansard*, third series, vol. 234, p. 426.
24. Franco, *Antonio Maceo*, vol. 1, pp. 159, 166–67.
25. Figueredo, *La revolución*, pp. 209–10; Franco, *Antonio Maceo*, vol. 1, pp. 164–65; Academia de la historia de Cuba, *Papeles de Maceo*, vol. 2 (Havana, 1948), p. 338.
26. Franco, *Antonio Maceo*, vol. 1, pp. 166–67; Figueredo, *La revolución*, p. 258.
27. Franco, *Antonio Maceo*, vol. 1, pp. 172–74; Figueredo, *La revolución*, p. 263.
28. Henry C. Hall to F.W. Seward, May 11, 1878, State Department Consular Despatches. NA.

6. *The Little War*

1. Gonzalo Cabrales, *Epistolario de héroes* (Havana, 1922), p. 183.
2. Reprinted in José Luciano Franco, *Antonio Maceo: apuntes para una historia de su vida*, vol. 1 (Havana, 1951), p. 178.

   For a discussion of Reverend Henry Highland Garnet, *see* Philip S. Foner, *The Voice of Black America: Major Speeches by Negroes in the United States 1797–1971* (New York, 1972), pp. 2, 77, 81–90, 154, 272, 307–16, 330, 380–84. José Martí's sketch of Reverend Garnet may be found in Philip S. Foner, ed., *Inside the Monster: Writings on the United States and American Imperialism*, trans. Eleanor Randall (New York, 1975), pp. 67–70.
3. "Entrevista a Maceo en 1879," *Revista de la universidad central de Las Villas* (Santa Clara, Cuba) 6, no. 1 (July-December 1963): 38–43.
4. Frank J. Webb, "General Antonio Maceo," *AME Church Review*, 14 (1897–1898): 113–14.

This is the third and final article in a three-part tribute to Maceo.

5. In reply to my inquiry, Alan C. Aimone, Military History Librarian, United States Military Academy Library at West Point, wrote on January 31, 1977: "An examination of our records failed to turn up any information concerning the employment of or even the possibility that Antonio Maceo was at the U.S. Military Academy during the period 1878–1880. This, however, does not mean that he could not have been here, since he may at the time have gone under a different name. The manuscript librarian checked circulation records and found nothing. If Maceo was a civilian it would have been possible to examine books in the library without charging them out."
6. Maceo to the President of the Provisional Government of Cuba, New York, June 5, 1878, Coronado Collection, yr. 1878.
7. Luis Estévez y Romero, *Desde el Zanjón hasta Baire* (Havana, 1899), pp. 13, 31, 41; F.A. Conte, *La lucha política en Cuba* (Havana, 1899), pp. 36–45.
8. Enrique Trujillo, *Apuntes históricos* (New York, 1896), p. 5.
9. *Ibid.*, pp. 5–10; Franco, *Antonio Maceo*, vol. 1, pp. 184–85.
10. Eusebio Hernández, "El Periodo Revolucionario de 1879 a 1895," *Revista de la facultad de letras y ciencias* 19 (July 1914): 6–8.
11. Franco, *Antonio Maceo*, vol. 1, pp. 187–89.
12. *Ibid.*, p. 208; Raúl Cepero y Bonilla, *Azúcar y Abolición: apuntas para una historia critica de abolicionismo.* (Havana, 1948), pp.192–93.
13. Octavio Bavastro to Calixto García, December 19, 1878, Guerra de 1878, Archivo National, caja 114, no. 10, 259; Calixto García to Maceo, New York, June 11, 1879, Coronado Collection, yr. 1879. Hereafter cited as AN. José Luciano Franco, *Ruta de Antonio Maceo en el Caribe* (Havana, 1961), pp. 26–28.
14. Laurence R. Nichols, "The 'Bronze Titan,' The Mulatto Hero of Cuban Independence, Antonio Maceo" (Ph.D. diss., Duke University, 1954), pp. 181–82.
15. García to the Revolutionary Committee of New York, August 5, 1879, Guerra de 1879, AN, caja 114, numero 10, 331.
16. Maceo to Arcadio Leyte Vidal, Kingston, August 16, 1879, in

Aguas Verdes, *Antonio Maceo, ideología política* (Havana, 1922), pp. 130–31.

17. Herminio C. Leyva y Aguilera, *El movimento insurreccional de 1879* (Havana, 1893), pp. 22–39.
18. Antonio Maceo, Proclamation, to the People of Cuba, Kingston, September 5, 1879, in *La Independencia* (New York), October 18, 1879.
19. Calixto García Iñíquez, *Mi diario* (Havana, 1928), p. 210.
20. Maceo to General José Lamothe, Port-au-Prince, September 23, 1879; Maceo to José Álvarez, October 2, 1879, Coronado Collection, yr. 1879.
21. Quoted in Franco, *Antonio Maceo*, vol. 1, p. 211.
22. Academia de la historia de Cuba, *Papeles de Maceo*, vol. 1 (Havana, 1948), pp. 15–16. The letter is dated September 23. 1879.

    For a general discussion of the views of the Haitian people towards the independence movement in Cuba and other parts of the Americas, *see* Laurore St. Juste, "Lutte de la République d'Haiti pour l'émancipation des peuples de l'Amérique," (M.A. thesis, University of Ottawa, 1954).
23. *See* Maneul Codina to Maceo, Port-au-Prince, October 15, 1879, Coronado Collection, yr. 1879.
24. Maceo to Máximo Gómez, Grand Turk, February 6, 1880, Coronado Collection, yr. 1880.
25. *Ibid.*
26. Codina to Maceo, Port-au-Prince, February 4, 1880, Coronado Collection, yr. 1880.
27. Maceo to Máximo Gómez, Grand Turk, February 6, 1880, Coronado Collection, yr. 1880.

    The Spanish consul in Haiti insisted that Maceo invented the stories concerning the assassination attempts as a means of arousing the people and weakening the government of Salomón. He insisted, moreover, that the charge that he was involved in a plot to kill Maceo was the "grossest calumny." The United States consul in Port-au-Prince also reported that "there were Haitians connected with this movement inimical to the Salomón government, who hoped thereby to involve that government in misunderstandings and differences with the Spanish, and thus the more easily succeed in the attempts which they were proposing to make for its overthrow." (Donna Marie Wolf, "The Caribbean People of Color and the Cuban Independence Movement," (PH.D. diss., University of Pittsburgh, 1973), pp. 342–44; Department of State, Consular Dispatches, No. 215, Port-au-Prince, December 31, 1879, AN. What makes this dispatch especially interesting is that it was by J.M. Langston, a leading black militant in the United States.)

However one interprets the incident, one thing is clear: it served to intensify the split between the government and the Cuban immigrants. In a decree published in *Le Moniteur* of Port-au-Prince of January 10, 1880, all Cubans were ordered to leave the country. (Jose Luciano Franco, *Ruta de Antonio Maceo en el Caribe*, Havana, 1961, p. 41.)

28. Jean Price-Mars, *La contribution haitienne à la lutte des Amériques pour les libertés humaines* (Port-au-Prince, Haiti, 1942), p. 42.
29. Emilio Rodríguez Demorizi, *Maceo en Santo Domingo* (Santiago, Dominican Republic, 1945), pp. 45–50.
30. *See* Maceo's letter in St. Thomas *Tidende*, January 24, 1880, quoted in *ibid.*, p. 50.
31. Evaristo Rodríguez to the Cuban Revolutionary Committee of New York, Puerto Plata, February 8, 1880, Correspondencia del Comité Revolucionario de Nueva York, Guerra de 1879, AN, caja 110, no. 2, 405.
32. Fernando Figueredo to Maceo, Puerto Plata, February 7, 1880; M.E. Chamberlain to Maceo, Puerto Plata, February 9, 1880, Coronado Collection, yr. 1880.
33. Rodríguez Demorizi, *Santo Domingo*, pp. 97–111.
34. *Ibid.*, p. 105.
35. *Ibid.*, p. 101.
36. *Ibid.*, pp. 99–100.
37. Wolf, "Caribbean People of Color," pp. 240–48.
38. Sociedad cubana de estudios historicos y internacionales, *Antonio Maceo, Ideología política, cartas y otros documentos*, vol. 2 (Havana, 1950), p. 195.
39. *Ibid.*, pp. 200–01.

40. Trujillo, *Apuntas*, pp. 28–40; Esteban García to Maceo, Port-au-Prince, October 7, 1880, Coronado Collection, yr. 1880; Nichols, "The 'Bronze Titan,' " pp. 199–202.
41. Rodríguez Demorizi, *Santo Domingo*, pp. 116–19; A. Audigno to Maceo, Cabo Haitiano, August, 1880, Coronado Collection, yr. 1880.
42. Maceo to Francisco Lamadriz, Turks Island, July 4, 1880; Maceo to Anthony Nusgrave, Governer of the Bahama Islands, Grand Turk, August 30, 1880; General Ulisses Heureaux to Maceo, Santo Domingo, August 2, 1880, Coronado Collection, yr. 1880; Sociedad cubana de estudios historicos y internacionales, *Antonio Maceo*, vol. 2, p. 182; Rodríguez Demorizi, *Santo Domingo*, pp. 121–22; Franco, *Antonio Maceo*, vol. 1, pp. 238–40.
43. Juan Bellido Luna to Maceo, New York, August 24, 1880, Coronado Collection, yr. 1880.
44. Juan Bellido de Luna to Maceo, New York, September 28, 1880, Coronado Collection, yr. 1880; Franco, *Antonio Maceo*, vol. 1, p. 240; Philip S. Foner, *A History of Cuba and Its Relations with the United States*, vol. 2 (New York, 1963), p. 287.
45. Maceo to Bellido de Luna, September 12, 1880, Coronado Collection, yr. 1880.

7. *Interlude*

1. Laurence R. Nichols, "The 'Bronze Titan,' The Mulatto Hero of Cuban Independence, Antonio Maceo," (Ph.D. diss., Duke University, 1954), p. 194.
2. Emilo Rodríguez Demorizi, *Maceo en Santo Domingo* (Santiago, Santa Domingo, 1945), p. 81.
3. José Luciano Franco, *Antonio Maceo, apuntes para una historia de su vida,* vol. 1 (Havana, 1951), pp. 217–18; Maceo to José F. Pérez, Puerto Cortés, October 9, 1882, "Maceo" *Revista de historia cubana y americana* 1 (1916): 92; Maceo to "Amigo Timoteo," Kingston, April 1881, Coronado Collection, yr. 1881.
4. Franco, *Antonio Maceo*, vol. 1, p. 246.

5. Eusebio Hernández to Maceo, Kingston, September 16, 1881, Coronado Collection, yr. 1881.
6. Maceo to José Dolores Poyo, Director of *El Yara* of Key West, June 1, 1881, published in *El Yara*, Key West, June 16, 1881.
7. Gómez to Maceo, San Pedro Sula (Honduras), July 23, 1881. Coronado Collection, yr. 1881.
8. Quoted in Franco, *Antonio Maceo* vol. 1, p. 247.
9. *Ibid.*, pp. 249–55.
10. Ramón Rosa was an outstanding intellectual. He and his fellow student, Marco Aurelio Soto, were greatly influenced by Justo Rufino Barrios who came to power in Guatemala in 1873 and instituted many liberal reforms, following the example of Benito Juárez in Mexico. In 1876, Soto became president and, with the assistance of Rosa as Minister General, carried out Liberal ecclesiastical and educational reforms.
11. Franco, *Antonio Maceo*, pp. 254–55.
12. Maceo to José F. Pérez, Puerto Cortés, October 9, 1882, "Maceo," *Revista de historia cubana y americana*, 1 (1916), 92.
13. Gómez to Maceo, San Pedro Sala, February 23 and March 25, 1883, Coronado Collection, yr. 1883.
14. Maceo to General Luis Bográn, Puerto Cortés, April 21, November 2, 11, 28, 1883, Coronado Collection, yr. 1883.
15. Maceo to Director of *El Yara*, San Pedro, June 13, 1884, Sociedad Cubana, *Antonio Maceo*, vol. 1, pp. 242–43.
16. Maceo to Anselmo Valdés, San Pedro, July 6, 1884, Coronado Collection, yr. 1884.

8. Revolutionary Activity, 1883–1887

1. *See* Jorge Mañach, *Martí: Apostle of Freedom*, trans. Coley Taylor (New York, 1950), and Félix Lizaso, *José Martí: Martyr of Cuban Independence*, trans. Esther E. Shuler (Albuquerque, New Mexico, 1953).
2. As a child, Martí had seen acts of such inhumanity committed against slaves that he could never forget them. In manhood he

wrote: "What man who has seen a Negro whipped does not ever consider himself his debtor? I saw it. I saw it when I was a child, and my cheeks still burn with shame." (José Martí, *Fragmentos: Obras Completas de Martí,* ed. Gonzalo de Quesada y Miranda (Havana, 1949), p. 34.)

3. José Martí, *Obras Completas,* vol. 1 (Havana, 1946), pp. 672–97. Fernándo Ortiz, *Martí y las razas* (Havana, 1950), pp. 13, 24–29, 63.
4. José Martí to Maceo, New York, July 20, 1882, Coronado Collection, yr. 1882.
5. Maceo to Martí, Puerto Cortés, July 29, 1882, Coronado Collection, yr. 1882.
6. Maceo to Ramón Leocadio Bonachea, Puerto Cortés, October 1883, Coronado Collection, yr. 1883.
7. Angel Maestre to Maceo, Vera Cruz, October 17, 1883, Coronado Collection, yr. 1883.
8. J. Luis Péñez to Maceo, New York, October 22, 1883, Coronado Collection, yr. 1883.
9. Maceo to Ramón Leocadio Bonachea, Puerto Cortés, October 1883, Coronado Collection, yr. 1883.
10. Maceo to Fernando Figueredo, Puerto Cortés, December 16, 1883, Coronado Collection, yr. 1883.
11. Gómez to Maceo, San Pedro, April 3, 1884, Coronado Collection, yr. 1884.
12. Maceo to Dr. Moreno, Tegucigalpa, May 2, 1884, Coronado Collection, yr. 1884.
13. Maceo to Bográn, San Pedro, July 20, 1884, Coronado Collection, yr. 1884.
14. Maceo to Antonio Pino and Figueredo Socarrás, Puerto Cortés, July 1, 1884; Maceo to Anselmo Valdés, San Pedro, July 6, 1884, Coronado Collection.
15. Máximo Gómez, *Diario de campaña* (Havana, 1940), p. 179.
16. José Luciano Franco, *Antonio Maceo, apuntas para una historia de su vida,* vol. 1 (Havana, 1951), p. 294.
17. Gómez, *Diario,* p. 183.
18. *Ibid.,* p. 179; J. Maynes to Maceo, Kingston, September 29, 1884, Coronado Collection, yr. 1884.
19. Gómez, *Diario,* pp. 180–83.

20. *Ibid.*, p. 185.
21. *Ibid.*, p. 187.

Some of Maceo's disappointments in New York were offset by a reunion with his brother José who had managed to escape after Rafael's death, and make his way to New York.

22. Franco, *Antonio Maceo*, vol. 1, pp. 303–04.
23. Martí to Gómez, October 20, 1884, original in Archivo Nacional; reprinted in Franco, *Antonio Maceo*, vol. 1, pp. 302–03. *See also* Eusebio Hernández, *Dos Conferencias* (Havana, n.d.), pp. 70–71.
24. Gómez. *Diario*, p. 183.
25. Mañach, *Martí*, pp. 231–32.
26. Maceo to Gómez, Vera Cruz, November 13, 1884; Maceo to Gómez, Mexico, December 24, 1884; Gómez to Maceo, New Orleans, November 26, 1884, Archivo Máximo Gómez, yr. 1884, AN; Gonzalo Cabrales *Epistolario de héroes* (Havana, 1922), p. 93; Coronado Collection, yr. 1884; Gómez, *Diario*, p. 187.
27. Maceo to Rodolfo Méndez and Carlos Varona, Vera Cruz, April, 1885; Maceo to Pedro Martínez Freire, Vera Cruz, April 14, 1885, Coronado Collection, yr. 1885.
28. Gómez, *Diario*, pp. 189–95; Trujillo, *Apuntes históricos*, pp. 16–17.
29. Hernández, *Conferencias*, p. 88.
30. Maceo to Gómez, New York, October 13, 1885, Archivo Máximo Gómez, yr. 1885, AN.
31. Hernández, *Conferencias*, pp. 96–97.
32. *Ibid.*, p. 98.
33. Maceo to Fernando López de Queralta, Kingston, January 4, 1886, Coronado Collection, yr. 1886; Enrique Trujillo, *Apuntes históricos* (New York, 1896), pp. 17–18.
34. Antonio Maceo, Proclamation To My Comrades and Conquerors of Oriente," n.d., Coronado Collection, yr. 1886.
35. Gómez to Maceo, Santo Domingo, December 23, 1885, Coronado Collection, yr. 1885.
36. Maceo to Gómez, Kingston, January 13, 1886, Sociedad cubana de estudios historicos y internacionales, *Antonio Maceo, ideología política, cartes y otros documentos* (Havana, 1950), pp. 288–89.
37. Maceo to Gómez, Kingston, January 16, 1886, in Cabrales, *Epistolario*, p. 94.

38. Maceo to Ernesto Bavastro, Colón, January 29, 1886, Sociedad cubana, *Antonio Maceo*, p. 290.
39. Maceo to Gómez, Colón, April 10, 1886; Maceo to Crombet, Colón, May 15, 1886; Maceo to the Emigrants of Key West, Kingston, June 17, 1886, Coronado Collection, yr. 1886; Gómez, *Diario*, vol. 1 pp. 210–15.
40. Maceo to General Francisco Borrero, Kingston, July 15, 1886, in Cabrales, *Epistolario*, pp. 163–64; Gómez, *Diario*, pp. 217–19.
41. Hernández, *Conferencias*, pp. 121–24; Maceo to Ernesto Barastro, Kingston, August 18, 1886, in Leonardo Gríñan Peralta, *La muerta de Antonio Maceo*, causas y consecuencias (Havana, 1941), p. 136; Maceo to Gómez, Kingston, August 28, 29, 1886; Gómez to Maceo, Kingston, August 31, 1886, in Cabrales, *Epistolario*, pp. 98–100, 121–22.
42. Maceo to Gómez, Kingston, August 31, September 1, 1886, in Cabrales, *Epistolario*, pp. 100–06.
43. Gómez to Maceo, Kingston, September 3, 1886, in Cabrales, *Epistolario*, p. 123.
44. Gómez, *Diario*, pp. 220–21.
45. Philip S. Foner, *A History of Cuba and Its Relations with the United States*, vol. 2 (New York, 1963), p. 311.
46. Gómez, *Diario*, p. 223; Franco, *Antonio Maceo*, vol. 1 p. 361.
47. Maceo to Fernando Figueredo, Kingston, November 24, 1886, Cabrales, *Epistolario*, pp. 162–63.
48. Maceo to Alejandro González, Panama Canal, December 21, 23, 24 yr. 1886, "Documentos historicos," *Revista de historia cubana y americana*, vol. 1 (1916), pp. 94–95.
49. Franco, *Antonio Maceo*, vol. 1, p. 356.

9. The Peace of Manganese

1. José Luciano Franco, *Antonio Maceo, apuntes para una historia de su vida*, vol. 1 (Havana, 1951), pp. 359–60.
2. Máximo Gómez, *Diario de campaña* (Havana, 1940), pp. 230–31, 238; Franco, *Antonio Maceo*, vol. 1, p. 361.

3. Maceo to Martí, Bas Obispo, January 4, 1888, Coronado Collection, yr. 1888; Franco, *Antonio Maceo*, vol. 1, p. 361.
4. Maceo to Martí, Bas Obispo, January 15, 1888, Coronado Collection, yr. 1888.
5. Franco, *Antonio Maceo*, vol. 1, pp. 362–63.
6. J.F. Echeverría, *Mis recuerdos* (Lima, 1S97), pp. 19–30.
7. Antonio Maceo, "Narraciones de Antonio Maceo," in Gonzalo Cabrales, *Epistolario de héroes* (Havana, 1922), p. 203.
8. *Ibid.*, pp. 203–04.
9. *Ibid.*, pp. 204–07.
10. The comment was made by Fidel Vidal de Santocildes. The source is Leonardo Griñán Peralta, *La muerta de Antonio Maceo, causas y consecuencias* (Havana, 1941), p. 45.
11. Manuel J. de Granda, *La paz del manganese* (Havana, 1939), pp. 15–16.
12. *Ibid.*
13. Morúa Delgado to Maceo, Vera Cruz, September 10, 1886, Coronado Collection, yr. 1886.
14. Eliseo Giberga, *Apuntes sobre la cuestión de Cuba* (Madrid, 1894), pp. 160–64; Juan F. Risquet, *Rectificaciones: la cuestión politico-social en la isla de Cuba* (Havana, 1900), pp. 102–04; Earl R. Beck, "The Martínez Campos Government of 1879: Spain's Last Chance in Cuba," *Hispanic American Historical Review* 56 (May 1976): 283.
15. Quoted in Franco, *Antonio Maceo*, vol. 1, p. 384.
16. Manuel de la Cruz, *Episodios de la revolución cubana* (Havana, 1926), p. 140.
17. Octavio Ramón Costa, *Juan Gualberto Gómez, una vida sin sombra* (Havana, 1950), pp. 110–16; Estuch Horrego, *Juan Gualberto Gómez, un gran inconforme*, 2nd. ed. (Havana, 1954), pp. 99–100; José Antonio Franco, *Ruta de Antonio Maceo en el Caribe* (Havana, 1961), p. 170.

    Gualberto Gómez's strongest critic was the mulatto Martin Morúa Delgado. For the debate between them, *see* Donna Marie Wolf, "The Caribbean People of Color and the Cuban Independence Movement," (Ph.D. diss., University of Pittsburgh, 1973), pp. 146–52.

18. Camilio Polavieja, *Relación documentada de mi política en Cuba* (Madrid, 1898), p. 109.
19. "Narraciones," in Cabrales *Epistolario*, pp. 209–10.
20. Manuel Sanguilly y Ariziti, *Páginas de historia* (Havana, 1929), p. 187.
21. "Narraciones," in Cabrales, *Epistolario*, p. 209.
22. *Ibid.*, pp. 210–11.
23. Emilio Bacardí y Moreau, ed., *Cronícas de Santiago de Cuba*, 7 vols. (Barcelona, 1908–1924), 6:82.
24. Great Britain. Public Records Office. Foreign Office, Havana, No. 277. A. De Crowe to Earl of Salisbury, Aug. 29, 1880; also quoted in Wolf, "The Caribbean People of Color," p. 133.
25. Granda, *La Paz*, p. 55.
26. *Ibid.*, p. 84; "Narraciones," in Cabrales, *Epistolario*, p. 213; Granda, *La Paz*, pp. 53–54, 60, 62–63; Franco, *Antonio Maceo*, vol. 1, p. 408.
27. Polavieja, *Relación documentada*, p. 114.
28. *Ibid.*, pp. 114–16.
29. Granda, *La Paz*, p. 69.
30. *Ibid.*, pp. 62–63.
31. *Ibid.*, p. 64.
32. *Ibid.*, p. 66.
33. *Ibid.*, pp. 68–68.
34. Polavieja, *Relación documentada*, p. 114; Franco, *Antonio Maceo*, vol. 1, p. 408.
35. Herminio Portell Vilá, *Historia de Cuba en sus relaciones con los Estados Unidos y España*, vol. 2 (Havana, 1939), p. 232.

10. Maceo and the Cuban Revolutionary Party

1. Enrique Trujillo, *Apuntes históricos* (New York, 1896), p. 49.
2. Maceo to José Miró, Kingston, November 2, 1890, in Gonzalo Cabrales, *Epistolario de héroes* (Havana, 1922), pp. 171–72.
3. "Datos Biográficos," in Cabrales, *Epistolario*, pp. 186–88; Academia de la historia de Cuba, *Papeles de Maceo*, vol. 2 (Havana, 1948), p. 230.

4. Maceo to Alejandro González, La Mansion, Costa Rica, April 26, May 4, 9, June 8, 1892, "Antonio Maceo," *Revista de historia cubana y americana*, 7 (1916): 96–99.
5. Carlos Jinesta, *Con Maceo en Nicoya* (Havana, 1912), pp. 19–20.
6. Philip S. Foner, *A History of Cuba and Its Relations with the United States*, vol. 2 (New York, 1963), pp. 317–23.
7. *Ibid.*, pp. 323–24. See also Trujillo, *Apuntes*, pp. 105–18, and José Martí, *La Cuestión Racial* (Havana, 1959).
8. Máximo Gómez, *Diario de Campaña*, vol. 1 (Havana, 1940), p. 238.
9. Foner, *A History of Cuba*, vol. 2, pp. 325–26.
10. Maceo to Tomás Padro Grinan, San José, August 16, 1892, Sociedad cubana de estudios historicos y internacionales, *Antonio Maceo, ideología politica, cartas y otros documentos*, pp. 402–03; Trujillo, *Apuntes*, p. 106.
11. L. Zaragoitia Ledesman, *Maceo* (Havana, 1949), pp. 266–67; Leopoldo Horrego Estuch, *Maceo Heroe y caracter* (Havana, 1952), p. 167.
12. José Luciano Franco, *Antonio Maceo: apuntes para una historia de su vida*, vol. 2 (Havana, 1954), pp. 23–24.

    In the two wars of independence, Mariana Grajales lost a husband and five sons. Marcos Maceo, Mariana Grajales' husband and Antonio Maceo's father, died in battle May 1869. Julio and Miguel Maceo were also killed during the Ten Years' War. Rafael was deported to Africa and died in prison. José, a major general in the war of 1895, was killed July 1896. Antonio Maceo died December 7, 1896. Only two sons, Tomás and Marco survived the war. Three of the four sons of Mariana Grajales by her first marriage were also killed. *See* Benigno Vásquez Rodríguez, *Precursores y fundadores* (Havana, 1958), pp. 63–66.
13. Jorge Mañach, *Martí: Apostle of Freedom*, trans. Coley Taylor (New York, 1950), pp. 307–08.
14. Salvador García Agüero, *Maceo cifra y caracter de la Revolución Cubana* (Havana, c. 1942), p. 16; José Martí, *Obras Completas*, vol. 1 (Havana, 1946), p. 701.
15. Maceo to González, "La Mansión," June 9, 1893, *Revista de historia cubana y americana* 7 (1916): 100–01.
16. Laurence R. Nichols, "The 'Bronze Titan,' The Mulatto Hero of

Cuban Independence, Antonio Maceo," (Ph.D. diss., Duke University, 1954), pp. 122–24; interview with José Luciano Franco, December 21, 22, 1976, Archivo Nacional, Havana, Cuba.

17. Trujillo, *Apuntes*, pp. 182–83; Manuel J. de Granda, *Memorias revolucionarias* (Havana, 1936), pp. 60–62.
18. Granda, *Memorias*, p. 71.
19. Maceo to Martí, San José, January 12, 1894, *Patria*, New York, March 15, 1894.
20. Three weeks later, in the January 6, 1894 issue of *Patria*, Martí published another tribute to "The Mother of the Maceos" in which he wrote, in part: "What, if not the unity of the Cuban soul, forged in the war, explains the unanimous and respectful tenderness, and the accents of indubitable emotion and gratitude with which so many have given accounts of the death of Mariana Grajales, the mother of our Maceos? What was there in this woman, what epic poem and mystery was there in this humble woman, what sanctity and devotion was there in her mother's bosom, what decorum and grandeur was there in her simple life, that when one writes about her it is from the depths of the soul with the gentleness of a son, and with the deepest affection?"
21. José Luciano Franco, *La Vida heróica y ejemplar de Antonio Maceo* (Havana, 1963), p. 81.
22. On April 24, 1923, *La Independencia*, published in Santiago de Cuba, carried a headline on its first page which read: "La repatriación de los restos de la madre de los Maceo." (The repatriation of the remains of the mother of the Maceos.) The subhead read: "After thirty years of internment in the city of Kingston, they are brought into the loving native land." The article told how a committee had been appointed to find the resting place of Mariana Maceo and have the remains returned to Cuba; how 23-year-old Antonio de Souza, chancellor of the foreign service of Cuba stationed at the Cuban consulate in Kingston had played a crucial role in locating the grave. The committee actually saw the registry in the Catholic Church of Kingston in which there was the inscription: "MACEO. On the 28 November 1893 was buried the body of Mariana Maceo, aged 85 years.—W. Spillmann SJ." Mariana's remains were returned to Santiago de Cuba on the Cuban vessel *Baire*.

    I am indebted to Dr. Celia Girona of the Foreign Service of Cuba for furnishing me with a copy of the April 24, 1893 issue of *La Independencia*.

23. Maceo to Martí, San Jose, January 12, 1894, *Patria*, New York, March 15, 1894.
24. Martí to Maceo, New York, April 20, 1894, in Cabrales, *Epistolario*, pp. 30–31.
25. Martí to Gómez, May 31, 1894, Martí, *Obras*, vol. 1, p. 179.
26. Martí to Gómez, May 25, 1894, *Ibid.*, vol. 1, pp. 185–88.
27. *Ibid.*, p. 186.
28. Martí to Maceo, June 18, 1894, *Ibid.*, pp. 182–83.
29. Martí to Maceo, June 22, 1894, *Ibid.*, p. 185.
30. Maceo to Enrique Trujillo, San Jose, August 22, 1894, *Epistolario*, pp. 174–75. For the background of the conflict between Trujillo and Martí, see Trujillo, *Apuntes*, pp. 93–104, 222–23.
31. Granda, *Memorias*, pp. 80–82.

    The assassination attempt was linked to an inflammatory article Loynez del Castillo, a protege of Martí, wrote in *La Prensa Libre* which infuriated the Spanish element in Costa Rica. Loynez was also the target of the assassins, and it was he who shot and killed the Spaniard who had shot Maceo.
32. *Ibid.*, p. 83.
33. Gómez, *Diario*, p. 278.
34. Cabrales, *Epistolario*, pp. 128–29.
35. *Ibid.*, pp. 57–58; Franco, *Antonio Maceo*, vol. 2, pp. 51–53.

11. The Second War for Independence Begins

1. José Martí to Antonio Maceo, December 25, 1894, Coronado Collection, yr. 1894.
2. Philip S. Foner, *A History of Cuba and Its Relations with the United States*, vol. 2 (New York, 1963), p. 348.
3. S.W. Paul to J.G. Carlisle, Secretary of the Treasury, Key West, January 21, 1895, United States Treasury Department Special Agents Reports, 1865–1915, Archivo Nacional (hereafter cited AN); Richard V. Rickenbach, "Filibustering with the *Dauntless*," *Florida Historical Quarterly* 38 (April 1950):231.
4. Jorge Mañach, *Martí: Apostle of Freedom*, trans. Coley Taylor

(New York, 1950), pp. 334–36; Félix Lizaso, *José Martí: Martyr of Cuban Independence*, trans. Esther E. Shuler (Albuquerque, N.M., 1953), pp. 238–40.

5. Horatio S. Rubens, *Liberty, the Story of Cuba* (New York, 1922), p. 74.

   Juan Gualberto Gómez, describing reaction to the Fernandina failure in Cuba, wrote: "And a singular thing: the failure at Fernandina which some thought would condemn the plans of the revolutionaries actually favored them extraordinarily. Previously some Cubans, although in favor of separation from Spain, had doubted the effectiveness of Martí's promises. They believed that nothing would come from this propaganda." But the non-believers, Gualberto Gómez continued, now looked at Martí and said in wonder, "Ah! This man is neither a dreamer nor a visionary, but rather a true organizing genius, with a strong and balanced mind, and an indisputable leader of men." (Juan Gualberto Gómez, *Por Cuba Libre* (Havana, 1922), p. 309.)

6. Máximo Gómez, *Diario de compaña* vol. 1 (Havana, 1940), p. 281; Flor Crombet to José Martí, Limón, January 27, 1895, Correspondencia diplomatica de la delegación de Nueva York, 1895, AN, caja 110, numero 1, 342; Crombet to Maceo, Limón, March 20, 1895, in Gonzalo Cabrales, *Epistolario de héroes* (Havana, 1922), p. 135.

   Maceo did write to Martí adjusting his figure down to $3,500, and indicating that he needed "no more than fifty rifles, fifty machetes, and fifty revolvers, with the corresponding ammuniton, to begin the trip." (Maceo to Martí, San José, February, 1895, AN, caja 116, no. 15, 102.)

7. Foner, *History of Cuba*, vol. 2, pp. 349–50.
8. Gómez to Maceo, February 27, 1895, Monte Cristi, February 27, 1895, Coronado Collection, yr. 1895.
9. Maceo to Martí, San José, February, 1895, AN, caja 116, no. 15, 102.
10. Maceo to María Cabrales, Limón, March 25, 1895, in Cabrales, *Epistolario*, pp. 73–74.
11. Gómez to Maceo, Monte Cristi, February 27, 1895, Coronado Collection, yr. 1895.
12. Maceo to María Cabrales, Limón, March 25, 1895, in Cabrales,

Epistolario, pp. 73–74; Franco, *Antonio Maceo*, vol. 2, pp. 199–200.

13. *Ibid.*
14. Manuel J. de Granda, *Memorias revolucionarias*, vol. 2 (Havana, 1936), pp. 88–92; Franco, *Antonio Maceo*, vol. 2, pp. 106–11; Maceo to María Cabrales, Alta Mar, March 27, 1895; Maceo to María Cabrales, En Campaña, April 30, 1895, in Cabrales, *Epistolario*, pp. 75–76.

    In the confusion of the landing process the sailor who had commanded the boat was shot by one of the Cubans. The Spanish press claimed that Maceo's men killed this sailor when he refused to follow their orders. Maceo declared it was an accident. (Maceo to Frederick Ramsden, the English vice-consul in Santiago, April 21, 1895, AN, caja 116, no. 15, 112.)
15. Maceo to the Forces of Oriente, April 20, 1895; to the Army of Oriente, April 21, 1895, AN, caja 116, no. 15, 115–18.
16. Franco, *Antonio Maceo*, vol. 2, p. 125; Cabrales, *Epistolario*, pp. 75–76.
17. Lizaso, *José Martí*, pp. 247–48.
18. José Martí, *Obras completas*, vol. 1 (Havana, 1946) pp. 271, 285–93.
19. Gómez, *Diario*, p. 336.

12. Cuban Revolutionary Strategy

1. *Diario de la Marina* (Havana), April 10, 1895.
2. *Ibid.*, March 31, 1895.
3. New York *World*, April 12, 1895.
4. N. Bashkina, "A Page from the Cuban People's Heroic History," *International Affairs*, Moscow (March 1964): 18. Twelve documents reprinted from the Russia Foreign Policy Archives. My emphasis. P.S.F.
5. Enrique José Varona, *De la colonia a la república* (Havana, 1919), p. 167; José Miró y Argenter, *Cuba: cronicas de la guerra; las campañas de invasión de occidente, 1895–1896*, vol. 1 (Havana, 1945), pp. 266–68; Miguel Angel Varona y Guerrero, *La guerra de*

independencia de Cuba, 1895–1898, vol. 2 (Havana, 1946), p. 1409.

6. Dorothy Stanhope, "The Negro Race in Cuba: Insular Society Draws no Discriminating Color Line," *New York Times*, September 16, 1900; "The Insurrection in Cuba," *Outlook*, June 1, 1912, p. 238; Charles E. Chapman, *A History of the Cuban Republic: A Study in Hispanic American Politics* (New York, 1927), p. 308.
7. Richard Vernon Rickenbach, "A History of Filibustering from Florida to Cuba, 1895–1898" (M.A. thesis, University of Florida, 1948), p. 80.
8. José L. French, "With Gómez in the Cuban Skirmishes," *National Magazine* 14 (1898): 18–40.
9. Murat Halstead, *The Story of Cuba* (Chicago, 1898), p. 122; George C. Musgrave, *Under Three Flags in Cuba* (Boston, 1899), pp. 61–62.
10. Calixto García to Tomás Estrada Palma, December 6, 1896, AN; Frederick Funston, *Memories of Two Wars* (New York, 1914), p. 143; Emilio Roig de Leuchsenring, *Cuba no debe su independencia a los Estados Unidos* (Havana, 1950), p. 24.
11. Gómez to Campos de Cuba, July, 1897, AN.
12. Gómez to Estrada Palma, August 11, 1896, AN.
13. French E. Chadwick, *The Relations of the United States and Spain: Diplomacy* (New York, 1909), p. 408.
14. *Algunos Documentos Politicos de Máximo Gómez*, ed. Amalia *Rodríguez Rodríguez (Havana, 1962), pp. 15–16.*
15. Gómez to Estrada Palma, August 11, 1896, AN.
16. Gómez, *Diario*, p. 133.
17. Antonio Maceo to Carlos Roloff, November 23, 1895, Coronado Collection, yr. 1895, AN.
18. Estrada Palma to Maceo, September 12, 1895, *Antonio Maceo: documentos para su vida* (Havana, 1945), p. 146; Maceo to Estrada Palma, September 22, 1895, Coronado Collection, yr. 1895.
19. Gómez to Estrada Palma, October 25, 1895, AN.
20. Miró, *Cuba*, vol. 1, pp. 126–28.
21. Philip S. Foner, *The Spanish-Cuban-American War and the Birth of American Imperialism*, vol. 1, 1895–1898 (New York, 1972), p. 26.

22. Gómez to Estrada Palma, November 22, 1896, AN.
23. Benigno Souza, *Máximo Gómez, el generalisimo* (Havana, 1936), p. 185.
24. Grover Flint, *Marching with Gómez, A War Correspondent's Field Note-Book kept during four months with the Cuban army*, introduction by John Fiske (Boston and New York, 1898), pp. 41–42, 45.
25. Thomas W. Steep, "A Cuban Insurgent Newspaper," *National Magazine* 8 (May, 1989): 147–49.
26. A.D. Hall, *Cuba, Its Past, Present, and Future* (New York, 1898), p. 83.
27. Richard Harding Davis, *Cuba in War Time* (New York, 1897), pp. 91–94.

13. The War in Oriente and Preparations for the Western Invasion

1. Frederick Funston, *Memories of Two Wars* (New York, 1914), p. 143.
2. José Luciano Franco, *Antonio Maceo, apuntes para una historia de su vida*, vol. 3 (Havana, 1957), p. 36.
3. New York *Herald*, June 7, 1895.
4. José Miro y Argenter, *Cuba: cronicas de la guerra; las compañas de invasión y de occidente, 1895–1896*, vol. 1 (Havana, 1945), p. 65; Gonzalo Cabrales, *Epistolario de héroes* (Havana, 1922), pp. 78–79.
5. Franco, *Antonio Maceo*,vol. 2, p. 141.
6. Miró, *Cuba*, vol. 1, pp. 67–82; Franco, *Antonio Maceo*, vol. 2, pp. 147–55; Laurence R. Nichols, "The 'Bronze Titan,' The Mulatto Hero of Cuban Independence, Antonio Maceo" (Ph.D. diss., Duke University, 1954), pp. 369–71; Juan Jerez Villarreal, *Oriente, Biografia de una provincia* (Havana, 1960), pp. 270–73.
7. Murat Halstead, *The Story of Cuba* (Chicago, 1898), p. 276.
8. Máxim Gómez to Tomás Estrada Palma, Camagüey, August 22, 1895, Archivo Nacional. Hereafter cited AN.
9. Antonio Maceo to María Cabrales, September 3, 1895, in Cabrales, *Epistolario*, pp. 83–84.

10. René E. Reyna Cossio, *Estudios histórico-militares sobre la Guerra de Independencia de Cuba* (Havana, 1954), p.16.
11. Gómez to Antonio Maceo, June 30, 1895; Maceo to Gómez, July 3, 1895; Maceo to Bartolomé Masó, July 14, 1895, Coronado Collection, yr. 1895.
12. Nichols, "The 'Bronze Titan,' " p. 360.
13. Maceo to Gómez, July 3, 1895, Coronado Collection, yr. 1895.
14. Salvador Cisneros Betancourt to Maceo, September 6, 1895; Maceo to Cisneros, September 11, 1895, Coronado Collection, yr. 1895.
15. Grover Flint, *Marching with Gómez. A War Correspondent's Field Note-Book kept during four months with the Cuban Army* (Boston and N.Y., 1898), p. 33.
16. Emilio Roig de Leuchsenring, *Máximo Gómez, el libertador de Cuba y el primer Ciudadano de la Republica* (Havana, 1959).
17. Maceo to Estrada Palma, September 22, 1895, Coronado Collection, yr. 1895.
18. Maceo to Estrada Palma, October 30, 1895, Coronado Collection, yr. 1895.
19. Maceo to Cisneros, September 8, 1895, in José Antonio Portuondo, ed., *El Pensamiento vivo de Maceo* (Havana, 1962), pp. 76–77.
20. Maceo to the Chiefs of the First Corps, September 24, 1895, Coronado Collection, yr. 1895.
21. Bernabé Boza, *Mi diario de la guerra, desde Baire hasta la intervención americana,* vol. 1 (Havana, 1900–1904), p. 15.
22. Miró, *Cuba,* vol. 1, p. 117.
23. *Ibid.*, pp. 118–19.
24. Juan Gualberto Gómez, *Los preliminares de la revolución de 1895* (Havana, 1913), pp. 13–17.
25. Miró, *Cuba,* vol. 1, p. 121.
26. *Ibid.*, vol. 1, p. 98.
27. Franco, *Antonio Maceo,* vol. 3, pp. 238–39.
28. *Ibid.*, vol. 1, pp. 98–99.
29. *Ibid.*, vol. 1, p. 102.
30. *Ibid.*, vol. 1, pp. 126–28; Maceo to Carlos Roloff, Secretary of War, November 23, 1895, Coronado Collection, yr. 1895.
31. Maceo to Manuel Sanguilly, Camagüey, November 21, 1895, original in Coronado Collection, yr. 1895; reprinted in Portuondo, *Pensamiento vivo,* pp. 83–84.

32. Maceo to Estrada Palma, October 30, 1895, Coronado Collection, yr. 1895.
33. Reyna, *Estudios histórico-militares*, pp. 16–17.
34. Miró, *Cuba*, vol. 1, pp. 99–100.
35. Maceo to Estrada Palma, November 21, 1895, Coronado Collection, yr. 1895.
36. *Ibid.*
37. Miró, *Cuba*, vol. 1, p. 117.
38. Maceo to María Cabrales, November 20, 1895, Cabrales, *Epistolario*, pp. 84–85.
39. Miró, *Cuba*, vol. 1, pp. 127–28.
40. Quoted in Roig, *Máximo Gómez, el libertador*, p. 18.
41. Miró, *Cuba*, vol. 1, pp. 129–34; Franco, *Antonio Maceo*, vol. 2, pp. 251–52.
42. Max Tosquella, "Baraguá-Mantua," *Bohemia* (Havana) (December 4, 1964): 8–9.
43. Miro, *Cuba*, vol. 1, pp. 139, 144–55; Maceo to Estrada Palma, November 29, 1895, Coronado Collection, yr. 1895.
44. Franco, *Antonio Maceo*, vol. 2, p. 253 and n.
45. Miró, *Cuba*, vol. 1, p. 139; Franco, *Antonio Maceo*, vol. 2, p. 258.

14. The Western Invasion

1. Máximo Gómez, *Diario de campaña* (Havana, 1940), p. 348.
2. Antonio Maceo to the People of Las Villas, Remedios, December 5, 1895, Coronado Collection, yr. 1895.
3. Colonel Campos y Feliú, *Españoles y insurrectos* (Madrid, 1900), p. 122.
4. Gómez, *Diario*, pp. 347–48.
5. José Miró y Argenter, *Cuba: crónicas de la guerra; las campañas de invasión y de occidente, 1895–1896*, vol. 1 (Havana, 1945), p. 151.
6. *Ibid.*, pp. 161–67; Gómiz, *Diario*, pp. 348–50.
7. José Luciano Franco, *La Vida heróica y ejemplar de Antonio Maceo* (Havana, 1963), p. 100.
8. Miró, *Cuba*, vol. 1, p. 170.
9. Miguel Varona y Guerrero, *La guerra de independencia de Cuba*, vol. 1 (Havana, 1946), p. 596.

10. Miró, *Cuba*, vol. 1, p. 170; Rene E. Reyna Cossio, *Estudios histórico-militares sobre la guerra de Independencia de Cuba* (Havana, 1954); José Luciano Franco, *Antonio Maceo, apuntes para una historia de su vida*, vol. 2 (Havana, 1954), pp. 277–78.
11. Miró, *Cuba*, vol. 1, p. 170.
12. *Ibid*., pp. 168–80; Reyna, *Estudios histórico-militares*, pp. 25–26; Franco, *Antonio Maceo*, vol. 2, pp. 277–78.
13. Grover Flint, *Marching with Gómez. A War Correspondent's Field Note-Book kept during four months with the Cuban Army*, (Boston and N.Y.,1898), pp. 41–42, 45, 151–56.
14. Miró, *Cuba*, vol. 1, pp. 224–25.
15. *Ibid*., pp. 226–31.
16. Colonel Camps y Feliú, *Españoles y insurrectos* (Madrid, 1900), p. 141.
17. Gómez, *Diario*, p. 351.
18. Miró, *Cuba*, vol. 1, pp. 258–63.
19. *Ibid*., p. 257.
20. Franco, *Antonio Maceo*, vol. 3, pp. 20–21.
21. "Máximo Gómez to the People of the West," Havana Province, January 10, 1896, AN.
22. Miró, *Cuba*, vol. 1, pp. 282–89; Gómez, *Diario*, p. 253.
23. Quoted in Franco, *Antonio Maceo*, vol. 3, p. 19.
24. José Rivero Muñiz, *Vereda Nueva* (Havana, 1964), pp. 84–94.
25. Miró, *Cuba*, vol. 1, pp. 288–90; Gómez, *Diario*, p. 254.
26. Quoted in Franco, *Antonio Maceo*, vol. 3, p. 19.
27. Murat Halstead, *The Story of Cuba* (Chicago, 1898), pp. 192–214.
28. *La Discusión* (Havana), January 1–7, 1896; Miró, *Cuba*, vol. 1, pp. 301–03.
29. *Diario de la Marina* (Havana), January 4, 6, 8, 1896; Franco, *Antonio Maceo*, vol., p. 27.
30. W. Rodney Long, *Railroads of Central America and the West Indies* (Washington, D.C., 1925), pp. 157–75; Laurence R. Nichols, "Domestic History of Cuba During the War of Insurrectos, 1895–1898" (M.A. thesis, Duke University, 1951), p. 121.
31. De Truffin to the Russian Envoy in Madrid, January 8, 1896, *International Affairs* (Moscow), March, 1964, pp. 119–20.
32. Quoted in Franco, *Antonio Maceo*, vol. 3, pp. 22–23.
33. Miró, *Cuba*, vol. 1, pp. 314–20.

34. *Ibid.;* Gómez, *Diario*, p. 353.
35. José Antonio Portuondo, ed., *El Pensamiento vivo de Maceo* (Havana, 1962), pp. 85–86.
36. Miró, *Cuba*, vol. 1, pp. 318–19.
37. Maceo to María Cabrales, Havana Province, February 14, 1896, in Gonzalo Cabrales *Epistolario de hérves* (Havana, 1922), pp. 85–86.
38. Miró, *Cuba*, vol. 1, pp. 315–16; Franco, *Antonio Maceo*, vol. 3, pp. 41–42.
39. Miró, *Cuba*, vol. 1, p. 320; Laurence R. Nichols, "The 'Bronze Titan,' The Mulatto Hero of Cuban Independence, Antonio Maceo" (Ph.D. diss., Duke University, 1954), p. 332.
40. Miró, *Cuba*, vol. 1, p. 321.
41. Flint, *Marching with Gómez*, pp. 112–13.
42. *Diario de la Marina* (Havana), January 15, 1896.
43. *Ibid.*, January 28, 1896. *See also* Diego Vicente Tejera, *Blancos y Negroes. Conferencia dada en Cayo Hueso en 7 de 1897* (Havana, 1900), pp. 18–19. Copy in Harvard College Library.
44. Franco, *Antonio Maceo*, vol. 3, p. 54.
45. Maceo to the Director of the Washington *Star*, Pinar del Río, January 27, 1896, in Portuondo, ed., *Pensamiento vivo*, pp. 86–87.
46. Miró, *Cuba*, vol. 1, p. 259.
47. *Ibid.*, pp. 344–45.
48. *Ibid.*, pp. 342–43.
49. Franco, *Antonio Maceo*, vol. 3, p. 55.
50. Miró, *Cuba*, vol. 1, p. 345.
51. *Ibid.*, p. 346.
52. Franco, *Antonio Maceo*, vol. 3, p. 56.
53. Miró, *Cuba*, vol. 1, pp. 345–46.
54. *Ibid.*, p. 346; Franco, *Antonio Maceo*, vol. 3, pp. 57–58.
55. Maceo to María Cabrales, February 14, 1896, in Cabrales, *Epistolario*, pp. 85–86.
56. Miró, *Cuba*, vol. 1, pp. 344–45; Franco, *Antonio Maceo*, vol. 3, p. 56; Nicholás Heredia, *Crónicas de la guerra de Cuba, 1895–1896*. Introducción por el doctor Enrique Gay-Calbo (Havana, 1951), p. XV. This is a reproduction of the original edition published in *El Figaro* in 1895 and 1896.
57. *International Affairs* (Moscow), March, 1964, p. 120.

58. Reyna, *Estudios histórico-militares*, pp. 126, 127.
59. Quoted in Franco, *Antonio Maceo*, vol. 3, p. 56.
60. Quoted in Franco, *Antonio Maceo*, vol. 3, p. 170.
61. Interview with Juan Marinello, who received this information from Picasso, Havana, February 14, 1967.
62. Portuondo, ed., *Pensamiento vivo*, pp. 87–88.

15. Weyler versus Maceo

1. José Miro, y Argenter, *Cuba: Crónicas de la guerra, las campañas de invasion y de occidente* (Havana, 1945), p. 18.
2. Antonio Maceo to María Cabrales, Provincia de la Habana, February 14, 1896, in Gonzalo Cabiales, *Epistolario de heróes* (Havana, 1922), pp. 85–86.
3. Miró, *Cuba*, vol. 2, p. 25.
4. *Ibid.*, pp. 36–42; José Luciano Franco, *Antonio Maceo, apuntes para una historia de su vida*, vol. 3 (Havana, 1957).
5. Miró, *Cuba*, vol. 2, pp. 42–55.

   In addition to having served in the Ten Years' War in Cuba, Weyler had participated in the Santo Domingo campaign of 1865, the Carlist Wars, the Moorish war, and the Philippine insurrection.
6. Miro, *Cuba*, vol. 2, pp. 56–57.
7. Valeriano Weyler y Nicolau, *Mi Mando en Cuba*, vol. 1 (Madrid, 1910), p. 101.

   The policy outlined in Weyler's order was not applied immediately to the entire island. The first order named only the provinces of Oriente and Camagüey and the jurisdiction of Sancti Spíritus. The second order, of October 21, 1896, designated only the province of Pinar del Río. In practice, however, an effort was made from the beginning to apply the *reconcentracion* policy to the entire rural population.

   For a discussion of the policy, its application, and its terrible effects, *see* Philip S. Foner, *The Spanish-Cuban-American War and the Birth of American Imperialism*, vol. 1 (New York, 1972), pp. 50–52, 110–18.

8. Miró, *Cuba,* vol. 3, pp. 178–79.
9. Weyler, *Mi Mando,* vol. 2, pp. 538–40.
10. Maceo to María Cabrales, Havana Province, February 14, 1896, in Cabrales, *Epistolario* (Havana, 1922), pp. 85–86.
11. Miró, *Cuba,* vol. 2, pp. 60–66.
12. *Ibid.,* pp. 74–84; Franco, *Antonio Maceo,* vol. 3, pp. 87–97.
13. Miró, *Cuba,* vol. 3, pp. 94–95; Franco, *Antonio Maceo,* vol 3, pp. 98–99.
14. José Antonio Portuoundo, ed., *El Pensamiento vivo de Maceo* (Havana, 1962), pp. 88–89.
15. *Diario de la Marina* (Havana), February 28, 1896.
16. Maceo to Estrada Palma, Cabañas, San Francisco, March 21, 1896, Coronado Collection, yr. 1896.
17. Miró, *Cuba,* vol. 2, pp. 128–30; Franco, *Antonio Maceo,* vol. 3, pp. 107–12.
18. Maceo to Estrada Palma, El Rubí, Pinar del Río, April 4, 1896, Coronado Collection, yr. 1896.
19. Maceo, Proclamation, Pinar del Río, March 16, 1896, Coronado Collection, yr. 1896.
20. Miró, *Cuba,* vol. 2, pp. 160–63; Franco, *Antonio Maceo,* vol. 3, pp. 128–30.
21. Miró, *Cuba,* vol. 2, pp. 117–78; Franco, *Antonio Maceo,* vol. 3, pp. 128–30.
22. Maceo to Estrada Palma, El Rubí, Pinar del Río, April 14, 1896, Coronado Collection, yr. 1896.
23. Weyler, *Mi Mando,* vol. 3, pp. 113–15.
24. Maceo to Gómez, April 14, 1896, Coronado Collection, yr. 1896.

    Maceo's contempt for the Spanish *trochas* was widely known. De Truffin reported: "Although being vigorously pursued, Maceo boasts that he is absolutely calm and . . . that he is not worried about the fortification line at all and will cross it whenever he likes." (De Truffin to the Russian Ambassador in Madrid, May 1, 1896, *International Affairs* (Moscow) March, 1964, p. 121.)
25. Laurance R. Nichols, "The 'Bronze Titan,' The Mulatto Hero of Cuban Independence Antonio Maceo" (Ph. D. diss., Duke University, 1954), p. 435.
26. *Diario de la Havana* (Havana), April 15, 1896.
27. Maceo to Estrada Palma, April 14, 1896, Coronado Collection, yr.

1896; Maceo to María Cabrales, April 17, 1896, in Cabrales, *Epistolario, p. 87.*

28. Miró, *Cuba,* vol. 2, pp. 196–204; Franco, *Antonio Maceo,* vol. 3, pp. 163–64.
29. Miró, *Cuba,* vol. 2, p. 232.
30. De Truffin to the Russian Ambassador in Madrid, May 1, 1896, *International Affairs* (Moscow), March, 1964, p. 121.
31. Miró, *Cuba,* vol. 2, pp. 24–51; Franco, *Antonio Maceo,* vol. 3, pp. 183–84.
32. London *Times,* June 6, 1896.

    The article opens: "With an army of 175,000 men, with materials of all kinds in unlimited quantities, beautiful weather, little or no sickness among the troops, in a word, with everything in his favor, General Weyler has been unable to defeat the insurrectionists."
33. Maceo to Estrada Palma, March 21, 1896, and June 27, 1896, Coronado Collection, yr. 1896; Magdalena Pando, *Antonio Maceo* (Gainesville, Fla.), pp. 15–16.
34. Pando, *Maceo,* p. 16.
35. *Ibid.,* p. 17.
36. For a discussion of the forces in the United States seeking annexation of Cuba or control over its economy, *see* Philip S. Foner, *A History of Cuba and Its Relations with the United States,* vol. 2 (New York, 1963), pp. 332–46.
37. *Ibid.,* pp. 348–59.
38. Henry A. Himley to Richard B. Olney, April 29, 1896, Richard B. Olney Papers, Library of Congress, Washington, D.C.
39. Emilio Roig de Leuchsenring, *Revolución y república en Maceo,* Havana, 1932, pp. 52–54, 62.
40. Franco, *Antonio Maceo,* vol. 2, p. 239.
41. Quoted in Roig de Leuchsenring, *Revolución y república* 1932, p. 51.
42. Walter La Feber, "The Background of Cleveland's Venezuela Policy: A Reinterpretation," *American Historical Review* 66 (July, 1961): 953.
43. For a discussion of the reasons for the failure of Latin America to offer aid to the Cuban revolutionists during the Second War for

Independence, *see* Foner, *The Spanish-Cuban-American War,* vol. 1, pp. 151–62.

44. Portuondo, ed., *Pensamiento vivo,* pp. 90–91.
45. José Luciano Franco, *La Vida heróica y ejemplar de Antonio Maceo* (Havana, 1963), p. 111.
46. *Journal of the Knights of Labor,* November 5, 1896.
47. *Ibid.*
48. *Ibid.*
49. Franco, *Antonio Maceo,* vol. 3, p. 175.

16. The Death of Maceo

1. Antonio Maceo to Tomás Estrada Palma, June 27, 1896, Coronado Collection, yr. 1896; José Miro y Argenter, *Cuba: Cronicas de la guerra; las campañas de invasión y de occidente, 1895–1896,* vol. 3 (Havana, 1945), pp. 12–13; José Luciano Franco, *Antonio Maceo: apuntes para una historia de su vida,* vol. 3 (Havana, 1957), pp. 255–56.
2. Miró, *Cuba,* vol. 3, pp. 12–13; Franco, *Antonio Maceo,* vol. 3, p. 176.
3. José Luciano Franco, *La Vida heróica y ejemplar de Antonio* Maceo (Havana, 1963) p. 112.
4. De Truffin to the Russian Ambassador to Madrid, October 14, 1896, *International Affairs* (Moscow), March, 1964, p. 122.
5. Miró, *Cuba,* vol. 3, pp. 82, 89–126; Franco, *Antonio Maceo,* vol. 3, pp. 316–30.
6. Miró, *Cuba,* vol. 3, p. 172; Franco, *Antonio Maceo,* vol. 3, p. 347.
7. Miró, *Cuba,* vol. 3, pp. 195–98; Miguel Varona y Guerrero, *La guerra de independencia de Cuba,* vol. 1 (Havana, 1946), p. 596.
8. Rafael Fermeselle-López, "Black Politics in Cuba: The Race War of 1912" (Ph.D. diss., American University, 1972), p. 9.
9. Varona, *La guerra de independencia,* vol. 1, pp. 598–602; Capitán Anibal Escalante Beatón, *Calixto García. Su campaña en el 1898* (Havana, 1938), pp. 40–47; Franco, *Antonio Maceo,* vol. 3, p. 185.
10. Máximo Gómez to Antonio Maceo, May 20, 27, 1896, Coronado

Collection, yr. 1896; Salvador Cisneros Betancourt to Tomás Estrada Palma, June 1, 1896, Archivo Nacional. (Hereafter cited AN.)

11. Franco, *Antonio Maceo,* vol. 3, p. 176.
12. Miró, *Cuba,* vol. 3, pp. 173–74.
13. Gómez to Estrada Palma, Camagüey, November, 1896, AN.
14. Franco, *La Vida heróica*, p. 114.
15. Miró, *Cuba,* vol. 3, pp. 173–74.
16. A.D. Hall, *Cuba, Its Past, Present, and Future* (New York, 1898), pp. 83, 123.
17. Maceo to Badomero Acosta, November 13, 1896, Coronado Collection, yr. 1896.
18. Portoundo, ed., *El Pensamiento vivo de Maceo* (Havana, 1967), pp. 99–102. For other letters, *see* Maceo to General Emilio Núñez, November 22, 1896; Maceo to Pérez Carbó, November 22, 1896; Maceo to Manuel Sanguilly, November 24, 1896, Coronado Collection, yr. 1896.
19. Franco, *La vida heróica,* p. 115; Franco, *Antonio Maceo,* vol. 3, pp. 389–95.
20. Franco, *Antonio Maceo,* vol. 3, pp. 394–96; Miró, *Cuba*, vol. 3, pp. 212–14.
21. Franco, *Antonio Maceo*, vol. 3, pp. 404–05.
22. In a book published in Havana in 1974 *(La Guerra en la Habana: Desde enero de 1896 hasta el combate de San Pedro),* Francisco Perez points out that there is no combat in Cuban military history with more historical confusion than that surrounding the events leading to Maceo's death. He points out that there are at least forty-seven different versions of the battle. In his own account, which is one of the most detailed, Perez notes that the first shot which wounded Maceo penetrated through the lower right jaw and ruptured the carotid artery near the chin. Maceo's jaw was fractured in three places, and according to Perez he died almost at the moment of being shot.

    For Perez's account of the battle, *see* pp. 129–75. *See also* Miró, *Cuba*, vol. 3, pp. 218–55; Franco, *Antonio Maceo*, vol. 3, pp. 408–10.

    In my conversation with him in Havana, December, 1976, Francisco Perez tended to minimize the importance of racism in the decisions that led to Maceo's return to the East, and implied that romance delayed his leaving.

23. Carol A. Preece, "Insurgent Guests: The Cuban Revolutionary Party and Its Activities in the United States, 1892–1898" (Ph.D. diss, Georgetown University, 1976), p. 42*n*.
24. Franco, *Antonio Maceo*, vol. 3, p. 419.
25. For the forces that led the United States into the war against Spain, the U.S.-Cuban military victory over Spain, and the snatching of real independence from Cuba after the defeat of Spain by the United States, *see* Philip S. Foner, *The Spanish-Cuban-American War and the Birth of American Imperialism, 1895–1902,* 2 volumes (New York, 1972).

    The full title of Leland H. Jenk's work is *Our Cuban Colony: A Study in Sugar* (New York, 1928).

17. Conclusion

1. *International Affairs* (Moscow), March 1964, p. 123.
2. Griñan Piralta, *La muerta de Antonio Maceo, causas y consecuencias* (Havana, 1941), p. 45.
3. Fernando Figueredo Socarrás, *La revolución de Yara* (Havana, 1902), p. 191.
4. *Diario de la Marina* (Havana), April 10, 1895.
5. José Antonio Portuondo, ed., *El Pensamiento vivo de Maceo,* (Havana, 1962), p. 7.
6. Although blacks formed a large proportation of the Liberating Army and quite a few rose to the highest ranks, no exact figures are available. In 1912, black leaders claimed that they had provided up to 85 percent of the soldiers during the Second War for Independence. One American historian, Charles Chapman, felt that these estimates were too high, but he did agree that "certainly the negroes had provided a majority of the Army of Liberation." More recently Rafael Fermeselle-López, in an unpublished doctoral dissertation at American University, concluded "that about 49 percent of the generals and colonels were blacks." ("The

Insurrection in Cuba," *Outlook,* June 1, 1912, p. 238; Charles E. Chapman, *A History of the Cuban Republic: A Study in Hispanic American Politics (New York, 1927), p. 308;* Rafael Fermeselle-López, "Black Politics in Cuba: The Race War of 1912" (Ph.D. diss., American University, 1972), p. 9. Perhaps the best way to answer this question is to say, as did the distinguished Cuban historian Sergio Aguirre, that the black soldier was the backbone of the revolutionary army, and made up to 70 percent of the fighters while only comprising about 32 percent of the entire population. (Sergio Aguirre, "El cincuentario de un gran crimen," *Cuba Socialista* Año II (December 1962), pp. 34–35.)

7. Cuba Libre. Misión Providencial. *El Programa de Maceo. Ideas de Maceo. Jefe de la raza negra en Cuba Insurrección*, New York, 1895.
8. Joseph Ki-Zerba, *Histoire de l'Afrique Noir* (Paris, 1972), p. 223.

   I am indebted to José Luciano Franco for calling my attention to this work.
9. José Luciano Franco, *La Vida heróica y ejemplar de Antonio Maceo* (Havana, 1963), p. 110.
10. Jorge Ibarra, *Ideología mambisa* (Havana, 1972), p. 52.
11. Quoted in Philip S. Foner, *The Spanish-Cuban-American War and the Birth of American Imperialism, 1898–1902*, vol. 2 (New York, 1972), p. 450.
12. Ibarra, *Ideología,* p. 73.
13. Reprinted in *Gramma* (Havana), December 27, 1976.
14. Enrique María de Hostos, *Obras Completas,* vol. 10 (Havana, 1939), pp. 159–61; Aristides Aguero to Estrada Palma, Lima, January 4, 1887, *Correspondencia diplómatica de la delegación cubana en Nueva York durante la guerra de independencia de 1895 a 1898,* vol. 2 (Havana, 1943–1946), pp. 77–80.

    Francisco Rosado joined Estrada Palma in New York where he translated articles from New York newspapers into Spanish for publication in the Cuban press.
15. José Maria Izaguirre to Estrada Palma, Managua, Nicaragua, December 18, 1896; Ramon Betances to Estrada Palma, Paris, December 18, 1896, *Correspondencea diplomatica*, vol. 9, pp. 71–72; vol. 6, p. 86.
16. José Luciano Franco, *Antonio Maceo: apuntes para una historia*

de su vida, vol. 3 (Havana, 1957), pp. 414–16; *Patria*, March 31, 1897.

17. Quoted in Mariano Rodríguez, "Conversación acerca de Maceo con José Luciano Franco," *Juventud Rebelde*, June 13, 1971.
18. *Ibid.*
19. New York *Journal*, December 14, 1896; Joseph E. Wisan, *The Cuban Crisis as Reflected in the New York Press, 1895–1898* (New York, 1934), p. 193.
20. The poem in Yiddish, "Antonio Maceo (Kubaner held)" is in *Shriftn fun Morris Rosenfeld*, New York, 1908, pp. 233–35. The English translation is by Aaron Kramer and was prepared especially for the present volume. Mr. Kramer, who has translated many of Morris Rosenfeld's poems, is himself a distinguished poet. For Aaron Kramer's translation of some of Rosenfeld's working-class poems, *see* Philip S. Foner, *American Labor Songs of the Nineteenth Century* (Urbana, Illinois, 1975), pp. 288, 315–20.
21. *Detroit Journal*, December 13, 1896.
22. "The Cuban Patriot," *The Freeman* (Indianapolis), February 20, 1897.

    The Christian Recorder, official organ of the African Methodist Episcopal Church, carried a poem, "The Colored Boys in Blue," in its issue of August 4, 1898 which dealt with black Americans who were fighting in Cuba after the United States entered the war against Spain. The concluding verse read:

    "Ye scions of a war-like race
    Renew the prestige of your sires,
    And by your valor win the place
    When glory flames with radiant fires,
    With those great heroes brave and pure,
    Men like Maceo, L'Ouverture."

23. A study of the Alumni Register of Lincoln University, the first black college in the United States, founded in 1854, reveals that a large number of black graduates in the early twentieth century had the first name of Maceo.

    Two prominent black Americans with the name Maceo as the first or middle name are Maceo C. Martin and A. Maceo Walker, both active in the world of banking and insurance. Another black American with the first name Maceo was not so fortunate in his experiences in this country. As a great black American, Paul Robeson, explained: "Maceo Snipes, a World War II veteran, went to vote in Taylor County, Alabama. One hour later he was killed on the doorstep of his home, within sight of his wife and children. His murderers walked away saying, 'We told you not to vote.' But the widow of Maceo Snipes told her children, 'When you grow up, you'll vote too.' " (Paul Robeson, *The Negro People and the Soviet Union: Address at Banquet Sponsored by the National Council of American-Soviet Friendship, Waldorf Astoria, New York City, November 10, 1949,* New York, 1950.) The courageous, defiant statement of the widow of Maceo Snipes to her children is reminiscent of the famous remark of Mariana Grajales Maceo, Antonio Maceo's heroic mother, who told her youngest child it was time he grew up and joined the battle for Cuban independence—this after having lost her husband and several of her other sons in the struggle for Cuban liberation.

24. S.F.C.C. Hanedoe, "Major-General Antonio Maceo: The Idol of Cuba and the Cuban Insurgents," *Colored American Magazine,* November, 1900.
25. *The Voice of the Negro* (Atlanta), November, 1904 and reprinted in Philip S. Foner, ed., *The Voice of Black America: Major Speeches of Negroes in the United States, 1797–1971* (New York, 1972), pp. 647–52.
26. Edmund David Cronon, *Black Moses: The Story of Marcus Garvey and the Universal Negro Improvement Association* (Madison, Wis. 1962), p. 58.
27. *AME Church Review* 14 (1897–1898): 119.
28. Carter G. Woodson, Preface to *Negro History in Thirteen Plays,* by Willis Richardson and May Miller (Washington, D.C., 1935), p. v.
29. Commandante Raúl Castro Ruz, *El ejemplo de los héroes nunca muere, Speech given on December 7, 1959, published by the Department of Public Relations of the Ministry of State,* Havana, n.d. p. 15.
30. "Discurso de Che sobre el General Antonio," recorded address in

honor of Antonio Maceo by Che Guevarra, 33 rpm record, Havana, Cuba.

31. This is what Fidel Castro said of Martí at his trial after the assault on Moncada.
32. The exploration of Maceo's thought is the theme of José Antonio Portuondo, ed., *El Pensamiento vivo de Maceo* (Havana, 1967). An excellent study of the changing historical approaches to Maceo in Cuba is Patricia Weiss Fagen, "Heroes of National Liberation: Antonio Maceo, An Historiographical Essay," unpublished paper presented at the American Studies Association Conference and New World Studies Conference, San Antonio, Texas, November 1975. The paper was later published under the title, "Antonio Maceo: Heroes, History, and Historiography," *Latin American Research Review 11* (1976): 69–93. These studies also render ridiculous Eldridge Cleaver's statement, cited above, that in Cuba today Antonio Maceo is relegated to the position of a man solely of brawn while José Martí, a white man, is credited with being the man of brains. (*See above* note 6, p. 271.)
33. *Granma Weekly Review*, October 13, 1968.
34. Franco, *Antonio Maceo*, vol. 3, pp. 415–16.

Bibliography

Manuscripts

Central University of Las Villas, Cuba:
  Francisco de Paula Coronado Collection, for the years 1872–1900
  Correspondencia de Antonio Maceo y Grajales, 1872–1896
Archivo Nacional de Cuba, Havana, Cuba
  Francisco de Paula Coronado Collection (items donated in 1947)
Máximo Gómez Collection
Great Britain. Public Records Office. Foreign Office, Havana, No. 277.
National Archives of the United States, Washington, D.C.
  Department of State, Consular Letters, from Havana to Washington, 1868–1896, Haiti, 1879–1880
  United States Treasury Department, Special Agents Reports, 1865–1895
Library of Congress, Washington, D.C.
Hamilton Fish Papers
Hamilton Fish Diary
Richard B. Olney Papers

Unpublished Theses and Papers

Fermeselle-López, Rafael. "Black Politics in Cuba: The Race War of 1912." Ph.D. dissertation, American University, 1972.

Fagen, Patricia Weiss. "Heroes of National Liberation: Antonio Maceo, An Historiographical Essay." Paper presented at the American Studies Association Conference and New World Studies Conference, San Antonio, Texas, November, 1975.

Nichols, Laurence R. "Domestic History of Cuba During the War of Insurrectos, 1895–1898." M.A. Thesis, Duke University, 1951.

Nichols, Laurence R. "The 'Bronze Titan,' The Mulatto Hero of Cuban Independence, Antonio Maceo." Ph.D. dissertation, Duke University, 1954.

Orum, Thomas T. "The Politics of Color: The Racial Dimension of Cuban Politics During the Early Republican Years, 1900–1912." Ph.D. dissertation, New York University, 1975.

Preece, Carol A., "Insurgent Guests: The Cuban Revolutionary Party and Its Activities in the United States, 1892–1898." Ph.D. dissertation, Georgetown University, 1976.

Rickenbach, Richard Vernon. "A History of Filibustering from Florida to Cuba, 1895–1898." M.A. thesis, University of Florida, 1948.

St. Juste, Laurore. "Lutte de la République d'Haiti pour l'émancipation des peuples de l'Amérique." M.A. thesis, University of Ottowa, 1954.

Wolf, Donna Marie. "The Caribbean People of Color and the Cuban Independence Movements." Ph.D. dissertation, University of Pittsburgh, 1973.

Books and Pamphlets

Academia de la historia de Cuba. *Papeles de Maceo*, 2 vols. Havana, 1948.

Aimes, Hubert H.S. *History of Slavery in Cuba, 1511–1868*. New York, 1907.

Alaiso y Saturjo, Eugenio. *Apuntes sobre los projectos de la abolición de la esclavitud en las islas de Cuba y Puerto Rico*. Madrid, 1874.

Aparicio, Raúl. *Hombradia de Antonio Maceo*. Havana, 1967.

Arnao, Juan. *Páginas sobre la historia de la isla de Cuba*. Havana, 1900.

Asprey, Robert. *War in the Shadows: The Guerrilla in History*. New York, 1975.

Bacardí y Moreau, Emilio, ed. *Cronícas de Santiago de Cuba*, 7 vols. Barcelona, 1908–1924.

Barrios y Carrión, Leopoldo. *Sobre la historia de la guerra de Cuba*. Madrid, 1882.

Bellido de Luna, Juan. *La anexioń de Cuba a los Estados Unidos*. New York, 1892.

Biblioteca Cuba. *Antonio Maceo, de la campaña*. Havana, 1916.

Biblioteca de la Sociedad Economica de Amigo del Pais. *Documentos manuscripts de interés*. Havana, 1885.

Boza, Barnabé. *Mi diario de la guerra desde Baire hasta la intervención*, 2 vols. Havana, 1900–1904.

Cabrales, Gonzalo. *Epistolario de héroes*. Havana, 1922

Cabrera, Luis Rolando. *El centenario de Maceo, 1845–14 de Junio–1945*, Havana, 1945. Translated by Beatrice M. Ash and Elda Lecrona, Havana, 1945.

Cabrera, Raimundo. *Cuba and the Cubans*. Philadelphia, 1896.

Camps y Feliú, Colonel. *Españoles y insurrectos*. Madrid, 1900.

Cardenas, Nicolas de. *Recuerdos de la guerra*. Havana, 1923.

Carranza, Araceli García. *Bibliografía de la guerra de independencia (1895–1898)*. Havana, 1976.

Carreras y Gonzales, Benito. *Páginas de la guerra de Cuba: historia de un guerrillero*. Havana, 1898.

Castellanos, Gerardo. *Panorama histórica*. Havana, 1934.

Castillo y Zuniga, Rogelio. *Para la historia de Cuba, autobiografi*. Havana, 1910.

Castro, Ruz Raúl. *El ejemple de los héroes nunca muere. Speech given on December 7, 1959, published by the Department of Public Relations of the Ministry of States*. Havana, n.d.

Cepero y Bonilla, Raúl. *Azúcar y abolición: Apuntes para una historia critica de abolicionismo*. Havana, 1948.

Chadwick, French E. *The Relations of the United States and Spain: Diplomacy*. New York, 1909.

Chapman, Charles E. *A History of the Cuban Republic: A Short Study in Hispanic American Politics*. New York, 1927.

Collazo, Enrique. *Cuba heroica*. Havana, 1921.

———. *Desda Yara hasta el Zanjón*. Havana, 1893.

Conte, F.A. *La lucha política en Cuba*. Havana, 1899.

Correspondencia diplómatica de la delegación cubana en Nueva

York durante la guerra de independencia de 1895 a 1898, vol. 2. Havana, 1943–1946.

Costa, Octavio Ramón. *Juan Gualberto Gómez, una vida sin sombra*. Havana, 1950.

Coute, Don José Ferrer de. *Cuba May Become Independent*. New York, 1872.

Crouch, Thomas W. *A Yankee Guerrillero: Frederick Funston and the Cuban Insurrection 1896–1897*. Memphis, Tenn., 1976.

Cruz, Manuel de la. *Episodios de la revolución cubana*. Havana, 1926.

Cuba Libre. Misión Providencial. *El Programa de Maceo. Ideas de Maceo. Jefe de la raza negra en Cuba. Insurrección*. New York, 1895.

Davis, Richard Harding. *Cuba in War Time*. New York, 1897.

Documentos políticos de Máximo Gómez. Havana, 1962

Domingo de Ibarra, Ramón. *Memorias revolucionarias*. Madrid, 1880.

Echeverría, J.F. *Mis recuerdos*. Lima, 1897.

Escalente Beatón, Capitán Anibal. *Calixto García. Su campaña en 1898*. Havana, 1938.

Estévez y Romero, Luis. *Desde el Zanjón hasta Baire*. Havana, 1899.

Facts About Cuba. Published under the Authority of the New York Cuban Junta. New York, 1870.

Figueredo Socarrás, Fernando. *La revolución de Yara*. Havana, 1902.

Flint, Grover. *Marching with Gómez. A War Correspondent's Field Note-Book kept during four months with the Cuban Army*, introduction by John Fisk. Boston and New York, 1898.

Foner, Philip S. *Abraham Lincoln: Selections from His Writings*, New York, 1944.

———. *The Spanish-Cuban-American War and the Birth of American Imperialism*, vol. 1, 1895–1898. New York, 1972.

———. *A History of Cuba and its Relations with the United States*, vol 1, New York, 1962; vol. 2, 1963.

———. ed. *The Voice of Black America: Major Speeches of Negroes in the United States, 1797–1971*. New York, 1972.

———, ed. *Inside the Monster: Writings on the United States and American Imperialism* by José Martí. Translated by Eleanor Randall. New York, 1975.

Franco, José Luciano. *Antonio Maceo, apuntes para una historia de su*

vida, vol. 1, Havana, 1951; vol. 2, Havana, 1954; vol. 3, Havana, 1957.
———. *La Vida heroica e ejemplar de Antonio Maceo*, Havana, 1963.
———. *Antonio Maceo en Honduras*. Havana, 1956.
———. *Ruta de Antonio Maceo en el Caribe*. Havana, 1961.
Friedlander, H.E. *Historia economica de Cuba*. Havana, 1944.
Funston, Frederick. *Memories of Two Wars*. New York, 1914.
García Agüero, Salvador. *Maceo cifra y caracter de la revolución cubana*. Havana, c. 1942.
García Iñíiquez, Calixto. *Mi diario*. Havana, 1928.
Garrigo, Rogue Eugenio. *Historia documentada de la conspiración de los soles y rayos de Bolivar*. 2 vols., Havana, 1929.
Giberga, Eliseo. *Apuntes sobre la cuestión de Cuba*. Madrid, 1894.
Gómez, Fernando. *La insurrección pro dentro*. Havana and Madrid, 1897.
Gómez, y Baez Máximo. *Diario de campaña*. 2 vols., Havana, 1940.
Granda, Manuel, J. de. *Memorias revolucionarias*. 2 vols., Havana 1936. *La paz del manganeso*. Havana, 1939.
Griñán Peralta, Leonardo. *La muerta de Antonio Maceo, causas y consecuencias*. Havana, 1941. *Antonio Maceo, Analisis caracterológico*. Havana, 1940.
Gualberto Gómez, Juan. *Los preliminares de la revolución de 1895*. Havana, 1913.
———. *Por Cuba Libre*. Havana, 1922.
Guerra y Sanchez, Ramiro. *La guerra de diez años*, vol. 1. Havana, 1950.
Hall, A.D. *Cuba, Its Past, Present, and Future*. New York, 1898.
Halstead, Murat. *The Story of Cuba*. Chicago, 1898.
Hernández, Eusebio. *Dos conferencias*. Havana, n.d.
Heredia, Nicolás. *Crónicas de la guerra de Cuba, 1895–1896*, introducción por la doctor Enrique Gay-Calbó. Havana, 1951.
Horrego, Estuch Leopoldo. *Antonio Maceo: Heroe y caracter*. Havana, 1952.
———. *Juan Gualberto Gómez: un gran inconforme*, 2nd ed. Havana, 1954.
Hostos, Eugènio María de. *Obras Completas*, vol. 10. Havana, 1939.
Ibarra, Jorge. *Ideologîa mambisa*. Havana, 1967.

Ibarra, Ramon Domingo de. *Memorias revolucionarias*. Madrid, 1880.
Jenks, Leland Hamilton. *Our Cuban Colony: A Study in Sugar*. New York, 1928.
Jerez Villarreal, Juan. *Oriente: Biografía de una provincia*. Havana, 1960.
Jinesta, Carlos. *Con Maceo en Nicoya*. Havana, 1912.
Johnson, Willis Fletcher. *The History of Cuba*, vols. 3–4. New York, 1920.
Kipple, Kenneth F. *Blacks in Colonial Cuba 1774–1899*. Gainesville, Fla., 1976.
Knight, Franklin Wills. *Slave Society in Cuba During the Nineteenth Century*. Madison, Wis., 1970.
Leyva y Aguilera, Herminio C. *El movimiento insurrecional de 1879*. Havana, 1893.
Lizaso, Félix. *José Martí: Martyr of Cuban Independence*. Translated by Esther E. Shuler. Albuquerque, N.M., 1953.
Long, W. Rodney. *Railroads of Central America and the West Indies*. Washington, D.C., 1925.
Malpica, Eduardo Rosell. *Diaro de campaña*. Havana, 1916.
Mañach, Jorge. *Martí: Apostle of Freedom*. Translated by Coley Taylor. New York, 1950.
Marquina, Rafael. *Antonio Maceo, heroe eponimo; estudio biografico*, Havana, 1943.
Martí, José. *Fragmentos: obras completos de Marti*, ed. Gonzalo de Quesada y Miranda. Havana, 1949.
———, *Obras Completas*, vol. 1. Havana, 1946.
———, *La cuestión racial*. Havana, 1959
Martinez-Alier, Verena. *Marriage, Class and Colour in Nineteenth Century Cuba*. London, 1974.
Miró y Argenter, José. *Cuba: cronicas de la guerra; Las campañas de invasión y de occidente, 1895–1896*, 3 vols. Havana, 1945.
Mora, Ignacio. *Diario durante la guerra de los diez años*. Havana, 1910.
Musgrave, George C. *Under Three Flags in Cuba*. Boston, 1899.
Nevins, Allan. *Hamilton Fish: the Inner History of the Grant Administration*. New York, 1957.
Ochando, T. *Martínez Campos en Cuba*. Madrid, 1878.

O'Kelly, James J. *The Mambi-Land, or, Adventures of a Herald Correspondent in Cuba*. Philadelphia, 1874.

Ortiz, Fernándo. *Cuban Counterpoint: Tobacco and Sugar*. Translated by Harriet de Onis. New York, 1947.

———. *Hampa Afro-cubana: Los negros esclavos*. Havana, 1916.

———. *Martí y las razas*. Havana, 1950.

Pando, Magdalena. *Grandes figuras de America. Antonio Maceo*. Gainesville, Fla., 1960.

Perez, Francisco. *La guerra en la Habana: Desde enero de 1896 hasta el combate de San Pedro*. Havana, 1974.

Pérez Moris, José. *Historia de la insurrección de Lares*. Barcelona, 1872.

Pezuela y Lobo, Jacobo de. *Diccionario geográfico estadístico de la isla de Cuba*. 3 vols. Madrid, 1863.

———, *Historia de la isla de Cuba*. 4 vols. Madrid, 1868–1878.

Piedra Martel, Manuel. *Campañas de Maceo en la ultima guerra de independencia*. Havana, 1946.

Pirala, Antonio. *Anales de la guerra de Cuba*. 3 vols. Madrid, 1896.

Polavieja, Camilo. *Relación documentada de mi política en Cuba*. Madrid, 1898.

Ponto y Dominguez, Francisco J. *Historia de la guerra de los diez años*. Havana, 1944.

Portell Vilá, Herminio. *Breve biografia de Antonio Maceo*. Havana, 1945.

———. *Historia de Cuba en sus relaciones con los Estados Unidos y España*. 3 vols. Havana, 1939.

Portuondo, José Antonio, ed. *El pensamiento vivo de Maceo*. Havana, 1962.

Price-Mars, Jean. *La contribution haitienne á la lutte des Amériques pour les libertés humaines*. Port-au-Prince, 1942.

Publicaciones de Secretaria de Educacion Direccion de Cultura. *Antonio Maceo. Disciplina y dignidad*. Havana, 1936.

Publicaciones del Archivo Nacional de Cuba. *Antonio Maceo: documentos para su vida*. Havana, 1945.

———. *Correspondencia diplómatica de la delegación cubana en Nueva York durante la guerra de independencia de 1895–1898*, vols. 2, 6, 9, 11. Havana, 1943–1946.

Quesada, Gonzalo de. *The War in Cuba; the Struggle for Freedom.* Washington, D.C., 1896.

Rea, George Bronson. *Facts and Fakes About Cuba.* New York, 1897.

Reyna Cossio, Rene E. *Estudios histórico-militares sobre la guerra de independencia de Cuba.* Havana, 1954.

Richardson, Willis. "Antonio Maceo." In W. Richardson and M. Miller, eds. *Negro History in Thirteen Plays.* Preface by Carter G. Woodson. Washington, D.C., 1935.

Risquet, Juan F. *Rectificaciones: la cuestión político-social en la isla de Cuba.* Havana, 1900.

Rivero, Mũniz José. *Verde Nueva.* Havana, 1964.

Roa, Ramón. *Con la pluma y el machete.* 3 vols. Havana, 1950.

Robeson, Paul. *The Negro People and the Soviet Union: Address at Banquet Sponsored by the National Council of American-Soviet Friendship, Waldorf-Astoria, New York City, November 10, 1949.* New York, 1950.

Robertson, William. *The Beginnings of Spanish-American Diplomacy.* New York, 1940.

Rodríguez Rodríguez, Amalia. *Algunos documentos politicos de Máximo Gómez.* Havana, 1962.

Rodríguez, Carlos Rafael. *La bases de desarrollo económica de Cuba.* Havana, 1956.

Rodríguez, Gabrial. *La España del siglo XIX.* 5 vols. Madrid, 1883.

———. *José Martí and Cuban Liberation.* New York, 1953.

Rodríguez, Mórejon, G. *Maceo homenaje que rinde el Ministerio de Defensa Nacional al Lugartenente General Antonio Maceo y Grajales.* Havana, 1946.

Rodríguez Demorizi, Emilio. *Maceo en Santo Domingo.* Santiago, Dominican Republic, n.d.

Roig de Leuchsenring, Emilió. *Antonio Maceo.* Havana, 1946.

———. *Ideario cubano: Máximo Gómez.* Havana, 1936.

———. *Máximo Gómez, el libertador de Cuba y el primer Ciudadano de la Republica.* Havana, 1959.

———. *Cuba no debe su independencía a los Estados Unidos.* Havana, 1950.

———. *Revolución y república en Maceo.* Havana, 1932.

Rosado, Colonel Pio. *Mi diario de la revolución.* Havana, 1899.

Rubens, Horatio. *Liberty, the Story of Cuba*. New York, 1922.

Saco, José Antonio. *Historia de la esclavitud de la raza africana en el nuevo mundo*. 6 vols. Barcelona, 1879.

Sanguilly y Arizti, Manuel. *Loma de Sevilla*. Havana, 1924.

———. *Páginas de historia*. Havana, 1929.

Sanguilly y Garrite, Manuel. "Antonio Maceo." In *Discursos y conferencias*, vol. 2. Havana, 1919.

Santovenia y Echaide, Emeterio. *Raiz y altura de Antonio Maceo*. Havana, 1943.

Sarabia, Nydia. *Historia de una familia mambisa: Mariana Grajales*. Havana, 1975.

Sociedad Cubana de Estudios Historicos y Internacionales. *Antonio Maceo, Ideología política, cartas y otros documentos*. Havana, 1950.

Souza, Benigno. *Máximo Gómez, el generalisimo*. Havana, 1936.

Tejera, Diego Vicente. *Blancos y Negroes. Conferencia dada en Cayo Hueso en 7 de 1897*. Havana, 1900.

Thomas, Hugh. *Cuba: The Pursuit of Freedom*. New York, 1971.

Trelles y Govín, Carlos M. *Bibliografía cubana del siglo XIX*. 8 vols. Matanzas, 1915.

———. *Matanzas en la independencia de Cuba*. Havana, 1919.

Trujillo, Enrique. *Apuntes históricos*. New York, 1896.

Ubieta, Enrique. *Efémerides de la revolución cubana*. 4 vols. Havana, 1910.

Varona, Enrique José. *De la colonia a la república*. Havana, 1919.

Varona y Guerrero, Miguel. *La guerra de independencia de Cuba, 1895–1898*. 3 vols. Havana, 1946.

Vázquez Rodríguez, Benigno. *Precursores y fundadores*. Havana, 1958.

Verdes, Aguas. *Antonio Maceo, ideología política*. Havana, 1922.

Vivanco, José Clemente. *Diario de campaña*. Havana, 1912.

Weyler y Nicolau, Valeriano. *Mi mando en Cuba*. 5 vols. Madrid, 1910.

Wisan, Joseph E. *The Cuban Crisis as Reflected in the New York Press, 1895–1898*. New York, 1934.

Wright, Irene Aloha. *The Early History of Cuba, 1492–1586*. New York, 1916.

Zambrana, Antonio. *La república de Cuba*. Havana, 1922.

Zamora y Coronado, José Maria. *Biblioteca de legislación ultamarina*, vol. 3. Madrid, 1845.

Zaragoitia Ledesma, L. *Maceo*. Havana, 1949.

Zaragoza, Justo. *Las insurrecciones en Cuba*. 2 vols. Madrid, 1872.

Articles

Aguirre, Sergio. "Esclavitud y abolicionismo." *Dialectica* 18 (March-June 1946): 12–20.

———. "El torno a la Revolucion de 1868." *Hoy*, 1945 (Año del Centenario Maceico) en el Magazine Especial del Primero de Mayo, "La Protesta de Baraguá," *ibid*.

———. "Frustración y reconquista del 24 de febrero." *Cuba Socialista* Año II (February 1962): 32–54.

"Antonio Maceo." *Revista de historia cubana y americana* 7 (1916): 91–101.

Aparicio, Raúl. "Esquema ideologico de Antonio Maceo." *Bohemia* (Havana), December 8, 1967, 10–12, 91.

Beck, Earl R. "The Martinez Campos Government of 1879: Spain's Last Chance in Cuba." *Hispanic American Historical Review* 56 (May 1976): 268–79.

"Documentos historicos," *Revista de historia cubana y americana* 1 (1916): 94–95.

"Documentos historicos." *Revista cubana* 3(1888): 533–34; 7(1902): 533–40.

"Entrevista a Maceo en 1878." *Revista de la universidad central de Las Villas* (Santa Clara) 6, no.1 (July-December 1963): 38–43.

Bashkina, N. "A Page from the Cuban People's Heroic History," *International Affairs.* Moscow (March 1964): 3–20.

Fagen, Patricia Weiss. "Antonio Maceo: Heroes, History, and Historiography." *Latin American Research Review* 11 (1976): 69–93.

Foner, Philip S. "A Tribute to Antonio Maceo." *Journal of Negro History* 60 (January 1970): 67–71.

Franco, José Luciano. "Facetas de Maceo Revolucionario, 1858–

1884." *Boletín Oficial de la Asociacion Nacional de Jubilados y Pensionados de Comunicaciones*. (November-December 1975): 2–3.

French, José L. "With Gómez in the Cuban Skirmishes." *National Magazine* 13 (June 1898): 38–40.

Gaspar, Jorge. "Influencia del Tabaquero en la trajectoria revlucionaria de Cuba." *Revista Bimestre Cubana* 39 (January-February 1937): 105–15.

Gates, Skip. "Eldridge Cleaver on Cuba. Interview by Skip Gates." *Yardbird Reader* 5 (1976): 200–12.

Hamedoe, S.E.F.C.C. "Major-General Antonio Maceo: The Idol of Cuba and the Cuban Insurgents." *Colored American Magazine*, November, 1900: 50–54.

Hernández, Eusebio. "El periodo Revolucionario de 1879 a 1895." *Revista de la Facultad de Letras y Ciencias* 19 (July 1914): 3–18.

Horrego Estuch, Leopoldo. "La Muerta de Maceo." *Bohemia* (Havana) December 8, 1967: 5–9, 113.

"Insurrection in Cuba, The". *Outlook*. June 1, 1912: 238.

Knight, Franklin W. "Origins of Wealth and the Sugar Revolution in Cuba, 1750–1850." *Hispanic American Historical Review* 57 (May 1977): 231–53.

La Feber, Walter. "The Background of Cleveland's Venezuelan Policy," *American Historical Review* 66 (July 1961): 940–59.

"Los Mambises." *Bohemia* (Havana) June 4, 1965: 102–08.

"Maceo." *Revista de historia cubana y americana* 2 (1916): 92.

Osa, Enrique de la. "Una interpretación materialista de la guerra de los diez años." *Bohemia* (Havana) October 8, 1961: 54–57.

Rickenbach, Richard V. "Filibustering with the Dauntless," *Florida Historical Quarterly* 38 (April 1950): 220–35.

Rodríguez, Mariano. "Conversación acera de Maceo con José Luciano Franco." *Juventud Rebelde*. June 13, 1971.

Schomburg, Arthur A. "General Antonio Maceo." *The Crisis* 38 (May 1931): 155–56, 174.

Stanhope, Dorothy. "The Negro Race in Cuba: Insular Society Draws no Color Line." *New York Times*, September 16, 1900.

Steep, Thomas W. "A Cuban Insurgent Newspaper." *National Magazine* 8 (1898): 145–49.

Tosquella, Mantua. "Baraguá-Mantua." *Bohemia*. Havana, December 4, 1964: 8–9.

Webb, Frank J. "General Antonio Maceo." *AME Church Review* 14 (1897–1898): 113–14.

Recordings

"Discurso de Che sobre el General Antonio." Address by Che Guevara in honor of Antonio Maceo, 33 rpm record, Havana, Cuba.

Index